Living the *good life*

Living the good life

How one family changed their world from their own backyard

Linda Cockburn

Hardie Grant Books

Published in 2006 by
Hardie Grant Books
85 High Street
Prahran, Victoria 3181, Australia
www.hardiegrant.com.au

National Library of Australia Cataloguing-in-Publication Data:

Cockburn, Linda.
    Living the good life: how one family changed their world
    from their own backyard.
    Includes index.
    ISBN 9 781 74066 312 0
    1. Cockburn, Linda — Family. 2. Alternative lifestyles —
    Australia. 3. Environmentalism — Australia. 4. Australia —
    Social life and customs. I. Title.
920.72

Cover and text design by Nick Mau, Mau Design
Edited by Alexandra Payne
Typeset by Pauline Haas, bluerinse setting
Printed and bound in Australia by Griffin Press

10 9 8 7 6 5 4 3

CONTENTS

Acknowledgements

I'd like to acknowledge the people who bartered with us over the six months, especially Elsie Roberts, who was our barter mainstay — without her, our adventure would have been a lot shorter. Thanks must also go to Marguerite River and Pete Smith — you're both wonderful. We couldn't miss out Janet Ernst, Dave Pearson, Phil Frayne, Paul Toon 'Tooney', Paul Keay, Heather and Marco, Caleb's 'old' teacher, Mrs Blackburn, and his classmates, whose joy in sharing our adventure, even the snail-cooking aspect, was a lot of fun. Also our patient neighbours Jeff and Carolyn Young, and Shane and Leah Miles and family. And to my mother for putting together those keenly awaited 'relief parcels'.

Thanks to Ehren who helped out wherever he could in as many ways as he could devise. Also to Leela who managed to smuggle in a few chocolate bars over the six months. You're both treasures.

Thanks goes to Alexandra Payne, who lent not just her editing expertise, but also invaluable support throughout the project. Also to the unrelated Steve Payne of *ABC Organic Gardener* magazine who deserves a big thanks for his ongoing interest and support during the adventure.

Throughout the experiment we received many supportive emails from people frequenting the website, offering advice on issues like chooks without eggs, and beans with maggots. It made us truly understand the concept of an online community.

To Trev and Caleb.

*And to our delicate and beautiful world, which took billions of years
to get where it is, and is being destroyed in the blink of an eye.
I hope humanity can offer it the ultimate emancipation soon.*

Linda Cockburn was born in New Zealand in 1968. Of her five siblings she was judged the least likely to garden due to a horror of accumulating dirt under her fingernails, but now she's managed to accrue at least a few kilos of exactly that. She recently made the mistake of pondering the ability to live in a domestically sustainable way on 2180 square metres, and spent the last five years working towards that goal, dragging Trev and Caleb with her.

Trevor Wittmer moved to Queensland from Melbourne 25 years ago, attracted by the endless summers and cheap land. For 20 of those years he lived the hippie dream – mud-brick house, solar power, wood stove, the bush. Eight years ago, through a mixture of tragedy and serendipity, he was fortunate enough to meet Linda. Trev has a background in forestry research.

Caleb Wittmer 'Caleb, do you think we can spend six months (that's 180 days) without spending a dollar?'
   'No, sweet things might run out.'
   'What other problems might we have?'
   'We can't get any toys for me, no Bionicles.'
   'Can you think of anything good about spending six months without a dollar?'
   'It would be fun – like biking to school, getting challenges at home and having days off from buying, and that's kind of fun.'
   Caleb is a fruit bat and as long as he is provided with enough watermelon, rockmelon, grapes, mandarins, mulberries, bananas and no pumpkin, he will be content.

Introduction

'We're going to try to go six months without spending a dollar.'

I smile, waiting for the inevitable response, which is a knowing grin and an array of, 'But how are you going to . . . ?' questions.

I'm prepared for being asked about shampoo, scrubbing brushes and soap. I'm even better at responding to questions about transport and tissues, but for a long time I didn't know how to respond to the one about toilet paper. I'd experimented with lamb's ears (the kind you grow), which, while soft, didn't have the required strength. Newspapers were not an option . . .

It seemed the last piece in the puzzle, but we didn't realise that this particular puzzle (our adventure in domestic sustainability) was a living thing, and we would need to keep building on it as we went.

I'm quick to point out that while we could opt out of certain things, we couldn't avoid taxes, rates, insurance or medical bills. We aren't about to be jailed for tax evasion or let a family member bleed to death or die of a strangulated hernia. Non-payment of rates might have drastic consequences and insurance is there just in case we lose the house, though ours is not inclined to go wandering. We would also need to remain connected to the phone and Internet, and have educational expenses funds for our seven-year-old son, Caleb. We didn't want to turn our back on the world, just reduce our environmental impact as far as possible without making our lifestyle unliveable.

Everything else is up to us to provide or to go without.

While there is a general push for industry and agriculture to adopt sustainable practices, the domestic area goes largely unnoticed. Severe droughts in 2004 provoked discussions about building higher dam walls, and when hot summers produced power shortages there was further talk about burning more coal and increasing infrastructure. Almost no one mentioned that we should learn to become more efficient with our water and power use. We looked into what the domestic sector was creating or using with respect to pollution, water, power and resources. The figures were frightening, and while this book will share some of that with you, it will mainly look at our contribution as a family, and how we reduced it, with only minimal impact on our way of life.

During our research, we were often confronted with information that was unremittingly negative and gave a message of hopelessness. This book is unremittingly positive in nature, and gives practical information on how we adopted a sustainable lifestyle without huge cost and without great sacrifice. It's more than just advice about using low-wattage light bulbs; it's an in-depth look at how we live and how we could be living. It's also an insight into how we went to an extreme we at first didn't intend to and don't recommend for everyone … and spent six months mostly self-reliant, or domestically sustainable, a term we prefer over self-sufficient, which implies 'going it alone' or turning away from the world. Domestic sustainability acknowledges the effects that overpopulation, consumerism and our current use of resources have on the environment, and seeks to reassess our way of life while embracing what it means to live within a community and its environmental limits.

But why would we want to undergo such an ordeal (although we think of it as an adventure), and just how do we think it's possible to do so? What are the expected outcomes?

Like most families we'd lost touch with the process of food creation, not just buying and artfully cooking the produce of others, but seeing it from seed to saliva. The cost of food was resented, because it represented a necessity that we no longer felt connected to and that forever needed replacing.

Both Trevor and I were working full-time, and Caleb was 'doing' daycare full-time too. I was often away nights, was forever behind the wheel of a car or in front of a computer, usually while eating junk food and wondering why I was getting so fat. We wanted a simpler life. But how could we? We'd already tried living off one income, and found it nearly impossible. Then I started researching aspects of our family's environmental impact and, somewhere on a highway in a car that looked like someone had dumped a rubbish bin full of junk food wrappers in, something gelled. We could live off one income if we could provide our own food and learn some of those forgotten skills like cheese-making; growing, threshing, winnowing and grinding our own wheat; making bean curd; and growing things like sesame seeds. We could even have a go at producing our own vegetable oils and growing our own coffee. We could grow our own meals, shampoo, scrubbing brushes and more.

We live on a 2180-square-metre town block, just over half an acre. Is it possible to feed a family on a suburban block? Later on you'll see the mathematical equations that say yes. But that's theory, what about practice?

Why is it so interesting to know if we can survive under our own auspices?

World events (and not just recent ones) make us wonder what would happen if the elaborate system we have spent thousands of years evolving disintegrated overnight. Could we survive? Have we the knowledge and the skills to adapt to changed circumstances? Are we 'progressing' ourselves into vulnerability? We know how to drive cars but most of us don't know how to fix them. We know how to cook a meal because we have the ability to buy food, we have the means to transport it to our homes, electricity to assist us in its preparation. Can we sustain ourselves without the huge human network? We've all learnt to refine our skills in select areas and have filtered out broader-based knowledge — this may be to our ultimate disadvantage.

We want to explore how a non-consumerist approach would affect our family. Can we survive without a new Bionicle toy (Caleb), the release of an eagerly awaited literary novel (me), a boutique beer (Trev)? Will we feel deprived? Will we have withdrawal symptoms? Will we develop other ways of obtaining pleasure within the boundaries of our 2180 square metres?

What will the impact be on our health? Will we be less stressed? Lower our cholesterol? Improve our liver function? Lose weight? (Trev has accused me of devising the most elaborate diet in the world.) What about our mental health? Will the six months leave us feeling invigorated or depleted? Will we long for the end of the six months or will we wish to linger in our 'sacred space' just a little longer? What will we take with us, what are the long-term ramifications of living on so little? And, as so many people ask, are we trying to go back in time or is this a movement forward?

The major impetus behind the experiment is concern for the health of the environment. By choosing to live in a sustainable way, we will reduce the production of greenhouse gas and reduce our use of disposable items and household chemicals.

Trev will continue to work in the 'real' world, while I'll stay at home. It could just as easily be the other way around. It also means that our son, Caleb, will experience things like picking caterpillars off cabbages and feeding them to the chooks, eating sugarpeas directly off the vines (and leaving chewed off stems for me to find later), collecting eggs and passionfruit, climbing mulberry trees, cracking fresh macadamias and developing an appreciation of the most important unit known to humankind — that of energy, not currency.

Overall there are five facts that led us to the conclusion that this experiment in domestic sustainability was a worthy pursuit:

1. It takes 9 calories of fossil fuel-based energy to provide 1 calorie of food in Australia.

2. Each day the average Australian family uses 15 to 20 kWh of electricity created primarily by burning coal, the production of which creates 5.5 to 7.3 tonnes of CO_2 a year.

3. In undeveloped countries the average daily water use per person can be as low as 30 litres. The world average is 139. In Australia — the driest country in the world — it's 300. But our use doesn't stop there; industry and agriculture consume much larger amounts on our behalf.

4. Most families turn over 200 litres of drinkable water into sewage a day. That's 73,000 litres a year.

5. Every litre of petrol used creates enough emissions to pollute 10,500 litres of air.

We no longer felt we could continue those same practices in good conscience.

We concluded early on that we can't change the way people live, but we can change the way we do. So we did.

This is our adventure.

january

1 January

We watch over Caleb's shoulder as he crosses off the first day on our six-month calendar.

'I wish it was already over', he says.

We agree. Not because we are dreading the next six months, but because we want to be able to say we have done it, we've succeeded — and it's a long time until we can. But it's a relief to finally begin what we've been saying we would do for three years. We don't really know whether we can do it or not. It's all very much speculation at this point and, now we've told everyone we are going to try, we're too embarrassed to fail. Most of what we will be doing has become par for the course. Managing water and power has been part of our daily lives for three years now. We know, bar unforseen climatic oddities, that we can go six months without relying on mains water or power. Transport — well we suspect we are going to miss the car, but we've been using bikes and feet for some time as well. Food — we've been providing our own at a rate between 5 per cent and 80 per cent, off and on, for six years, but never at such a high sustained rate. Can we do it? It's the late-night question gnawing at our sleep. We don't know.

'What's for dinner, Mum?'

'Nothing.'

'Oh, great!'

It's his favourite meal, made up of things we always have plenty of. This one is made from large wedge chips, boiled eggs, homemade mayonnaise, chives, parsley, mushrooms, grated carrot and peanuts. At other times we've substituted asparagus, pumpkin, sweet potato, corn, cashews, squash, whatever is currently prolific. It's our version of takeaway — high fat and fairly fast.

3 January

We're down to the last three rolls of toilet paper. Caleb and I are making inroads into the Christmas chocolate, and have polished off the ice-cream. Trev has discovered that his home-grown tobacco could be marketed as nicotineless, and his elderflower champagne, which he scientifically tested for alcohol content by filling a mug, sculling it and waiting for a buzz (none came), is alcohol-less. He shrugs and says it doesn't matter, but Trev is a man of oral pleasures — alcohol and tobacco are two very ritualised aspects of this. While it won't cause us to fail, it is obviously a disappointment. I make the requisite number of oh, no, oh, darlings before moving off.

If you feel sorry for Trev, you are not alone. Many people greet Trev for the first time with, 'You poor man'. It's a running gag around the house: 'It's OK Trev, I might not feel sorry for you, but lots of others do'.

There is a belief that the eccentric idea of six months without spending a dollar is all mine and that I'm a train pulling Trev and Caleb along a rough track with many torturous bends, with a sign at each one saying things like 'no McDonald's', 'no airconditioned rides to school', and now this new torture for Trev, a low-alcohol, low-nicotine, no red meat, only snails diet. I'm a witch.

Trev, however, feels embarrassed about this, even though he recently said to Caleb, 'The next bright idea that Mum has, let's shoot her'. (Caleb agreed.)

Nothing

So-called as it uses ingredients we always have on hand or in the garden, plus it makes us smile when we ask each other what we'd like for dinner and the other says, 'Nothing'.

1 onion, chopped

4 or 5 mushrooms, sliced

500 grams potatoes or sweet potatoes, or a mix (newer the better)

6 hard-boiled eggs, peeled and halved

2 carrots, grated

generous handful roasted peanuts

chopped chives

chopped parsley

2 tablespoons mayonnaise

1 teaspoon ground cumin

Pan-fry the onion and mushrooms in a little oil until lightly browned, then set aside. Microwave the potatoes until nearly cooked, then gently pan-fry until golden and crisp. Combine all ingredients and serve warm. Exchange any of the ingredients for anything you prefer, or have too much of.

Serves 3 to 4.

This is a team effort and we are all willing members. Caleb demonstrated that conclusively when, yesterday, I wiped sweat from brow and said, 'Oh bugger this experiment, let's get in the car and go for a swim'.

'No, Mum!' he replied, 'We'll fail our six months'.

Trev and I have our own environmental, personal and even financial goals to achieve through the experiment. Caleb, though keen on the idea, needed an additional goal. He's been promised a $200 do-what-you-like-with-it shopping trip if he helps us get to the end. The kind of help I'm after is the 'eat what you are given' variety. It's given him something to work towards.

Sometime during the day, Trev suggests our next experiment be one of complete self-indulgence — how much food, drink and resources can we squander in six months. I point out that there are plenty of others already conducting their own experiments on this without needing to replicate them. I suggest we try our current experiment in every state — Tasmania here we come! I ignore the dirty looks.

4 January

Trev conducts Phase II of alcohol testing the elderflower champagne — two mugs provide a medium-level buzz equivalent to beer. I think he's deluding himself. He is, nevertheless, somewhat appeased.

Elderflower champagne

Don't use yellowed elderflower heads as they make Cat Piss Wine.

25 very fresh elderflower heads
10 litres water
2 lemons, quartered
1 kilo sugar
1 packet wine maker's yeast (7 grams)

Combine elderflower heads, water and lemons and soak overnight in a carboy (a plastic drum with an airlock, made especially for fermenting). Strain liquid and pour back into carboy. Dissolve sugar in sufficient additional warm water, and add this and the yeast to the liquid. Stir well. Leave to ferment until bubbling stops (around a week). Bottle, adding a teaspoon of sugar to each. Leave two to three weeks before drinking.

Makes around 10 litres.

Recently our power creation has not been meeting up with our consumption. It's a predictable effect of high humidity and high temperatures reducing solar PV (photo-voltaic) efficiency (by 0.5 per cent for every degree over 25) and increasing the time the fridge needs to run to maintain 5 degrees. Especially as we are all sweating profusely and continually opening the door, mainly to rest our heads in the freezer for a moment before searching for something cold. We've tracked down a sheet of heavy plastic to make a barrier over the front of the opened fridge — something that will allow us to access the contents through cut slots, and yet not let the heavier cold air 'flop' out onto the floor when the fridge opens. I spent ages fastidiously taping the plastic sheet to the fridge only to discover it prevented the door from closing. I moved it back an inch or so, whacking it on in any old way. Meanwhile, Trev is on the roof cleaning the solar panels with a squeegee. Then he spends a blistering several hours working out how to lower the solar panels into a more efficient 'summer' angle. Our installer had told us it wasn't necessary and, before long, Trev discovers that the installer believed it so unnecessary he didn't bother to make it possible. Hence the several blistering hours up top.

I turn up in time to help wriggle along underneath and pop the bolts that Trev can't reach.

5 January

Woke up stuck to the sheets and prepared to have a day of lethargy. The humidity has sucked all good intentions from us, and the heat has inflamed tempers. I ask Caleb to pull the plug on the bath before I leave the house and then I race down to the end of the greywater hose. I stand there for several steaming minutes waiting for it to start running. It doesn't. I return to the house to do it myself. He's forgotten, but he's keen to clamber over me with sweaty hands, bump his nose into my headache, and wrench at my neck, which has felt like it has been resting at right angles to my body for several days now. To add to it all, Trev tells me the way I'm holding my head makes me look like my father. I am not impressed.

Trev is also making repeated comments on his imminent demise — the blood tests are back. The medical receptionist tells me my results are normal, but the doctor wishes to talk to Trev about his. She will not elaborate. The doctor will give him a call — but this is several days on and, while I'm sure he will not die, his blood pressure is rising. 'Kidney cancer!' he cries. 'Malfunctioning liver!'

I suspect high cholesterol and, considering he experimented with battering and deep-frying goat's cheddar cheese this morning, it makes more sense than proclamations of a multitude of cancers and organ failures.

Trev jeopardises what health he has left by standing out in the heat to finish off fencing the 'south paddock', as he calls the steep, rocky slope just below the house: around 25 square metres of lab lab, sorghum, pigeon pea and nasturtium. It has stirred up his AF (Atrial Fibrillation), a condition where the impulse to the heart goes awry and the atrium quivers instead of pumps, resulting in an erratic pulse. While it only makes him feel weak and won't kill him, if his blood sits around in the atrium too long, the next good pump could send out a clot which might.

Over indulgence in alcohol, dehydration and mega-loads of caffeine are triggers, and today he demonstrated his ability to sweat by wringing out his shirt on the verandah — it couldn't have been any wetter if he had been swimming in it. Then he puts it back on and goes back out.

Apart from the heat and frayed tempers, our first five dollar-less days have been a breeze. Last night's dinner was eggplant and tomato ratatouille followed by plum and vanilla custard. All, bar the bartered cornflour, sugar and vanilla essence, is ours.

I have a vanilla orchid growing in the hope of producing our own; unfortunately it grew a large spider. I picked up the pot, the spider made a bolt up my arm, I dropped the pot, and the poor vanilla has remained in intensive care on the verandah ever since. I was looking forward to the first flowers, which I would need to hand-pollinate, then would collect the pods, wrapping them in plastic where they 'sweat' before placing them in alcohol where they exude their particular fragrant deliciousness. It's something that will happen one day, but not perhaps with this orchid.

6 January

We received the medical test results in the mail: Trev has almost twice the recommended level of cholesterol, more than four times the recommended level of triglycerides and his urea is off the charts, which could indicate either kidney problems or a diet high in protein. I calm him with a lullaby of 'Well, you did eat a leg of pig all by yourself over Christmas'. My cholesterol was a tad high, but then I too felt obliged to make the most of the last week.

Trev cleared the last sediments of elderflower champagne from the carboy and made his first ginger beer — I'm looking forward to a good quaff. One of my addictions has been Coca-Cola. Six days without and I could do with a substitute.

We woke to a shower of 3 or 4 millimetres, which would have seemed a brief blessing except we looked up the Bureau of Meteorology radar and saw the great ship *Heavy Rainfall* drifting just south of us, unfurling a brief flag of drizzle in a token gesture. We missed out. The humidity does not abate. Trev seems to have the wet look as a permanent part of his attire. After a night in which sleep played only a small part, he declared an all-day sleep-in. But instead he has helped milk the goat, fed everyone breakfast, devised an ingenious weeding tool made from recycled material and used it extensively, cut himself, bled profusely, bottled wine and made us both a great cup of coffee. He is still muttering about having missed out on good rain. He is walking a thin line. We've had a complicit agreement after years of angst and long tirades on our meteorological luck, or lack of. Nothing infuriates Trev more than missing out; nothing infuriates me more than the repetitious comments. Summed up: 'We really have to suffer before it rains' — 'When they say it rains in the South-East, we're not in the South-East we're in the Wide Bay; when they say it will rain in the Wide Bay, we're in the South-East' — 'When they say it will rain on the coast, we're inland; when they say it will rain inland, we're on the coast' — ad infinitum, ad nauseam.

Having said that, I'm moved to tears of rage when it's been dry for a long period. We watch the radar with glee as a storm moves our way then disappears within one frame, only to reappear a frame later, continuing its rampage south, north, east or west of us. Still, we are better off than some, and vastly more fortunate than people such as those in areas of Chile who get an average of 1 millimetre of rainfall a year and rely on fog harvesting for domestic water.

Trevor has projects; I potter. I add a little bit of mulch, weed a little here, plant a few seeds, pull, water, trim. I forget where things are for a week, rediscover them half-dead and have to try to revive them. I grasped — no, embraced — the permaculture concept of letting weeds grow on barren ground, for to pull them out only encourages more. My motto is 'weeding is feeding'. Most things I weed go straight to Possum the goat, who picks fastidiously through them for anything worthwhile. What she turns her nose up at, the chooks are then entitled to. If I weeded the entire block at once, she would be overwhelmed with delicacies and leave nothing for next week. Impeccable logic but I could be accused of being a lazy gardener.

PERMACULTURE

Bill Mollison, the father of permaculture, coined the phrase in the 1970s from an amalgamation of the words 'permanent' and 'agriculture'. Permaculture is the 'harmonious integration of landscape and people, providing their food, energy, shelter and other material and non-material needs in a sustainable way. Without permanent agriculture there is no possibility of a stable social order'.[1]

Ethics
- Care for the Earth.
- Care for people.
- Distribute surplus.
- Reduce consumption.

Principles
- Everything works at least two ways.
- See solutions, not problems.
- Cooperation, not competition, in work, communications and economics.
- Make things pay.
- Work where it counts.
- Use everything to its highest capacity.
- Bring food production back to cities.
- Help make more people self-reliant.
- Minimise maintenance and energy inputs to achieve maximum yields.[2]

Part of permaculture is letting things go to seed and go a little wild. I haven't planted a pumpkin in years, and have succeeded, by being so casual about the whole thing, in breeding up a fantastic cross between a jap and a butternut. Chillies can grow in perversely awkward spots, as do eggplants, basil, coriander, lettuce, kale, sorghum, millet, sunflowers, pigeon pea, potatoes, peanuts, beans, pak choi and a multitude of inbred tomatoes. My system could not be called that. I'm stingy with water, preferring a survival of the fittest regime that culls all but the hardiest. I am lackadaisical with fertiliser, instead spreading the worn-down mulch from the goat pen with its decaying black marbles of goat and chook poo, a sprinkle of dolomite, a dash of fish sauce and it's all over. My recipe for the half-hearted gardener (Trev prefers the term half-arsed).

In my pottering, I leave things half-done when something else that needs doing catches my eye. I might return to pick up the first job, or find myself on yet a different course in a different part of the garden. I might chance upon the first task with an 'Oh, that's right' with only a 50 per cent chance that I might complete it. My only saving grace is my book of lists. I make one daily — everything I can think of that I can do, and lots I probably won't but, hey, let's add them anyway. I love crossing them off and refer to them often. Without my book of lists, starting this experiment would still be a dream. Trev finds my work methods frustrating; I see his need to fulfil each project with the utmost precision, punctiliousness and patience, following each one to its full completion before embarking on the next, as anal. So when he finds 2 kilograms of plums sitting on the bench, unwashed and un-refrigerated, and sighs heavily, it's a sign for me to back out slowly and spend another hour hiding in the garden. Without Trevor I wouldn't get half the things I want to do done.

Mowed the lawn today — that is, what's left of it. We sold the petrol mower a year or so ago and found a little push mower to run over the nature strip, which is a misnomer if ever I heard one. It's home to a few ants, a couple of species of grass and that's all. It's a 30 by 4 metre area that I regularly mow, if only to try to get the elastic grass under control; if I let it grow too high, it simply bends over and snaps back on passing.

Plants have various abilities to convert sunlight into energy — grass is relatively low in the scheme of things, and humans have yet to find a way to eat it without first passing it through a cow, after which its energy value is yet again reduced. I have a hard heart and a sharp tongue when it comes to lawns. Lawns are a hangover from our English forebears' preference for manicured blobs of green. I wonder if it wasn't, even then, a symbol of wealth: 'Hey, look everyone, I'm so bloody wealthy I can afford to have large expanses of fertile soil dedicated to growing something as useless as grass'.

In England they have a climate that is grass-conducive; in Australia, we don't. Hence my hardening arteries take a thrashing every time I drive down a road and see cramped suburbanites taking their pet snake for a spin around the front lawn, watering for hours, pampering it with various chemicals to keep it green, killing subterranean lawn grubs and striking with venom those unwanted plants they call weeds. Trevor has an alternative hypothesis: it's a primeval desire to keep the grass low so that no predators can sneak up on us and eat us.

CAPTURING THE SUN'S ENERGY

The basis of life on our planet is the ability of plants to utilise sunlight. There are a number of limiting factors involved: first, only around 25 per cent of solar energy makes it through our atmosphere. Plants typically photosynthesise less than 2 per cent of what does, and then only if there are sufficient nutrients and water available. The rest is lost as heat in evaporation or transpiration.

Different ecosystems are able to 'trap sunlight' or convert solar energy (via photosynthesis) into organic matter or calorific energy (called net productivity) at different efficiencies. For example, the amounts of kilocalories 'trapped' per square metre, per year, for five different types of plants/ecosystems are:[3]

sugar cane	25,000
tropical rainforest	15,000
coastal marsh	12,000
lucerne	15,000
lawn	6800

We reduce the amount of energy 'trapped' by clearing land, paving roads, building housing and so on.

When solar energy is considered as calorific energy, one square metre receives on average:

3750 calories of energy per hour

90,000 calories per day

32.8 million calories per year.

If that one square metre had plants growing on it all the time, it would be able to convert sunlight into energy at approximately 1 per cent efficiency, so on average it would convert:

37.5 calories per hour

900 calories per day

328,500 calories per year.

We have 2180 square metres. According to this we should be creating 1.962 million calories a day. But not all of the 2180 metres is productive. We have roofs, paths, mulched or fallow areas, even, dare I say it, a few ornamentals. If we were to assume that at any given time 500 square metres are productive, that would give us a total of 450,000 calories of plant energy harvested a day.

Parts of each plant are inedible – for example, we eat the squash but the rest of the plant is eventually fed back into the system as compost material and soil nutrients.

We estimate that only 5 per cent of an average plant is edible: 450,000 calories a day therefore becomes 22,500.

If we eat nothing other than primary producers (I'm talking plants, not farmers), we are 10 per cent efficient at converting the food into useable energy (most is lost in heat and movement and the tremendous strain of thinking).

So what starts out as a large sum of energy is in fact very little by the time it moves through our inefficient harvesting system.

Despite this, our block should theoretically support us in food and leave enough excess to barter for goods that we can't produce ourselves.

8 January

Caleb ate the last of the chocolate today, the edible kind at least. Trev still has his 85 per cent cocoa stuff left (it will be safe from us). I feigned disinterest as Caleb ate it while secretly hyperventilating. I have a sweet tooth. I made toffee, the kind Trev said he hasn't eaten since his mother made it for him. We recall school fairs where for 5 cents you could buy a patty-cake paper full of toffee with an iceblock stick, or stacks of toffee that had been shattered out of the pan like amber glass and wrapped in gladwrap. Trev is devouring it at great speed. Caleb is disinclined to partake of our sticky memories.

Desserts have quickly become one of my priorities. I make a lemon and passionfruit flan, chocolate custard with the last of the cocoa and a five-egg yolk passionfruit gelato. My chocolate angst melts away – my sweet tooth shall have its say.

We've grown sugar cane and crushed it to use the juice to sweeten fruit cordials before, but now we haven't the space or electricity to grow or crush enough and then render it down to a crystallised form. So we barter for sugar, but it then becomes part of the energy equation: 1 kilogram of raw sugar is 4000 calories; it takes 0.5 square metres to grow it, and uses 1315 litres of water. We still grow sugar cane but as a windbreak and we harvest the tops as 'cow candy' for the goat. Energy is the defining measurement of success in our experiment. Living sustainably is about generating enough energy to fuel ourselves and our 21st-century appliances by trapping sunlight from a suburban block and reducing our CO_2 emissions to sustainable levels as a result of that. Even though we have called this 'six months without spending a dollar', we consider currency a lesser indicator of success.

We cracked open a watermelon yesterday; it almost takes up the whole fridge. Written on its side in wobbly letters is 'CALEB'; having seen them sitting in the garden, he thought to claim this one as his own. It won't be too many more days before it's eaten. Watermelon has always been his favourite food. I'll never forget going shopping with him when he was two. He became 'the watermelon felon' — the child caught pink-faced in the supermarket trolley. He ate through the plastic and submerged himself in it before I'd realised. I was a good shade of pink too when I'd presented the remainder at the checkout and admitted it had once weighed a good deal more.

He went through such a watermelon-eating phase that it wasn't unusual to find pink poo at the bottom of the potty. He tried a fresh fig today. I told him he'd love it; he didn't look convinced. I told him it was the coolest fruit in the world because it's really an inside-out flower he is eating, and that a tiny little insect must crawl inside a little hole in the end to pollinate it — how cool is that? His suspicion does not lessen.

'My brain tells me it's probably not a good idea', he informs me.

'Tell you brain to go park somewhere else while you try it', I cajole.

Then, giving in, I say the only thing I know will work.

'Caleb, if you eat that fig, it is guaranteed to make you fart — a lot.' He eats it. He decides it's not that bad at all.

Trev and I don the gardening gloves and tackle some major weeding. Trev, who hates weeding, endeavours to make the job interesting by devising another new weeding appliance. He tells me it's his way of maintaining interest in the job. I see it as procrastination: he spends half a day banging around in his 'recycling centre' — where he is known as 'the recycling king' — and emerges triumphant with a cool contraption (and Linda will be so astounded she will fail to recognise that Trevor is using avoidance strategies). I make the mistake five minutes into the job of asking him if he knew what a particular weed was. We spend the next 40 minutes looking it up and failing to find it. Trevor enjoys weed identification far more than extraction. Considering the state of weeds at the moment, it could be confidently said that I too enjoy anything better than weed removal. Every time I close my eyes I see red caustic creeper, cobblers pegs, milk thistle and asthma plant.

I have been christened the Naked Gardener after a recent unplanned streaking episode. I knelt in a colony of jumping ants, all of whom decided to lose themselves somewhere in my dress. They became distressed by the odd jerking movements of the mountain they were climbing and bit it numerous times before it divested itself of its clothing and ran, screaming, to the house. At the moment the only one going naked around here is Caleb, who, at six, is aware his last days of un-inhibition are upon him. And it's hot.

After four long nights of stick-to-the-blanket heat, the cool change seeps into the bedroom and we wake to find someone has filled up the rain gauge with 37 millimetres — hey, what a joke, and look! They've filled both wheel-barrows and topped up the tanks. Neat trick.

10 January

I wake to find Trev shaking his head in quiet dismay. It's his first day back at work. He'd plugged in the electric bike's battery charger, turned it on, and it promptly went up in smoke.

Trev resorts to his low-tech version. He brushes off the cobwebs and pumps up the tyres. As he leaves I yell out my regular line — 'Don't run over any trucks!' Our next-door neighbour is accompanying him for the exercise — Trev is going to get more than he bargained for. While the trip to work won't be too bad with a nice breeze behind him, by the afternoon the cyclone hanging off the coast will provide a rip-roaring bluster for him to ride home against.

The electric bike is still under warranty and I organise a replacement. It should be here in a day or two.

Not having Trev at home and on holiday feels like the end of mine too. No more excuses for lethargy. It's still early when I barter flour with Elsie, who is kind enough to drive to the top of the block and beep so I can run up to do the egg swap. Elsie is 80 and has been bartering for our orange-yolked eggs for a year or so now. She doesn't like driving and can't walk down the steps for a visit but we natter via email fairly frequently — the Internet is now her second home, no agility problems there.

I knead the bread, running off now and then to feed the goat, and watch Caleb roll his own mini-loaf. He decides it's a pizza base, which he inexpertly juggles. Each time he throws it up he yells, 'It's on the house!' and it lands on a different part of it, picking up dust and dirt. I bite my tongue. He is enjoying his game, and we are not yet so desperate for food that the 50-gram piece he is playing with is so important that I have to rant at him. He gives me enough other worthwhile causes to rant — I let it pass.

'Hey Mum?'

'Yes?'

'It really is on the house — see up there, it's stuck.'

Two and a half metres above our heads I can see his pizza peering down from the rafter where it will remain as midnight-feast material for passing cockroaches.

I sigh, 'Caleb, I'll show you how to measure out a level teaspoon'.

We make six loaves, eight mini-loaves, half a dozen cinnamon scrolls (which do not last out the day), two goat's cheese pizzas, a passionfruit and lemon custard tart and a plum shortcake. At Caleb's suggestion we make four Harry Potter wands from skinny dough sticks, bake them and then dip them in icing sugar. White, with green on each end, he takes them down to share with the kids down the road. They look more like oversized matchsticks than wands, but are eaten regardless. We've managed to make baked goods for the next fortnight with only one firing up of the oven, making it efficient utilisation of a big power user. The bake-off uses 4 kilograms of bartered flour, which, like the sugar, has its own energy equation to add to our system.

Producing 1 kilogram of flour uses 1350 litres of water. Based on our usage of 5 kilos of flour a fortnight we're 'using' 482 litres of virtual water per day — a total of over 87,000 litres over the 181 days. As each kilo requires approximately 6 square metres to grow, that's 390 square metres. For six months of flour we'd need to use 18 per cent of our block.

Without the water component we could do it. We have previously grown, harvested, threshed and winnowed, and milled our own wheat, resulting in a 15-muffin feast. They tasted great, but the work involved was formidable. A group of teenage boys arrived just as they came out of the oven and five months of work was laid to waste in five minutes.

VIRTUAL WATER

Imagine walking around a supermarket where every apple, every litre of milk, every item on the shelves has a label showing how much water it took to produce. At the checkout there are two totals on the docket: the cost of the groceries and the amount of water used to produce them. When we pop a lettuce in the supermarket trolley, we might not be carting around the 23 litres of water it took to grow it, but we do carry the shared responsibility for its use.

In the last 10 years there has been an increased awareness of household water use, with urban water usage dropping off. We're now being introduced to a new term: 'virtual water', the amount of water used per person per year in Australia, not just domestically, but also our estimated share of the water required to provide consumer goods and services.

The total amount of water used in Australia for domestic purposes is around 12,000 gigalitres a year – enough to fill the Sydney Harbour 18 times. (One kilolitre (kL) equals 1000 litres; 1 gigalitre (gL) equals 1000 million litres – around 444 Olympic swimming pools.) And, while significant at 8 per cent of total water use, the 12,000 gigalitres used in Australia for domestic use are far less than that used by agriculture, which consumes around 70 per cent.[4]

Agriculture is water-intensive: it takes 1350 litres to grow a kilo of wheat, 900 litres for a kilo of maize, 1000 litres for a litre of milk, 500 for a kilo of potatoes, 140 litres for a cup of coffee and 500 for two eggs.[5] A kilo of rice becomes a great deal heavier when we take into account the 2000–7000 litres it takes to grow in Australia. Figures vary, but it's a generally accepted 16,000 litres for a kilo of beef, while there are estimates of up to 100,000 litres for the feedlot variety.[6]

It seems unbelievable, but once you work out how much grain it takes to 'grow' a kilo of beef, the figures start to make more sense. Vegetarianism is one way we can drastically reduce our water usage.

We also wear vast amounts of water in our clothing: 1 kilo of cotton takes between 7000 and 29,000 litres to produce. A cotton t-shirt requires 760 litres, a 100 per cent cotton queen size sheet uses 6000 litres, and pillowcases, 150 litres.[7] Nudism and sleeping on a dirt floor are other ways to reduce your environmental impact (and your reputation).

We fill our homes with water in the form of consumer goods, from mining the steel in our saucepans, through to the electricity used to manufacture it (mining accounts for 3 per cent of Australia's annual total water usage, while electricity and gas account for 6 per cent). Electricity is generated not just from coal, but by turning water into steam, so every time we turn on the TV we are using water.

It is estimated that an Australian's 'virtual use' of water is about 1.2 million litres per year. But other sources would bring that estimate much higher; the UN Food and Agriculture Organisation estimated a daily cereal diet of 2700 calories per person requires 4300 litres of water per day. Annually that's 1.5 million litres of water derived either from rainfall or irrigation just for a vegetarian diet. Rubbery statistics – you can't always trust them – but they do point us in the direction of being able to say, without too much prevaricating, that our lifestyle requires a hell of a lot of water.

An average vegetable grower in Australia uses 460,000 litres of water to make $100 profit, the fruit grower, 200,000 litres. Dairy products, with their water use incorporated from grain growing, use 500,000 litres; cotton, 760,000; rice, 1,850,000; and pasture a whopping 2,780,000.[8] It makes the focus on household water use look like trying to save a teaspoon full of water out of an overflowing bath. However, the amounts of agricultural water include both irrigation and naturally occurring rainfall, whereas, for the most part, household water is sourced from dams and not from water harvested onsite.

While it might not seem there is a great deal you can do about your share of virtual water use from agriculture and manufacturing, there is. In Australia, we throw away 3.3 million tonnes of food a year. This is an accumulation of everyone's uneaten dinners and the 'left too long in the back of the fridge' mouldy things. Planet Ark estimates that they represent 2000 gigalitres of water use. Take these steps to reduce your virtual water use:

- Buy fresh food more often and in smaller amounts.
- Plan meals ahead to make best use of what's in the fridge.
- Chooks are a great way to use food waste. (Having a Trevor is even better. Trevors can combine the last three nights' dinners into a grey-brown slop, microwave it, cover it in chilli sauce and declare it the best thing Trevor has ever eaten.)
- Grow your own food using water-efficient gardening methods.
- Buy organic produce; organic farms typically use less water.
- Volunteer to plant trees for Landcare and other community groups. Trees are not just about tying up CO_2, but are intrinsically linked to groundwater and riparian (waterway) health.
- Support water-efficient crops by eating them.
- Support companies like Banrock Station – drink their wine. At Banrock Station they use environmental management systems, and support 900 hectares of wetlands and 600 hectares of mallee woodland in the sensitive Murray–Darling Basin. They have donated $2 million since 1998 to Landcare Australia and many other projects around the world. Some of these projects have helped save the regent parrot, freckled duck and green and golden bell frog. I'll drink to that.

- If your favourite wine doesn't come with an environmental policy, write to them and ask why not. This goes for all other food and beverage producers. Consumer-driven corporate social responsibility – they've given it a name now. And it works. Major chicken producers stopped feeding hormones, the egg industry markets free-range chook eggs, not because they think it's healthier or more humane, but through consumer demand.
- Boycott companies with known poor environmental practice, and make sure they know what you're up to.
- Buy products that are designed to last. Ask if they are repairable. With electronic or white goods, generally the length of the warranty and the price are an indication of longevity.
- Choose to repair before buying new items.
- Buy clothes designed to last longer than the current season's fashions.
- Don't buy white clothes, or clothing that requires harsh detergents or chemicals to keep clean.
- Repair clothes. (I know I've been guilty of tossing out shirts that are only suffering a lost button.)
- Recycle clothes, drop them into your favourite charity bin.
- Buy recycled paper products, it's not just trees you're saving, but water. Estimates put it at a saving of 31,400 litres per tonne of recycled paper.

Dinosaur water

It's up to 2 million years old, covers an area of 1.7 million square kilometres (22 per cent of Australia), is between 100–3000 metres deep and stores 64 million gigalitres of water: the Great Artesian Basin.

It's one of the largest aquifer systems in the world and Australia has the tap running on it, in an estimated 1200 megalitre daily flow. Up to 95 per cent of the water that runs in open bores is lost to evaporation and seepage.

Each year around 570 gigalitres are pumped for grazing and, to a lesser extent, mining. As levels drop, so does pressure. In Queensland only 252 out of 519 natural artesian springs are still flowing. The Basin, which extends from South Australia through to the Northern Territory, is being accessed to such an extent that 24 per cent of groundwater-management areas are being used at 70 per cent to 100 per cent of sustainable yield.

In 1999 the federal and state governments, in conjunction with pastoral bore owners, started turning off the taps with the introduction of the Great Artesian Basin Sustainability Initiative. In 2003 there were still 892 uncontrolled bores, mainly in New South Wales and Queensland.

Dinosaur water is part of every Australian's virtual water use.

Trev remarks that there is no room in the fridge. I'm quite proud of the fact. We have a great range of food, so there is no going hungry, yet. Trev would like to see us going desperate for food at least for a short time; he wants to know how we will handle it. I can see his point; it's not going to feel enough of a success if we just breeze through the six months. I look into the garden and into the future and tell him, 'You might not have to wait that long'. If we do get desperate, there are always the arrowroot tubers to eat, the bamboo shoots to hack off, lilli pilli berries to pick and carrot tops to munch on. Even cobblers pegs (*Bidens pilosa*) are supposed to be high in iron and palatable when young. All are legitimate food, but they've been put into the last-resort food group along with snails, though Trevor sees those as quite the opposite.

12 January

The bike battery charger is still not here.

While Trev was at work he had the brilliant idea of pulling some pine sap from a tree to see how it goes as an alternative to chewing gum, another of the lost habits he's been tussling with. Observing Trev do this, his workmates ribbed him with 'starving and reduced to eating pine gum already' jokes. He explains his chewy replacement idea, having already spat the sap onto the ground in disgust. They banter with him.

'Somebody could *buy* a packet of chewy and give it to you ...'

They've also tempted him with, 'Well, if an extra beer was paid for and it was just sitting there, someone would have to drink it'.

It's been the theme of the week: people are arriving on our doorstep with food and even an 18-pack of toilet paper. They come with the best of intentions, not wanting to see us starve or go without. We've even had an offer of chocolate via mail from someone who visits our website frequently. We explain that, if we did accept, it would compromise the integrity of the experiment, and we really want to explore the whole self-denial thing. Thanks all the same, and your kindness has not gone unnoticed etc. etc. A friend accuses me of deliberately not making it easy for ourselves. However, I feel that we have already made various concessions that could impinge on our integrity. The cheese we are eating was made months before the experiment (it takes that long to mature). We finished off the bought goat food in the first week before starting on our own. Perhaps only small things, but we are very conscious of 'cheating'.

The peach-faced lorikeets are having a glorious time eating sorghum and millet, the rainbow lorikeets the sunflowers and, as Trev and I have discovered, the king parrots are enjoying the blue lake climbing beans, fresh from the trellis. For the last few days I've been doing a haka around the block scaring the bloody things off. As a Kiwi, I feel completely at home with the haka, especially the tongue-projecting part. But I am feeble; I cannot compete with their numbers, their stealth and their quiet skill in denuding plants of their protein. I suspect I will be spending the rest of the day adorning the sunflowers with paper-bag hoods, until they stand like rows of condemned men.

Trevor is seen in the garden with a Bart Simpson grin and a homemade shanghai. I value my eyesight too much to take a closer look. Though I resent the theft I wouldn't like to see the birds dead. With Trev's level of accuracy they should be safe.

13 January

Trev arrives home puffed out but triumphant. He has scored. From the roadside he has retrieved an 80-centimetre-long square steel bar.

'But that's not all!' he exclaims, pulling a yellow flannel from his back pocket.

'But, that's not all, there's more!' and he flourishes an unopened packet of 150 cottonwool balls.

I am embarrassed. It's stupid of me, but I am. Last week it was a book of dog stories for Caleb, two drill bits and a tea towel. It cries poverty, and I am loath to look like we are poor. I have theories on this; I call it 'penurism', the fear of poverty. No one has it more than those with money. They have a greater fear of losing it. They want so little part of anything to do with poverty that they reject its symptoms with vigour and its sufferers with disdain, if not horror. Part of that mentality is reflected by our public face: we don't want to appear poor — there's something wrong with you if you are. I am embarrassed about my embarrassment. I accept the proffered gifts without visually shuddering.

Mental note: Picking up stuff off the side of the road is a method of recycling. Recycling is good. Therefore picking stuff up off the side of the road is good.

15 January

I've lain awake all night thinking of things to feed Possum (the uninvited birds are getting the better of our crops). She likes pumpkin (it's 9 per cent protein), chopped up fine with a sprinkle of copra and a splash of make-anything-palatable molasses. I'll have to track down more fodder trees, and try her on the ice-cream bean tree again. She used to like it, but has been spoilt with better tucker and now looks at me pityingly when I present an armload. We've grown 6 kilos of soybeans. They're in glass jars and are waiting for me to get around to making tofu. If we're desperate, the 37 per cent protein level will be a great way to tide over any shortfalls. First, however, they must be cooked — a quick way to a high power-usage week. The figures and foods go around and around in my head. Possum is a problem. She requires around 200 grams of protein in her diet per day; a non-lactating adult requires 30–40 grams.

Trev and I gather some of the prolific male pumpkin flowers that are out in full bloom. In the kitchen I make a light batter with wholemeal and corn flour. I blend around 150 grams of the fetta cheese that is softer and creamier than it should be with chopped onions and chillies. I've never done this before, but it doesn't take long to figure out how to stuff the flowers with the mixture, press them closed, dip them in batter and then drop them in hot oil. I display them artfully to a bemused Trev. They are fantastic. We try Caleb on them, but he's too neo-phobic to eat battered flowers with goat's cheese. Even so, we've added it to the list of popular food items around here. Trev gets desperate to find something Caleb will eat for breakfast other than the usual boring things. He ends up battering and deep-frying a boiled egg. I'm not surprised to find it still sitting on the plate.

After breakfast it's an early morning burst of energy for watering, weeding and pulling up comfrey leaves and thistles and putting them in the liquid fertiliser bucket where they break down, becoming a health tonic for various plants.

I feed the chooks some whey, a handful of copra, kitchen scraps, millet and warrigal greens. By the time I've changed their water, picked a kilo of cherry tomatoes and chopped down a large armful of pigeon pea for Possum, I am sweating profusely. The day kicked off with a feeble blast of heat that's grown stronger by the minute, and by midday we're up to 70 per cent humidity. It's time to take refuge in the house. I prepare kilos of bananas for drying, gather a bucket or so of passionfruit and freeze the pulp in ice-cube trays.

Serendipity strikes. The bananas I prepared for drying are not very sweet, so I dip them in lemon juice to stop them going too dark, then roll them in raw sugar, before placing them in the solar oven. I checked on them an hour later to find the sugar has absorbed water from the atmosphere and they were sitting in a large amount of sugary syrup. I drained it off, and Trev had the idea of trying it out as a cordial — banana and lemon cordial. It's delicious. Caleb, who is getting used to plain water, will have a respite. I will replicate that failure again.

Liquid fertiliser

No hard and fast rules here. It's good to start with a 20-litre (or bigger) lidded bucket. Add water until three-quarters full. Fill a cloth bag with weeds, especially ones like comfrey, nettles and other high-mineral herbs. Throw in a few handfuls of chook poo or other manure (if you're caught short while in the garden, pee in the bucket — it's all good stuff). Suspend the whole smelly mess in the water and add a dash of fish sauce in the form of a ready-made organic liquid fish fertiliser. Lid the bucket then give it a few days to a week to break down. Dilute the resulting brew in more water until it's tea-coloured. Pour over unsuspecting (but no doubt grateful) plants.

16 January

Made another 1.5 kilos of fetta cheese today — not sure it is up to the usual standards; the curd was a little too soft. I tried to ameliorate the flaw by putting it under the press overnight. I have large steel pots of 10–15 litre capacity. I use them like a double boiler, inserting a small one into the larger, which is partially filled with boiling water. The snugger the fit the less water needs to be heated, therefore increasing the efficiency.

The unpasteurised milk is poured in and heated to around 70 degrees and held there for 15 minutes. It's then a question of trying to cool the pasteurised milk down as fast as possible. Out goes the hot water, in goes the cold, along with as many ice cubes as I can fit, and the process goes into reverse. Once the temperature hits the 32-degree mark, it's in with the culture — for fetta and cheddar it's the *Mesophilic lactococcus lactis* subspecies *cremoris* and the *Lactococcus lactis* subspecies *lactis* respectively. Around a quarter of a teaspoon is all that's needed. I blend it in with a sterilised whisk, then add the rennet (in this case a non-animal variety). It's amazing how little is required: 1.6 millilitres, which has been diluted in 10 times its own volume of water, spread over as much of the surface area as possible and whisked into a frenzy for an uninterrupted minute or so, during which my arms ache and, invariably, the phone rings. Then it's left to coagulate. Within minutes, it has become custard-like in texture, but don't stir! Let it go another 60–90 minutes before cutting the curd. A sterilised knife slices it up into cubes 1 centimetre in diameter. It's left to sit a further five minutes before being stirred; the stirring drives more of the whey from the curd and makes it firmer. Leave it an hour (maintaining the same temperature) and stir it again, and then once more an hour after that. The nature of cheese-making is that it's not difficult, or even time-consuming — most of the time it's a case of walk away for an hour and do something else.

Finally, the curds and whey are poured or ladled into lined cheese hoops. I place a board across one of the pots and set the cheese hoops on this so the whey drains into it and becomes tomorrow's chook food.

 Cheese-making was invented as a way to store milk for long periods of time. You were 'a big wheel' if you had a large wheel of cheese. It meant you had many cows; those with many cows were obviously richer than all those 'small wheelers', and therefore more important within the community.

Amazingly, only 10 per cent of the original milk is now curd, so a litre makes approx 100–120 grams. Either I invert the hoops twice in the first hour and then leave till morning or, in the case of a soft curd cheese I've managed to mismanage, lightly press till morning and hope for the best.

Normally it wouldn't be a bother that this cheese is too soft, except this time it's for barter. We already have the 2 litres of sunflower oil and 9 kilos of raw sugar in advance. We're blown out by how much we get in return. Originally we had proposed a calorific equivalent to tie in with our overall energy equation but, as 2 litres of sunflower oil is over 17,000 calories (and around $6), we'd have to supply 4 kilos of fetta, which would take 40 litres of goat milk. Of course, there is always more to the equation. It's taken a lot of calories to feed the goat so she can create the milk we use to make the cheese. Then of course some of that gets fed back to the chooks in the form of whey, further complicating the total calorific equation. We can't begin to figure all the ins and outs, so we revert to approximate cost value, in which case the people with whom we barter feel they're doing well and we feel we are too. Producing 2 litres of oil is arduous and time consuming — we've tried. The 9 kilos of sugar is the same story. It seems amazing that something that requires around 11,800 litres of water to grow could cost so very little. Nutritionally, it has little value; we should stop using it, but our sweet tooths prevail.

Sunflower oil

Sunflower seed is approximately 30 per cent oil, has no cholesterol and is high in vitamin E.

Take a cupful of seed (the black sunflower seeds have higher oil content than the confectionery seed). Heat them in the oven until warm as this will increase the oil yield. Place them in a cheesecloth bag. Use a press with a pressure of 4 tonnes (Trev modified a $20 car jack with welding and elbow grease). Press the seeds in small batches. Collect the oil and let it rest until the sediment has dropped to the bottom. Repeat this process until all the oil is collected. Allow settling overnight. Without disturbing the sediment, draw off the oil using a plastic syringe. Bottle. Appreciate how little 4 litres of oil costs!

Caleb asked me today why it is that everything is made in China. I'd like to say he was at someone else's place when he observed this phenomenon but, no, he was going through next year's school paraphernalia.

'There are a lot of people in China, and a lot of them are very poor, and because they are very poor they will do anything to keep their families fed, and so they end up working for very little, sometimes only a few cents an hour, so they can make things very cheaply and then send what they make to rich countries like Australia, where people, like us, with lots of money, like to buy things cheap. Doesn't seem very fair does it?'

'No.' He puts his fake sable paintbrush down. 'We shouldn't do it.'

I leave the conversation there. Recently, while researching recycling, I found a website showing very distressing images of Chinese people working in 'computer recycling centres' — in other words, slums, where children scramble up hills of computer junk from western countries, and their parents crouch on the ground surrounded by the hulls of monitors, jumbles of wires and broken glass, extracting various parts and, at night, burning the wires to retrieve the copper, thereby releasing and breathing in toxins such as dioxins. The conditions were brutal, the people were blank-eyed and unsmiling.

Caleb had looked over my shoulder at the website and we discussed what was happening in the photographs. He is perturbed by it. And he should be, but I wonder whether too much understanding is good for him. Caleb is becoming an environmental 'warrior' (read tyrant). We once drove past a bakery that had all its lights blazing despite the fact it was closed. He noted this, telling us how bad it was and we agreed. A month later we walk in there to buy something and he marches up to the counter and tells them, 'You shouldn't leave your lights on at night, you're wasting power'.

They looked confused, looked past him and asked us what we'd like.

And watch out should anyone attempt to provide us with one of those almost weightless stretches of plastic in which one can legitimately place the smallest item for its brief trip back to the car.

'We do not use plastic bags, *thank you.*' His glare is quite unsettling.

I want him to be aware of, not oblivious to, the injustice in the world. Yet at the same time I myself find it hard not to be overwhelmed by the huge discrepancies in what different countries call an average lifestyle, and wonder if he's old enough to be burdened with these complications, which regularly prove too much for most adults. Then I think of the children who don't have to live with the concept, but with the reality. Upon his little shoulders can rest a little more.

CONSUMERISM VERSUS HUMANITARIANISM

Consider the priorities in global spending in 1998:[9]

GLOBAL PRIORITY	$US BILLIONS
Basic education for everybody in the world	6
Cosmetics in the United States	8
Water and sanitation for everyone in the world	9
Ice-cream in Europe	11
Reproductive health for all women in the world	12
Perfumes in Europe and the United States	12
Basic health and nutrition for everyone in the world	13
Pet foods in Europe and the United States	17
Business entertainment in Japan	35
Cigarettes in Europe	50
Alcoholic drinks in Europe	105
Narcotic drugs in the world	400
Military spending in the world	780

Today I served Caleb pancakes with the plum jam we're all into right now. We lay out on the trampoline and talked about nothing much at all. When I leave he calls out, 'Thanks for giving me some attention, Mum'.

Smart bugger — but I do tend to leave him to his own devices a lot. I'm always around, but it's usually doing something other than filling in his every second. If he gets bored, I feel guilty, but I wait till he inevitably rediscovers both his brain and something to do.

The passionfruit vine is definitely on the wane. It's dying back at an alarming rate, doing something it should have done in winter, but didn't. Now it's bearing prolifically while doing the deciduous thing. I'm not yet sure if it's a permanent death or one of those temporary anomalies. I pick all the passionfruit that are halfway ripe and the scattering of those on the ground and de-pulp them. I get around a litre, which I freeze for later. Normally I'd make passionfruit butter, which is a favourite of ours, but without good old high-fat cow's butter, it's not going to be.

Passionfruit butter

50 grams butter
3/4 cup sugar
1 cup passionfruit pulp
2 eggs, beaten

Melt the butter in a double boiler. Stir in sugar and juice until the sugar has dissolved. Add eggs. Stir until the mixture thickens (this can take half an hour to an hour). Pour into sterilised jars.

Makes approx 500 grams and tastes fantastic as a sauce on ice-cream.

It's difficult, but not impossible, to make goat's butter. The milk is naturally homogenised due to the smaller sized globules of fat, which disperse more readily and are less likely to rise to the top than the fat in cow's milk. It can be done, but that would leave us with a lot of skim milk — and Caleb needs all the fat he can get. Plus the butter tends to go goat-flavoured after a week. We're still in a reasonably early milk with Possum. She came into milk in September when she kidded Vanilla and Chocolate. When we started milking her for ourselves in November (having found V and C a home), we were getting up to and sometimes over 4 litres a day; now we've settled in to the 3-litre average, which suits us fine. We drink a litre a day; the rest is kept frozen or refrigerated until we have 10 litres, when we turn it into cheese.

The taste of goat's milk is different from cow's. It's sweeter, though I'm told that different goats have different tastes and you should always taste the milk of a goat you are intending to buy. We didn't, and we were lucky, though she does have small teats, a sloped rump and a bellow that can be heard near and far. Not all goats are as noisy as Possum — it's the breed. Chalk that up to experience. But having said that, Possum is a nice goat, as affectionate as she is demanding. When I grab her brush, she rushes to stand on a nearby platform and closes her eyes ready for the pleasure of having her back brushed, and especially, ohhh yes, right between the horns. When I bend down to fetch the eggs in the laying box there's often a little nibble on my ear, or she'll gently grab my shirt and give it a pull or, on a hot day, Trev becomes a living salt block, much to his amusement.

20 January

Cool yet humid day — had a burst of energy and cleaned out all the various chook pens, collected the poo and spread it around plants lacking a little oomph: at this point, most of the zucchinis, watermelons and rockmelons. Yesterday we finally had enough of the constant bickering going on in the goat-cum-chook pen between the two new chooks and Light and Dark Orange, as we refer to them, who are the long-time residents. They've been heckling the two newcomers without mercy since they first arrived. We had hoped it would settle down, but no luck, and, while they have laid an egg each, they still aren't on the lay. We figure the stress of so much workplace bullying has taken its egg production toll, and we moved Light and Dark Orange into a vacant chook pen. Today Dark Orange kept appearing in the garden, having freed herself from what I had always considered an escape-proof pen. She'd squeezed through a tiny break Possum had made in the wire. I've stuffed a fertiliser bag in the hole until I come up with a better idea, which probably amounts to telling Trev about it.

Wash Day today — we use a twin-tub. People always seem aghast at the idea, but it beats any other machine for water use every time. Our practice is to use one 35-litre tub of water for four consecutive loads and, when they've all been through, drain the dirty, soapy water, pour in another 35 litres of clean water to which we add a few drops of tea tree oil, and then rinse them through. The first wash for all the delicate clothes, progressing through to Trev's work gear and the towels.

With 75 litres of water to wash around four loads of washing, a top loader would use around 600 litres. It's certainly more time-consuming with a twin-tub, yet we don't stand around watching it; we do nearby jobs and keep an ear out for the end of the cycle. We've saved tanks of water using this method. It takes 150 litres a week to do the washing where we once used 1200. We get our clothes clean by using solar hot-water and a homemade gel that is fragrance-free, uses no optical brighteners and is made from a small amount of Sunlight soap, washing soda, herbs and lots of water. The transition from the top loader to the twin tub was not an arduous thing. We both admit to enjoying getting 'closer' to the process of getting clothes clean. We could also be considered quite mad.

Laundry gel[10]

---

100 grams Sunlight soap, grated
120 grams washing soda
water
bunch sweet-smelling herbs and leaves such as lemon verbena, tea tree and eucalyptus

Fill a bucket with hot water to the 8-litre mark. Add the herbs and leaves. Place the grated soap in a pot with another litre of water. Heat while stirring until the soap has melted. Add the washing soda. Quickly add the mixture to the bucket of scented water and continue to stir until the mix is well blended. Allow to cool and set.

1 to 2 cups per load washes effectively in warm to hot water.

Sprayed the citrus with white oil for sooty mould in some vain hope that it might also help with citrus leaf miner. It's another homemade recipe. The grapefruit is suffering badly from lack of nutrients, gall wasp, leaf miner and scale. (Actually, I've been trying to kill it off for a few years now. Quietly that is.) It's also the citrus that gets the worst of the fruit fly. In my book that should mean 'the chop', but Trev is fond of grapefruit.

Homemade white oil

1 tablespoon vegetable oil
1 teaspoon soap

Blend the two together and then dilute with a litre of water. Spray onto affected plants, taking care not to apply during the heat of the day or in bright sunlight as it may burn the leaves. The soap allows the oil to penetrate the insects' protective coat, which effectively suffocates them.

We do have a fruit tree death happening at the bottom of the garden, the cause of which is known. Last week the council came around killing off the leucaena that grows wild on the side of the road. Mains Road land. However, one larger leucaena was hiding in with one of my mulberries, a little higher up on our block. I'd been chopping it back and feeding it to the goat for quite some time. The council managed, in their exuberance, to kill both. It was one of Possum's favourites.

Caleb discovered a new computer game and has only surfaced four or five times today, usually to babble on about what is happening in it; a case of smile sweetly, nod my head and offer him more food. Today it's been hot chocolate and plum jam on toast, followed by banana smoothie and watermelon. I gathered a kilo of yellow pear and sweet bite cherry tomatoes, four lonely eggs, a kilo of plums (nearly the last), and a large bucket of millet and sorghum heads. Later I'll dash out for greenskin and golden zucchini, carrots, leeks, capsicum and a handful of beans. These will be sliced, along with a few onions and potatoes from the cupboard, before being dipped into a small quantity of wholemeal batter and pan-fried till golden, served in a stack with a heavy-handed pour of the freshly made chunky tomato and chilli sauce, which Caleb will gracefully decline, and topped with fresh parsley and chives. For dessert it's a chocolate mousse, made mostly to use up some of the extra ricotta cheese getting around. What I like about our dinners is that I can confidently say, 'You know, Caleb, 20 minutes ago your dinner was still growing'.

'Yeah, I'm watching *Doctor Who*, Mum.'

21 *January*

Hot. Caleb and I walk to the local shop and back after the owner rings with a computer problem. I try to make the walk interesting by giving him the pedometer to wear, but his dainty steps don't always register on it. We play our usual games, plus a few new ones. We have a stand of hibiscus trees that has grown in the shape of arches. We walk through at the same time and into another world. Each time we do there is a different game to play; either we are both invisible and can't see each other, tripping over each other, or Caleb has a twin and I must interrogate both Calebs to try to decide which is the correct one. Once discovered, the 'impostor' falls to the ground and can be 'seen' shooting sparks from his ears and arse. Today we are transported into the world of *Doctor Who*; I'm the doctor, of course, and Caleb is Sarah Jane Smith. We play our roles as we search for the missing intergalactic rock that will save the universe. When we arrive at the shop we are sweating profusely. I fix the owner's computer problem in 20 seconds and Caleb and I walk back home. Caleb begins to lag, declaring himself hopelessly dehydrated. I cheer him up with another familiar game. It has its roots in simple counting: 'How many four-wheel drives can we count before we get home?', but it changed over time, when Caleb decided counting them wasn't as fun as shooting them. Occasionally I see someone wave to him as he does. We get back home and invest time in some serious re-hydration.

I spend several hours in the garden watering and feeding the goat and chooks, and then retreat to the house. Trevor made a declaration this morning.

'I can't stand this, I can't wait for it to be over. I am a gourmand, I like my food. I drive into service stations to fill up the work vehicle and I have to walk past hot chips.'

He's only half serious, but I don't laugh.

'I drive past the pie van and then the peanut van in Nanango. I'm hungry all the time.'

I'm annoyed. I have been making nice meals, taking pains to give him variety, spice, 'meaty' meatless meals and lots of them. He makes his own breakfast, makes his own lunch. There is plenty of food — if you're hungry, take more.

'Still', he says, 'we won't give up'. It's difficult for him; the dens of iniquity have been taking their toll, luring him from the roadside.

'Yesterday', he says, 'I walked into the smoko room and someone had left a packet of full-strength cigarettes on the table. I was seriously tempted to take one'.

On the brighter side, he's passed the 1000-kilometre mark on his 'leccy bike'.

Strangely, except for a few stray twinges of Vanilla Coke fantasies, I've not missed anything really. A couple of times I've felt the urge to jump in the car and take Caleb somewhere. But that's mostly guilt inspired.

I go nowhere. I have not felt the cool of an airconditioner. I have not said, 'Oh bugger this, it's hot and I can't be bothered cooking, let's go grab something' in, heck, 20 days.

The chooks are not getting any better at pushing out oval, calcium-covered oblongs: one from each of the three pens today, and Trev has resigned himself to a cull. The old chooks are eating lots of our resources, but are not paying their dues.

The parrots are making headway into every high-protein seed we have, so Caleb and I try our hands at making a scarecrow. As I couldn't find any suitable stiff material, we assembled him from a pair of old pants with the legs sewn closed, stuffed him full of newspaper, and then did the same with the arms and waist of my old black shirt. We stiffened his resolve a little with a piece of PVC pipe stuck down his neck, a bag stuffed with newspaper for a head, sunglasses, sunhat and, due to his indolent nature, sat him on an old chair, where he slumps forward dejectedly, no doubt pondering what it was his maker was thinking of when she stuffed his right leg so full, while his left leg is such a shrivelled meatless thing. We've yet to see if the parrots care a fig ... oh yes, they're eating those too.

Dinner was a bang-up meal of pancakes layered with chunky tomato sauce, goat's cheddar sauce, onion fried with fresh ground coriander, garlic chives and parsley. Caleb ate a sliced zucchini raw; it's the only vegetable bar carrots he likes.

Tomorrow will be the dawning of a new era — it will be the first time we cull the chooks, cull being an interesting word that sounds very much like what happens, especially if you're a Kiwi. This has been the subject of many a late-night debate. I was the first to raise the concept, the first to raise concerns, and probably would be the very last to raise the axe. I did, in all honesty, offer to do the deed, as I know Trevor is dreading it, but I never, in all honesty, expected him to accept.

22 *January*

Today I selected the victims, judging them by their lack of feathers and the lack of lustre in their combs as being the oldest in the flock. Trevor did the deed quickly, and with a freshly sharpened machete. I fed those on reprieve lots of juicy titbits to distract them from the execution. Caleb came to witness, but managed only the briefest of seconds before fleeing to the house. I watched him on the way past, his hand over his mouth, gagging. Trev did the plucking, gutting, and cooking of the poor old things and later that night Caleb was happy to chew, and I mean a real case of major mastication, on the bits of chook now nestled in fried rice. Fully aware of what and who it had once been, he said it was nice and there was no point wasting good food. I just wish he felt that way about vegetables. My share found itself ostracised on the side of my plate and Trevor, who's not keen on wastage either, wore down his teeth on them instead.

There is heavy rainfall north and south of here, but we're deep into a dry patch.

Trev and I weighed ourselves and were happy to find we have both lost weight. Trev 2 kilos and I'm not far behind. Already my food consciousness is changing. I don't just go for the sweet and fatty food (there isn't much), but select instead what we have an avalanche of. Caleb gets all the best bits. I have no doubt this is the kind of attitude pioneers had. It's a constant preoccupation with amounts of food, and whether the children are getting enough. I'm always trying to gauge what I am entitled to eat when I open the fridge. I like the figs — they're mine. Caleb loves watermelon, so Trev and I hold off and let him eat as much as he likes. Trev is going orange around the gills from all the pawpaws. He's always been good at eating leftovers and gluts. For me it's a new thing. I'm becoming attracted to different foods; I sometimes crave a plum — before it would have been an ice-cream or soft drink. It's been only 22 days. But, as they say, new habits require just 20 days to take. I have never been into self-denial — my self-discipline is a wasted and shrivelled organ — and yet now, when the rules have been made and the degree of embarrassment if we fail secured (I had to go public, otherwise I'd never be able to shame myself into going this far), I seem to be able to handle it. Already I've gone 18 days longer than I've ever managed to go without spending money. With luck on our side we will still be at it next month, and perhaps several kilos lighter yet again. The world's most elaborate diet has begun.

24 January

First day of school. It's up at 5.30 am to milk the goat, feed the chooks, make breakfast and lunches, back out to water the garden, read Caleb a chapter of *Charlie and the chocolate factory* and reassure him for the 200th time that there's no point worrying about what will and will not happen at school until it does.

'I mean, I could worry about a bee flying into my mouth when I walked around talking, but it doesn't stop me talking does it?'

'Nothing would', he replies.

Today is a big day in Caleb's world. I plonk him on my bike, where he perches, complaining about getting serious wedgies, and I walk him to school offering soothing words about how there's no point in worrying, but he won't buy a word of it. He's just like me; my preaching will not overcome my practice ...

I bike back home on my $2 retrieved-from-the-dump treadly. I enjoy coasting down the hills, and even stand on the pedals to build up speed for the big climbs. I'm panting by the time I make the big hill up to the house.

I have a great garden day. I plant snake and blue lake beans and carrots; plant out tomatoes and eggplants; weed; feed the chooks titbits; and give Possum a nice long brush. I make Caleb some passionfruit cordial, and make up pikelet batter and refrigerate it for later. I make a kilo of flat bread mix and begin rolling and cutting the pieces, gently cooking them on both sides. Tonight will be kebab night. The beans are on the simmer. I recall saying to Trev a while back, 'We'll have to have vegetarian kebabs tonight, I don't have time to cook the beans'.

'Hate to tell you', he smiles, 'but most people consider beans to be vegetarian'.

'Oh yeah.' My spicy bean mix is meant to be a meat substitute; obviously it's worked well, at least in my head.

I bike back the 2 kilometres to school, and pick up an ecstatic Caleb.

'It's been fantastic!' he says.

I sit him on the seat and push him most of the way home while he tells me about his day. At home I make him pikelets with plum jam and pour him a passionfruit drink. We sit out on the trampoline under the trees and eat them and read more of *Charlie and the chocolate factory*. This is a big reason why we're doing what we are. Caleb was 18 months old when I went back to work with a government-funded project as a computer trainer, travelling around south-east Queensland visiting people in their home to teach them the basics of internet and email (and in the process gaining an unwarranted reputation as a remover of viruses). It meant a week away from Caleb to begin with and then continued to be two to three nights a week spent in motel rooms for the next three and a half years. I left home at 7 am and either didn't come home or not till well after dark. Then he'd crawl all over me for cuddles or treat me like dirt for deserting him in daycare for up to 10 hours a day. We quickly realised that Trev was the only one who could drop him off at daycare without him screaming, 'Mummy, mummy, mummy!' all day. Ten out of 10 on the guilt scale. Life was about hurrying, being late, high stress levels and sitting in a motel room at night talking to him on the phone, his wee voice asking me where I was and when I was coming home. Or refusing to speak to me. He was feeling abandoned. Every time I stayed away I came home with a present. But it didn't make up for all the missing out he was doing. Finally, the day came when it ended. We all made great sighs of relief and paid the last of what had been the considerable expense of around $26,000 in daycare fees over the period.

During that time we'd been putting as much time and money as we could afford into building up the garden, installing solar hot-water, solar panels, rainwater tanks and the composting loo, dreaming about being at home all day, going nowhere, speaking to no one unless we chose to and doing things with Caleb. Finally those days have come. Well, for most of us, anyway.

A while back, when Caleb was exercising his right not to behave, I threatened him with daycare. Should have seen him run to do what he was asked. It was a good demonstration of how much it meant to him to be at home too. On Mother's Day last year he crawled into bed at 5 am and gave me a cuddle and a handmade pressie and whispered in my ear, 'I don't want you ever to go to work again'.

I'm doing my best. While I'm at home I do very little socialising, apart from school drop-offs, a yak over the fence to the neighbours and a bit of front-yard bartering. I don't feel isolated. I don't crave 'going' somewhere (going somewhere equals spending money), apart from the local library, which is at the bottom of the longest, steepest hill in town, and the idea of having to lug a pile of books back up it on a hot day has seen me going though my bookshelves and rediscovering all the books I'd bought but not read over the last five years.

Vegetarian kebabs

Filling

2 cups kidney beans, soaked overnight

2 teaspoons ground coriander

2 teaspoons ground cumin

salt and pepper to taste

toppings such as onion, tomato, pineapple, grated carrot,
cheese and fresh herbs

sauce such as chilli sauce or hommus

Chapattis

2 cups plain flour

1 teaspoon salt

$^1/_2$ cup water

oil (or butter)

Simmer beans for 45 minutes. Drain. Use a stick blender to blend the beans with a little water until you get a paste that is thick but still chunky. Add coriander, cumin and salt and pepper to taste, then set aside.

To make chapattis, sift flour into a bowl and add salt. Add half the water and mix with your hand to form a dough. You may need to add more water depending on the flour used. Knead well. Divide dough into six balls (for larger chapattis to serve three) or eight (for smaller chapattis to serve four), and roll each out into a thin circle on a floured surface. (For a perfect circle, you can place a sandwich plate on top and cut around with a knife.)

Heat a pan over moderate heat. Brush pan with oil or butter and cook chapattis one at a time until golden brown on each side.

To serve, smear bean mix down the centre of a chapatti, then add toppings and sauce. Roll chapatti firmly and cook in a sandwich press. Eat while hot.

It seems like a lot of work, but if you make more than required you can assemble meals for the next three days in less than three minutes. The bean mix tastes like spicy mince to me. (Trev guffaws loudly in the background.)

Serves 3 to 4.

25 January

Discovered that the coffee jars someone gave me are not suitable for preserving – I now have 8 kilos of off plums, peaches and apples. I am not very happy. Caleb is with me when I make the discovery.

'We're going to starve! Oh no, this is bad, this is really bad', he laments.

While it doesn't mean starvation, it's a complete waste of food – emergency fruit that was to tide Caleb over if we had a shortfall or a lack of variety. I wonder if I should give it to the chooks, or whether it will kill them. I've looked up botulism and now I'm worried about dipping my finger in and licking it. Trev, however, reckons it tastes OK. He thinks anything with mould on it means Roquefort. I'm watching him closely for signs of paralysis, staggering and slurring.

I bartered fetta cheese for a tray of mangoes and some grapes. This should tide us over until the next lot of watermelons come on. We're going to be swimming in them soon. I have failed in the succession planting. I planted them around two weeks apart for a period of two months, but failed to note that the different varieties had different maturation times, so now they're all going to be coming on at once.

Today has been showery, so I thought I'd make a dash for school during a lull, and managed to bike straight into the heaviest shower of the day. I arrived soaked but exhilarated. 'Hi, I'm here for the wet t-shirt competition – where's everyone else?'

Caleb sits on the bike while I push it home. He likes to slouch there, hands free, wobbling the bike dangerously in his efforts to shoot more four-wheel drives.

I baked today – four loaves, eight mini-loaves, 20 cinnamon scrolls, four jam roly-poly buns, two pizzas and a caramel pumpkin dessert, which, later on, is covered in a thin sticky toffee sauce and served up to lots of yum noises.

It's continuing to shower, but is amounting to very little, enough to get the ground damp and little else. The rest of Queensland, as usual, is getting more than we are. I gird myself for the forecasts of weather evil that Trev will espouse.

Cinnamon scrolls

2 tablespoons butter
2 tablespoons cinnamon
2 tablespoons brown sugar
500 grams plain flour
2 teaspoons dried yeast
2 tablespoons sugar
around 1 cup water

In a microwave zap the butter, cinnamon and sugar until melted. Set aside to cool.

In a bowl combine the flour, yeast, sugar and enough water to turn it into a dough. On a floured bench knead the dough until smooth and elastic. Return it to the bowl, cover with a tea-towel and set in a warm place until the dough has roughly doubled in size.

Preheat oven to 180°C. Knock the dough back, then roll out until it is a rectangle around 1 centimetre thick. Spread the melted cinnamon mixture across the dough. With a sharp knife cut the dough into 3-centimetre strips. Roll each strip into a scroll and place on a greased baking tray. Bake until just golden, then whip them out and wait as long as you can before burning your lips on one. A decent smothering of more butter is always good.

Makes approximately 10 to 12 scrolls.

26 January

Trev is espousing.

It drizzles; I gather up food for Possum, who manages to eat it as fast as she can, hops back into her house and peers at us up on the verandah, bellowing occasionally in case we forget to bring her more. Thank god for all the pigeon pea. A native to India, it's a high-protein leguminous plant that, when inoculated, fixes soil nitrogen. It handles the heat and is relatively drought-resistant. I pick a 5-litre bucket of cherry tomatoes, and check out the other 5 kilos in the fridge. It's time I got out a big pot and made pasta sauce. But after my previous failures I have botulism stories running through my brain. Botulism can shield itself from high temperatures and live in the absence of air but, thankfully, it doesn't like high-acid environments like tomatoes. I steel myself and sort through them; the slightly blemished, the over-ripe or the misshapen are all tossed into the pot, blended with pepper, salt, sugar and vinegar, brought to the boil, left to simmer for 20 minutes or so, then thickened with a tad or two of cornflour. Normally I'd have added onions and capsicums and herbs but, as they are low acid and I'm feeling paranoid, they will be added to the pasta dish fresh. If you think I'm over the top, try out the story of the woman who dipped her finger into a jar of canned carrots, decided it tasted odd so didn't feed it to her guests. Two days later she was close to death with respiratory paralysis. On writing 'carrots' on a piece of paper, they identified the cause and gave her the antidote; she didn't die. Not so lucky was the mouse who was fed some of the suspect carrots and subsequently keeled over, as did the mouse who was fed a sample of the afflicted woman's blood; death was almost instantaneous. Great stuff.

Rainy weather is good weeding weather; they are easy to pull from the softened ground. Trev and I go out for a weed pull and a snail gather. Trev is keen for another go at the gourmet gastropods. I want to get some ground ready for spring onions, Hungarian wax capsicums and more beans. Perfect weather for planting. We figure we'll pick a nice lull in the drizzle, only to find ourselves half an hour later labouring in a downpour. Already wet, we plough on through till Trevor's radio is in danger of drowning. We pull back, retreating to the verandah where Possum spies us and bellows, as if to say, 'Get back down here and feed me more!'

Trev cleans off the snails we gathered and puts them in his snail box, a well-ventilated area from which they cannot escape nor touch the ground. In a week they'll be ready to come out for the next stage in their journey to escargot.

I'm sure he'd eat worm brain stew if only they gave it a French name. At dusk I go on a snail-harvesting mission expecting multitudes of huge snails, but find only a few. What has happened? Between Trev and the chooks, are snails on the endangered list?

We have a tortured history with snails. In the flood of 1999 we had a plague of them, eating everything edible and even a few inedible things, like the mail.

We called a war counsel. We were not prepared to use poisons for all the usual reasons, such as the possibility that birds will eat the poisoned snails, or that traces of poison could enter the soil. Trevor invented the Ex-snailibur, a piece of dowel with a wedge stuck to the end.

When Caleb went to bed, we donned our safety gear (torches and shoes so as not to get gummed up in the remains of our fallen enemy), armed ourselves with an Ex-snailibur each, then stomped off to crush them in what turned out to be quite a therapeutic means by which to reduce the snail population and avoid the negative ions emitted by the TV.

We invited all those who dined with us to join in this activity. Our somewhat-anxious guests soon discovered that snail extermination was almost addictive and came armed with their own versions of the Ex-snailibur. We adopted the motto 'Friends who slay together, stay together'. Not sure they would have been quite so keen if I'd suggested we pick them up, put them in a bucket and meet up the following week for a chewy, gooey meal.

We also made the mistake of telling local children that if they collected snails we would pay them 2 cents a snail. We were presented with a full 10-litre bucket and a request that we please count them ourselves. They ended up crushed and placed in the liquid compost bucket to provide extra calcium, and got stuck in my watering can for the next six months.

At one stage, I tried to discover if the bright green faecal matter of the snail could possibly be the next big thing, like worm castings, but no one seemed to know its nutrient content. All I knew was they did a lot of it. Given that they also like large amounts of paper (considering the half-eaten remains in the letterbox), they could be a welcome addition to the composting world.

I guess the snails were the first problem we came across that we could give a positive slant to. I would never have thought, five years ago, that I'd find myself taking an interest in the nutritional value of snails.

NUTRITIONAL VALUE OF SNAILS[11]

Based on 100 grams of edible snail meat:

Energy (cal)	80.5
Protein (g)	16
Water (g)	79
Fibre (g)	0
Fat (g)	1
Available carbohydrate (g)	2
Magnesium (mg)	250
Calcium (mg)	170
Iron (mg)	3.5
Vitamin A	1.5%
Vitamin C	1.5%

Snails also contain traces of zinc, copper, potassium and iodine, and 9 of the 10 essential amino acids

Trevor has confiscated the off fruit, claiming he will make cider vinegar out of it. I bah humbug it, but let him sidle out the door. It will be interesting if it works, but somehow I doubt it. Hopefully the fumes aren't toxic.

The rain has settled in and is determined to make some headway into the soil. I'm looking forward to hearing it on the roof all night — gentle, steady, soaking rain. Tomorrow it will be a joy to see the tanks overflowing, the rain gauge's open mouth gargling on glorious rain and to sink a garden fork in and see how far it goes.

Trev and Caleb stood at the door lamenting our inability to go buy a few videos, chips, soft drink and other munchies. Then Caleb announced in a giant-sized voice, 'When this is over, I am going to buy a bottle of lemonade with my money ... No, I'm not, I'm going to buy bottles of every kind of lemonade there is!'

Trev told me today that he has had to sit next to a guy he works with and watch him eat takeaway. I'm sure the person in question is as unsettled by this as Trevor obviously is. I'm not sure I could handle that too well. As it is, I had a huge craving for chocolate today and ended up settling for very hot chocolate custard with mango. Caleb and I devoured it. It's a cool and rainy day — we should be lying around reading books, not outside weeding and gathering snails.

27 January

We had to bring Possum up under the house to milk her this morning; it's too wet and mucky in her pen. I cleaned out her house yesterday afternoon, as she had stood in it all day, looking out at the rain, periodically lifting her tail and doing the half squat without thought of the consequences. Goats are supposed to be intelligent, but either they don't care if they lie in their own poo or they are incredibly dumb. Trev has made a Possum-house scraper, and I use this to scrape the said poo into a bucket and plonk it around plants. I did this yesterday and twice again this morning. I even layered her flooring with newspaper to try to make it more comfortable, but she just went on and did more. Then she bellows at me, looks up at the house and says, 'I've eaten grain, half a fat pumpkin, pigeon pea, arrowroot, lab-lab, but give me MOOOORRRE!'

Trev and I finally agree that, while we make and eat award-winning cheeses and yoghurts and enjoy fresh unpasteurised milk, she is getting to the point of intolerable. She needs other goats and to stop thinking we're the herd without horns. It's not fair on her either; though she is spoilt rotten, I'm sure she would be happier on a bigger block. We'll hang her out till the end of the six months and then think hard about what we will do.

We've had 38 millimetres in the last 24 hours, which has the tanks overflowing again, and the soil moisture is good. You can almost hear those dry roots sucking. Caleb and I make a break for school and discover halfway there that his school jacket is only partially waterproof. I don't have one and am beginning to feel so constantly damp that I'm in danger of going mouldy. It continued to rain steadily until I threw the bike in the bushes at the top of the block and made a squelching run for the house. The moment the door closed behind me, someone turned off the tap. Change of clothes number two for the day.

Took advantage of soil moisture and planted (what seemed like) several thousand onion seeds, daikon, squash, rockmelons, sugarbaby watermelon, lemon cucumber, chillies and pak choi. I am woefully behind with planting carrots and onions. I've had so many failures getting them to germinate during the hot weather. They don't like temperatures above 25 degrees and this time of year we don't get many days that drop below that. There will be a gap, during which I will have to admit failure and serve no carrots or onions for quite some time. We still have around 4 kilos of our onions in the cupboard, but we are onion fans, and I'm not sure how long they will last. There are plenty of leeks and carrots still growing, and several thousand carrots sprouted a week or so ago. But they take a long time to mature, and the newest sprouting is still three months away from eating. Thankfully, someone finally gave me the clue I needed to get germination happening. I cover the sown soil with wet hessian so the seeds don't get washed away, the sun doesn't curdle their little hearts, and the moisture is retained.

I better go sow several thousand more carrots, beans and millet, do some weeding, and throw more food at the goat.

28 January

I smell a rat. Unfortunately, it's literal rather than figurative and it's festering somewhere in the walls. The only room it is noticeable in is our bedroom and, as the day heats up, the stench becomes unbearable. I light one incense stick after another. We've already searched the roof space. Nothing there. Under the house, nothing there either. We contemplate setting up a mosquito net on the verandah until the miasma clears.

'How many days does it take a rat to decompose?'

'Depends, I guess, on the size of the rat.'

Last night I heard something on the verandah and, by the vague light of the moon, I thought I saw a cat sitting there. It scurried the moment I arrived. Now I'm wondering. Then there's the pumpkin in the garden showing signs of having been gnawed at with bigger-than-mouse-sized teeth. Rats are attracted to the grain that inevitably spills when we hand-grind it. I hate rats, but worse than rats are the brown snakes they attract and we have only just removed one of those. We set the rat traps.

31 January

Caleb crosses off the last day of the month and declares, 'I've had enough of this experiment, let's stop'.

'Why, what is it you'd like to buy?'

I know he was surfing the Lego website only 10 minutes previously and has seen the new range.

'Oh, nothing really.' He smiles coyly.

'Oh well, then why stop if we don't want to buy anything?'

'I could probably think of something', he says, tapping his front teeth, which are loose. He's not lost a single tooth so far; what's the bet the whole lot will go in the six months and the toothfairy will come with money that will burn a hole in his pocket the size of Mars. The other day we were talking chocolate. Nothing too desperate, just thinking of eating whole buckets of it, when he says, 'It's all right, Mum, just wait till the Easter Bunny gets here. I reckon he'll give us lots'.

'Oh, um, yes, I'm sure he will.' Furtive glances are exchanged over his head. Then simultaneously we both nod. Who are we to ruin this particular fantasy?

I'd failed to think of such consumer-ridden events as Easter.

Trev stayed at home with AF — not surprising as he worked out in the glaring sun all day yesterday and finally came in shivering — usually the first sign of sunstroke. It was almost inevitable that it would trigger AF, and it did.

Over the weekend he has welded up (from scraps, a little bit of this and a little bit of that) a bike seat and handlebars for the back of my bike. Now I can plonk Caleb on it and bike him to school in half the time. Only I'm scared. How will the bike handle? I don't want to crash with both of us on board. How will I successfully manage steep slopes, loose gravel and the constant flow of 80-kilometre-per-hour traffic? We take it for a test run.

'Whooooooohooooo!' he screams from the back.

'Stop wobbling, sit still, hold on, keep your feet on the pegs, if I say jump, jump!'

We manage a circuit of the street and survive. He's currently 25 kilograms, a considerable weight to add. Trev accompanied us to school, riding his mountain bike so as not to have me at too much of a disadvantage. We made it in 10 minutes, instead of the usual half-hour walking. We walked some of the uphill parts. And, apart from a few admonishments for shooting four-wheel drives (not that there is anything wrong with that apart from the lack of hands on handlebars and the extra wobble factor), it was uneventful.

Trev says as we walk up one hill, 'So now we're off the experiment, Mummy and I can go out and spend money today. What do you want to get?'

Caleb is horrified. 'You're not going to give in!'

'But you said you wanted to stop.'

'It's all right,' he says, 'we can keep going'.

Trev and I race each other home and arrive out of breath. I've been watching his rear end — it's considerably smaller than usual. It's even fitting inside a pair of shorts he'd bought years ago that turned out to be a few sizes too small. I tell him he looks younger, and he does. He calls me saggy pants, because all my pants suddenly are. He doesn't seem to be aware that I have given him a compliment, and he hasn't returned it. He hides away in his recycling centre, coming out only to make himself tomato soup with fetta, snails and flecks of chilli powder floating in it. He yums and hums to himself with pleasure, while I find it, suddenly, at the sight of the snails, just too early in the day to eat.

I spend several hours hammering a board to the side of Caleb's Bionicles bed, then hammering nails into it and dangling bits and pieces of Bionicles off the nails in an effort to put them into some kind of order. It will make it easier to assemble them, and might increase his interest level. Right now he's going through a watch TV and play computer games phase, and I'm not prepared to let the phase last very long. I can't buy him new Bionicles, but maybe this will do the trick. I'd rather not lay down the law, but lure him away with an activity in which a few brain cells can bang against each other. Yesterday I read him the chapter about Mike Teevee in *Charlie and the chocolate factory*. Brilliant, those oompah loompahs really got it right. I've already explained to him that when he watches TV his brain activity is less than if he was asleep. He merely bends his head around me so he can watch some tacky cartoon.

During the day I harvest what sorghum and sunflowers the parrots have left. Then water gardens, feed chooks, weed, sweep, mow the lawn and make 2 litres of yoghurt. I could live on it. A cup of yoghurt, a tablespoon of honey, a dash of vanilla, some ice, use the stick blender, and — *voila* — a meal (otherwise known as lassi, a delicious Indian yoghurt drink). I then bike back and pick Caleb up.

Dinner tonight is Celebratory Make-in, the opposite of Takeaway. Kebabs again — vegetarian-style with spiced beans and chilli sauce. The end of the first month and we have had rain, eaten well, lost weight and our consumer addictions have not prevailed. Still, there seems, when we look at the calendar on the fridge, to be an alarming amount of squares yet to be crossed off. Anything could happen between now and then.

Trev's rave

It's funny about snakes. You seem to know they're there just before you see them. Maybe it's a peripheral vision thing, something that the subconscious registers before the conscious, slipping it an inkling of precognition, or maybe it's some sort of stunted second sight, but that's how it was with the brown in the garden.

Linda had seen it around a few times and it worried her. She's a Kiwi, and most Kiwis like snakes even less than Australians. Maybe it's because they don't have them over there, and get brought up on tales of giant Australian serpents dropping from the trees or springing out of the plumbing, every one of them capable of inflicting the fatal bite, probably 200 times over. She'd wanted to get rid of it for a while, had even gone to the extent of getting the Snake Man out, but it had given him the slip. This made me pretty happy. I'd been telling her since the day we met that I was the snake man; everybody, when I lived out bush, used to get me to identify or get rid of their snakes. If there was going to be a snake man around, it was going to be me. Now it was time to put my money where my mouth was.

I was walking past the goat pen, just about level with the plum tree, when I saw it stick its head out past the wooden boundary of the garden bed we called Caleb's garden, or Caleb's bed. This was to cause some confusion and panic later, when I told Linda I'd seen the brown snake in Caleb's bed. We had beans growing thickly in Caleb's bed, so there was plenty of cover. The snake and I saw each other at the same time and stopped, both stock still, both as happy as each other about this meeting. I groaned. Now I was going to have to get rid of the bastard.

Previously, I'd only seen it down at the bottom of the block, and could convince myself that it didn't really want to come and tangle with the humans and if we left it alone, it would return the favour. I could no longer maintain this fiction. It was only a matter of time before there was a closer and potentially nastier encounter.

I went and told Linda the news.

'Caleb's bed!' she squawked, 'what do you mean Caleb's bed?'

We both knew the time for hoping it would go away had ended. We headed into the garden and down to the scene of the sighting. I was still in denial.

'It could be anywhere now. It's probably shot through back down to the bottom', I said, all the while poking around among the bean bushes with my hand. Linda was not convinced. We circled the bed a couple more times and were just about to head off again when Linda said, her voice tense with excitement and fear, 'There it is. It's looking at me. There, right where you had your hand a minute ago'.

I came around to where she was standing and, sure enough, there it was, its black, dangerous-looking eyes staring back at us. Snakes haven't got real good eyesight, but it knew we were there, and that something was afoot.

'Shit!' I said to Linda. 'Keep an eye on it, I'll go put overalls and boots on.'

Here, surely, was a sign of incipient old age. The truth was, it had been more than 10 years since I'd caught a dangerous snake and if, when I was 30 or so, it had been something of an adrenaline rush and (if the stories my erstwhile neighbours tell about me are to be believed) something I'd do naked, now I was scared, and wanted all the protective clothing I could get. I regretted there was no armour in the cupboard.

I dressed as described and went to look for a good forked stick. Every snake catcher has his favourite method and will spend a lot of time telling you why it's the best way to go, and why your way is so dangerous it's a wonder you've lived to tell the tale. I'll just say I like the forky stick and leave it at that.

I cut my stick just long enough to keep me out of strike reach, and with enough fork to pin the head and leave some room for my fingers when the time came to pick it up, but not allow the snake to pull its head free. By this time the adrenaline was fairly buzzing – not a feeling I really like, which is why

I never took to things like abseiling or betting on the horses. I also grabbed a tomato stake just in case and a fertiliser bag to put the snake in and headed back to where Linda was watching with eagle eyes and some trepidation.

I started beating the bush a bit trying, as it were, to flush the prey.

'There it is!' Linda said, pointing to a spot to my right.

I laid my tomato stake on the snake's back, trying to stop it while I pinned its head, but it got free and turned back into the bean bushes.

'It's around this side now!' said Linda, the thrill of the chase clearly evident in her voice.

I tried the same trick with the tomato stake and this time slowed it down it well enough to enable me to get the forky stick and pin its head. Now for the scary bit. With the snake firmly pinned, the idea is to reach down, grab it behind the head and slip it into the bag. I've never had one suddenly pull its head out from under the stick and have a go at me, but there's a first time for everything. I looked down at the writhing – and by this time thoroughly pissed-off – creature, took a deep breath and picked it up. They're beautiful animals, this one a deep, burnished copper, smooth and cool. I sometimes worry that I, in my fear, squeeze them too hard when holding them, but they have a protrusible glottis, which means they can push their windpipe, protected by heavy cartilage, right out of their mouths. This is handy when swallowing large prey. I held it pretty tight.

Linda had watched all this with some concern of her own, predisposed as she is to fear that the worst will happen to me and it'll be ambulance time any second. However, she was ready with the bag and brought it over, which required a fair bit of courage on her part. Given how she feels about snakes, it's a wonder she wasn't up on the verandah.

'Hold the bag open', I told her. 'I'll drop it in then grab the bag and tie it up.'

This can be a tricky operation in itself; you don't want to muck around once the thing's inside. She held out the bag and I lifted the snake up to put it in tail first. I was just about to let it go when Linda, pre-empting me by a second or so, dropped the bag. Could've been nasty.

'Don't worry, it won't jump out at you. And it won't bite you through the bag. Let me get it in and then let go.'

I dropped the snake into the bag, quickly took it from Linda and tied it up with a piece of twine. By this time I'm shaking like a leaf, but it's done now, so I also feel pretty proud of myself, especially with Linda looking up at me and saying stuff like 'My hero'. Well, maybe she didn't actually say that, but I could tell she was thinking it.

Now all that remained was to take it somewhere it could live in peace, but not come back to our place. I've heard various things about how far to take them away. We settled on a bit of farmland next to a creek about 3 or 4 kilometres away, which should be far enough. I've also heard relocation never works, and they never survive it.

One way or the other, we haven't seen it back here. We can only hope it's a happy-ever-after thing.

february

1 February

Someone told me the function of eyebrows is to stop the sweat from getting in your eyes, but mine are inadequate for the job. By the time I haul myself back up the hill from the early morning garden water, I need goggles for any real effect.

I mention homework and Caleb disappears into the toilet. I listen to him strain for a few minutes before knocking on the door. But his pants aren't down around his ankles, and the toilet seat isn't up. He's sitting on it, swivelling as far as he can in order to reach his portable tape deck. I can hear Elvis Presley singing from the Lilo & Stitch soundtrack. He swivels back around and says, 'Excuse me, I'm after some privacy here'.

At least he recalls the exact phrase I use on him in similar circumstances, even if it never works. I suggest his bedroom might be a better place to seek privacy and he relocates. As he passes the table, I grab his homework and relocate it within his vicinity, making strong suggestions (read threats) connecting the use of computer games with the completion of homework. It works; we do it together. He eats, mumbling between bites of plum jam toast, a hot chocolate and the side of a mango. He is gaining weight; I am losing it. This is as it should be.

We leave for school. Our second day riding. As I pull away I ask, 'Have you got your feet on the pegs?'

'Yes', he says.

I hear three weird clicks. I jump off the bike, whirl around and see Caleb's horrified face. His foot is bent the wrong way, stuck through the spokes of the bike and hard up against the frame. He begins to scream. His shoe has half twisted off; I twist it the rest of the way, freeing him. He's on the footpath and going hard on the pain thing.

'Don't touch it!' he screams as I try to get a good look, pulling away. It's not broken, and barely is the skin, but there are burst capillaries and a lot of pinched white flesh.

We don't go to school today. Caleb is restored to his normal happy self within minutes. I occupy him with the drill, a piece of wood, nails and a hammer. I resign myself to assisting him to further organise the Bionicle bed.

We read from Roald Dahl's *The witches* — one of which I have half-convinced him I am. (I was doing well in all the signs until the blue spit bit was mentioned.) I enjoy having him at home. He missed out so much those first years when I spent the waking half of my life at work. We make a pact together: from now on, even though it takes 30 minutes instead of 10, we will walk to school.

I leave him lying on the trampoline playing with Lego while I feed whey and grain to the chooks, and catch giant-sized brown grasshoppers (surely they are locusts) with the secateurs and throw them, still living, into the chooks' pens, where the birds raise dust fighting over the tasty morsels. If they are locusts, you can cook them in a variety of ways, according to two NSW agricultural officers who have published a recipe book containing such arthropodian delights as chocolate-covered locust and Coonabarabran stir-fry. Those areas most affected by plagues have been advised, 'If you can't beat them, eat them'. This is, so far, information I have kept to myself. Trevor is just as likely to be tempted by the idea of locust-flavoured popcorn. The western world does not indulge in entomophagy (the eating of insects), though the concept of microlivestock, as an American university calls the farming of insects, as a low-cost, low-energy way of providing high-quality protein is being looked at seriously. For instance, a cricket contains 13 grams of protein, 10 milligrams of iron and 76 milligrams of calcium. Crickets are said to be nice deep-fried, and in Mexico you can buy them canned. I do see insects as protein, but only for chooks. I catch cockroaches in oiled jars and toss them to the chooks the next day; fruit fly are microwaved and go the same way. One thing I have learnt is if you have a pest, try to find a way to make it useful. Protein is useful, insects are protein, therefore insects are useful. If you can get to them before they fill your rockmelon with maggots, so much the better.

Tonight it's an entrée of banana capsicums stuffed with fetta and nutmeg, battered and deep-fried, followed by a serving of steamed vegies with a yoghurt, coriander and cumin sauce.

2 February

Caleb refused the ratatouille. I refused to feed him anything else. He managed four mouthfuls before gagging on a piece of eggplant. This happens far too often, and the best meal of the day goes uneaten. The only vegies he likes are cucumber, raw carrots, zucchini, corn and potato. I don't even grow corn: it is too hungry, the parrots eat it off the cob before we do, it's not particularly nutritious and it takes a lot of space to grow a small amount. He goes to bed moaning about how hungry he is. I offer him a drink, but no food. I have guilt, but I also have stubbornness. He must learn to eat what we eat. Trev and I found the ratatouille absolutely delicious. I know eggplant is not a child-friendly food, but it's a nutritious one. My foot is down.

3 February

At the moment I'm walking a bit like John Wayne, but it's only nappy rash. Caleb and I biked to school yesterday after all — Trev pop-riveted some guards on the back of the bike so Caleb can't get his feet caught in the spokes, at least not without trying very hard. It was hot, over 80 per cent humidity, so I wore a skirt instead of the usual pants. By the time I'd done the repeat journey I'd given myself a wonderful case of nappy rash. I had a shower and attempted to sound like I was singing a strangled opera rather than screaming. I won't be wearing a skirt on the bike again.

We had a storm last night and netted a total of 16 millimetres. Fantastic, didn't have to get out there first thing for the morning water.

I've made a disturbing dissection. My beans look great till just about the time they flower and then they keel over. Their stems look gnarled and ugly. I got out the pest and diseases book and find it may be bean fly. I grab a sharp knife and an affected plant, and do some explorative surgery — and, yes, there are maggots in the stems. We've not had them before, and I wonder why it is they choose now to decimate all my beans. I look up remedies and find most of them prescribe poison, which would cure the problem, but make the beans inedible at the same time. Catch 22. I discover that the snake beans are the most bean-fly resistant, though it'll be a while before they mature. I planted them around Christmas and they take 90–120 days to mature. We don't rely on any one food, so we can do without till then. Just. I have 6 kilos of dried soybeans, plus a kilo of pinto, red kidney and Madagascar beans from prior harvests, which can fill a bean gap. I had hoped to be able to save them for a dire necessity.

I gather close to a kilo of elderberries and turn them into a cordial that tastes like a cross between grape and tomato juice. It has a tremendous amount of vitamin A and is high in vitamin B17, the controversial cancer cure. Caleb doesn't like it much. I wonder if it's too late to turn it into ink. I have a fountain pen that sucks up ink. I've made lilli pilli ink, but it's not as strongly coloured as I had hoped. Elderberries might be better. I like the idea of using a non-disposable pen, something you can get attached to, is environmentally friendly and classy, and ultimately saves money.

I pulled up a few peanut plants, dried out the nuts in the solar oven, shelled them, pan-roasted and salted them, and then lightly chopped them as a garnish for tonight's dinner, which is sure to be a favourite with Caleb, who hates any form of pumpkin. Pumpkin and soy bean stew, which has a pasta sauce stirred through with plenty of cumin and coriander, liberally sprinkled with the roasted nuts and topped with a mint and yoghurt dressing. I make enough for dinner and Trev's lunch the following day. It is 100 per cent our own, no bartered goods included. I feel a degree of satisfaction that is hard to describe. Caleb manages four mouthfuls before the gag reflex kicks in.

'Listen, Caleb, last week you ate green pancakes, what's so bad about this dinner? It's delicious.'

'People have different tastes, you know.' It's his stock answer.

After dinner he is lying on the couch and I lie down with him for a cuddle. I put my ear against his chest and listen. What I hear is the sound of alarm bells ringing. I extricate myself from the cuddle and tell Trev, 'Caleb's heartbeat is erratic, misses here, there, everywhere'.

'Doctor?'

'Yes.'

4 February

I pull the silver cover off the car, the one we put on it when we parked it for the duration. The first thing I do when I start the car is flick on the air-conditioning. Caleb is in the back seat looking excited. We're on the road, zipping around corners. Going up a steep hill, I call back to Caleb, 'Hold on, keep your feet on the pedals!'

He laughs. 'This hill's really steep, my legs hurt', he joins in.

'Really makes you sweat, all this exercise.' We giggle.

We walk through the shopping centre. I'm looking at all the signs saying rockmelons $1.50 per half, $1.15 a bag of onions. It seems incredibly cheap. It's just before lunch and Caleb is hungry. The last time we were here, he was looking at hot chips and burnt the end of his nose pressing it against the hot metal of the bain-marie. He looked like, and was called, Rudolph for a week. We both hurry past the hot chips.

We walk out of the doctor's an hour later. I have a letter of referral to a paediatric cardiologist — Caleb's heartbeat is abnormal. It's not that much of a surprise. I've already been to the doctor twice suspecting something is wrong, only to be told, 'No, he just disrupts his heartbeat when he breathes heavily. Sinus arrhythmia'.

Of course, my mother's psychic in New Zealand predicted this a year or so ago, in what is the best long-range diagnosis I've heard. The appointment will be in Brisbane, sometime in the next couple of weeks. I'm not sure if that means we can 'take the day off' from the six months. At the moment, I'm more worried about Caleb than I am about six months of self-denial. I was going to take him back to school, but I grant him the rest of the day off and stipulate no computers or TV — he potters around with Lego.

6 February

It's poos-day, and thunderboxes are go! Once every four to six months Trev and I change the toilet chamber over on the composting loo. While it sounds like it would be a disgusting job, the material has been thoroughly broken down over the time it has sat out under the warm sun.

After five months, there is remarkably little compost material. We estimate around 15–20 kilos. Aerated, with a few nice enzymes thrown in, it's a thick cake with virtually no smell. It is often full of soldier fly larvae. This is a good sign, as they are great poo eaters, tend to reduce the bulk of the compost very quickly and are unlikely vectors for disease (they do not frequent the kitchen). The job requires the decomposed poo to be buried in a hole and covered. We wash out the chamber, haul it back under the house and connect it back up to the black polypipe under the toilet. The latest batch, from the upper compartment, is then placed out in the sun to begin the big breakdown. Then we go have a nice long shower.

Before our composting toilet, we reduced our toilet water usage by investing in a few bricks to fill up the cistern, reducing its overall capacity so a full flush used less water. We also bought a small weighted gadget for $10, which allowed us to regulate the water further still. The toilet would only flush while we held our finger down; as soon as it was removed, so was the gush.

We adopted the motto: if it's yellow, let it mellow; if it's brown, flush it down. Caleb adopted one of his own: if it's yellow, let it mellow; if it's brown, just let it sit there and stink.

While the saving in water was no doubt significant, we still knew that water was being used in the processing of raw sewage and this feeling of unease was doubled once we'd changed over to the rainwater tank and we were on a restricted water budget.

We decided to investigate composting toilets. Of all our installations I think I was most excited about this one. During my product research we were informed that they don't smell. While I wasn't convinced, we felt compelled to try one out.

We purchased the Nature Loo Classic in August 2003, and it took Trevor a fairly industrious day to install it. About two seconds later it was christened by us all; we'd been loo-less for the majority of the day. Trevor also mounted a 6.2-watt solar panel to the roof to trickle charge a car battery that powered an electric fan, used to extract smells and vent them above the house. The first thing we discovered is that it really doesn't smell at all. In fact we were enthusiastic about the change in morning ritual, which, before the composting loo, was Trevor walking into the toilet and coming out 10 minutes later to loud and mournful complaints about the smell wafting through the house — but no more. The toilet smelled *less*. When people start making delicate little shudders when we mention it's a composting loo, I like to make a delicate little shudder of my own and say, 'So much better than a water toilet, seeing your own poo floating, how disgusting!' We have a young visitor who likes to lift the lid, peer down and whisper, 'Swek, are you there Swek?' He means Shrek.

Our conclusions were entirely positive, though it did take an initial few reminders for everyone to put the seat back down afterwards to avoid any insects using the receptacle for their own devices. The toilet looks entirely normal except it doesn't have a cistern. When it comes to dealing with the downstairs part, it's not as offensive as you might think. We move the contents of the current waste compartment off the down chute every four months or so, and from there it sits out of sight for another four months before it is emptied under the fruit trees.

THE CISTERN STINKS!

Up until the 1950s the Australian outhouse was not uncommon. It was built a discreet distance from the home and ensured frostbitten feet during winter. Did it smell? Probably, I'm too young to remember, nor do I remember the carefully cut segments of old telephone book sewn together and hanging from the wall where the toilet roll now does.

The outhouse, often not much more advanced than a hole in the ground, was far from perfect: raw sewage could seep into groundwater and contaminate it with a proliferation of dangerous organisms carrying such deadlies as polio and dysentery. One gram of faeces can contain 10,000,000 viruses, 1,000,000 bacteria, 1000 parasite cysts and 100 parasite eggs. No doubt the flush toilet seemed a more sanitary and efficient solution to these problems, but out of sight it was also out of mind. Most of us know little about what happens beyond the flush.

Every minute in Australia 60,000 litres of drinkable water is mixed with excrement, urine and wads of loo paper, and is forced by a modest wall of water through an s-bend. At that rate, we're polluting the equivalent of an Olympic swimming pool of water and flushing it down the toilet every 16 minutes.

Across Australia that's 304 gigalitres a year requiring treatment, or 8.8 billion litres daily.

These amounts are hard to visualise and are best brought down to a personal equivalent: each person flushes an average of 16,000 litres of drinking-quality water per year. Per family, that's an average of 200 litres of water a day.

Sewerage treatment

On the Gold Coast there are 163,000 sewered households. Each year it costs $413 per household for wastewater treatment – a total of over $67 million.

There were 7.5 million households in Australia in 2002. If we assume that 7 million of these are sewered, and the costs are similar to that of the Gold Coast, we are looking at spending $2.9 billion each year on sewerage treatment in the 9000 sewage pumping stations and 800 sewage treatment plants in Australia. It's worth asking ... what sensible country (also the world's driest) would mix effluent with drinking water and then spend big money trying to extract it?

But wait, there's more.

In an anaerobic system, such as the flush toilet, the speed of decomposition is very slow. Once it has taken place, the end product is not a plant food but a system contaminant consisting of ammonia, methane and hydrogen sulphide.

John Foss, spokesperson for the Surfrider Foundation (Surf Coast), says, 'There are currently 141 public sewage outfalls discharging human effluent and industrial waste into the ocean around Australia at a rate exceeding 3 billion litres per day. Elevated nutrient levels may cause eutrophication, the excessive growth of algae, which depletes oxygen levels in the water and may suffocate marine organisms'.[1]

The average person's faeces have a decomposed weight of around 25 kilograms per year. Not much.

Dam walls are built higher and animal habitats and waterways destroyed so we can use 16 kilolitres of water to flush what would eventually amount to 25 kilos of humus.

There's no doubt about it, the cistern stinks . . .

Alternatives to flush toilets

If a long drop in your backyard sounds horrific, there are a host of composting or waterless toilet systems. Companies in Australia manufacture and sell systems (made to Australian standards) such as Bio Loo, Dowmus, Clivus Multrum, Rota Loo and Nature Loo. The systems use no water, are sanitary and do not smell (most use a small exhaust fan to draw smells through a pipe and are vented above the house). Stuart Elliot from Nature Loo says people can be put off composting toilets because of 'bad experiences at roadside or national park composting toilets', explaining that, 'these toilets can smell if they are not properly maintained and ventilated, and often this is the case because power to the fans gets stolen or vandalised. Also, there is a perception that they can only be installed in a high-set home. There are now imported and locally made models that work on slab floors and work very well'.

Composting loos require differing amounts of maintenance. Continuous systems, like Clivus Multrum, involve new material being constantly added, while the oldest material can be raked or shovelled out. Batch systems, like ours, use alternating chambers, and new material is not continually added to the composting chamber. The chambers need alternating every four to 12 months.

Composting toilets are designed to look like their flush cousins, with only the cistern missing. The bowl is a different shape to minimise marking, and the tube is usually dark, so little can be seen of the toilet's contents without the use of a torch. Urine or leachate is not held in most systems; instead it is drained away from the pile. Some composting toilet systems are not suitable for colder areas as the material may take longer to decompose. Generally the systems do not use electricity, chemicals or moving parts, so there are no issues with breakdowns, except for the ventilation fan (it's good to keep one spare).

The gardener's reward

The raw material is broken down by micro-organisms, and thermophilic action (heat), which kills pathogens and viruses. The length of time itself renders most possible vectors for disease harmless. As the composting system is aerobic, microbes, which require an oxygenated environment, are able to break down the compost into a useful plant food. The humus is covered in pores, which shelter nutrients, water and air more than soil can, and it releases nutrients gradually as it breaks down.

When emptying a composting toilet the 'humanure' is required, by law, to be buried. To be on the safe side, it should not be used on vegetable beds, but buried under a tree and covered in mulch.

In many less squeamish cultures, humanure is a useful source of topsoil on food crops. In the past Japanese farmers would vie for travellers' excrement by building comfortable roadside privies and, once it was composted, they would use the deposits to enrich their soil.

According to composting toilet manufacturers, installing composting toilets in households is a slow-growing trend. Stuart Elliot of Nature Loo wonders 'why the government doesn't recognise the benefits of composting toilets and provide incentives to people who install them'.

As John Foss says, 'Recycling human and industrial waste is the only way that Australia can manage sustainable population and agricultural and industrial growth into the future'.[2]

Any way you look at it, it's time we got our shit together.

7 February

The days are following a distinct pattern. Up at 6 am, grind grain, feed chooks and milk the goat prior to wiping the sleep from our eyes. Connect to the net, download email, drink a hot cup of chai (I like the ritual of chai tea in the morning, but soon all the spices will be gone and I will have to start drinking the home-grown herb teas instead), do the minimal amount of cleaning up required to not be considered a complete pig, and then rush back down for an early morning water — how else do you keep seedlings alive in this kind of weather?

Chai tea

This recipe makes a large quantity of tea and spice mix, to last many cups of chai.

5 teaspoons ground cinnamon

5 teaspoons ground ginger

2 teaspoons ground cloves

3 teaspoons ground cardamom

5 allspice (pimento) berries, ground

$^1/_2$ teaspoon peppercorns

10 bay leaves

10 tablespoons black tea

Mix all ingredients together. To make enough chai for four, place a heaped teaspoon of the mix in a litre of water and bring to the boil in a pot or microwave. Let it sit for five minutes before straining into cups. Add milk and sugar to taste and reheat in microwave (if you're like me and need to blister the lining of your mouth, that is).

Later I check for eggs and feed the goat. First thing, Possum usually gets half a pumpkin roughly chopped with a machete. Chooks get weeds and I make sure all their water is clean and full. I generally come back to the house sweating, stand at the top of the stairs cursing (did I or did I not turn off the tap), and make a quick trip back to find that, yes, I did. (Worse when I wake up in the middle of the night wondering that, and can't sleep till I find the torch and trip over cane toads as I go down to make sure. This happens more frequently than I would like.) Then it's inside for a bit of guilt-assuaging housework, thankless and horrid task that it is, and it's either bread-baking day, cheese-making day or laundry day. But, of course, there is also 'dig over a garden bed and mulch' day, 'cover fruit fly susceptible things in bags' day, and 'liquid fertilise with my lovely big bucket of stinky animal poo, plant and occasional decomposed snail gloop' day (a shower usually follows soon after). Then there are the planting-out days, the harvesting days, the 'pick another 5 kilos of tomatoes and then try think of something truly original to do with them' days. Sweep paths, feed the goat, wait till she roars at me, then feed her again, feed her more when that doesn't seem to bring her to bursting point. Start cooking dinner, sometimes as early as lunchtime. Of course, on school days, it's all about finding the time to organise Caleb's breakfast, lunch, books and last-minute show and tell, and bike him there, and bike back and then there again, and then back again. When he's back it's about feeding him and watering the garden. Trev gets home, we milk the goat, dinner is made, served, and I immediately start thinking about what tomorrow's dinner is going to be, while still contemplating tonight's dishes.

Having said all this, Caleb accused me this morning of sending him off to school so I can sit at home and watch TV.

'But, Caleb, when have you ever seen me turn the TV on?'

'I don't see you do it, because you wait until I'm at school.'

This weekend Trev covered a lot of the sorghum with mosquito and bird nets. We need to get it to seed. A while back, we bartered with Ehren, Trev's 21-year-old son, for some wheat. We still had plenty of our own seed, but could see we might have shortages ahead with all the feeding-frenzied parrots. We asked for a 5-kilo bag in exchange for a pumpkin, some tomatoes and capsicums. He arrived not long after with a 40-kilo bag over his shoulder.

'The shop that sold 5-kilo bags wasn't open', he said, smiling.

We're still feeding him and offering him food from the garden, and will be for a while longer till we pay the $20 off. He also bought around the scythe, which is Trev's belated Christmas present. It has a 'bush' handle, is old, worn and groovy, and Trev practises his 'golf swing' with it on the easement between the neighbours and us. It's an addition to our collection of antique tools. We have the chaffcutter, which we advertised for in the local paper and bought for $120. It needed repairs; Trev built a new wooden 'in ramp', removed rust, sharpened the blades and now we use it all the time. It makes short work of wheat stems, sorghum, sugar cane and grass, turning it all into useable mulch, quietly and efficiently, while giving us a nice cardiovascular workout. Plus, it's a pleasure to use something that is made so beautifully and has class (beats those horrible power-guzzling, ear-killing motorised brutes).

Our neighbour Shane from down the road was shown the chaffcutter masterpiece and remarked that his dad had an old corn kerneller in the chook shed at home, were we interested? Yes, what does it do? Takes the husks off macadamias, the corn off cobs and sunflower seeds from the heads. The following week he showed us a digital movie of it. The corn kerneller was sitting dejected in a half-collapsed chook pen.

A week later Trev helped Shane out with some concreting and the kerneller was ours. (We call it the Colonel.) It no longer worked; its gears were worn and tended to seize. Trev lavished it with love and oil, then manufactured a few parts, and a month later it was sanded, wire-brushed, stained and beautiful. A flywheel circulates two opposing plates into which the unsuspecting cobs are dropped. A light grinding later, the kernels drop down a chute and onto a narrow platform, which is agitated back and forth by the movement of the flywheel. The cobs move down the chute and drop out of the end, while the kernels drop through a screen onto a lower level and are funnelled into a bucket. The only problem is that the cobs of corn we are growing are the Golfball variety — tiny, too small for the Colonel. But it works for the sunflower heads, and we're looking forward to using it on the next crop of macadamias.

Today is liquid fertilising day. Out with a bucket, a cup to measure out the stinky liquid, and the hose at the ready to dilute the muck. I used to use a watering can, but it was forever getting plugged up with goop, so now it's the bucket technique. If it were Trev doing the job, he'd have found a more efficient way of doing it. But I run around splashing plants and pouring it around the root zone, bucket after bucket. The soil is dry, the air is wet and the sun is blazing. I gather eggs, half a dozen today, and go back upstairs to grab a couple of ice-cream containers full of whey to distribute among the chooks. I feed Possum again, and cut down a few sunflowers, giving a fat head to each of the three chook pens. Water the onions, carrot, squash and cucumber seedlings, and harvest the dried coriander seeds. Upstairs, they're stripped off the bush for further drying before being ground into powder and stored. I de-pulp a bucket of passionfruit and make cordial, freezing some for when Caleb gets home from school. I make a chocolate mousse for dessert, and two jars of pasta sauce. I contemplate the kitchen, which is never clean for long before it goes into production mode again, and the pile of dishes appears, like magic, waiting for me and my loofah. I dream of a clean kitchen, the kind only takeaway or dinner out allows for.

8 February

Trevor stayed away last night in Pechey. It's a work commitment, and while he's away he will need to spend money. He is torn by this, and seems to think we are threatening the experiment's integrity by having to pay for his room in a motel, and his meals for a day, even though he will be reimbursed by the organisation for which he works. I feel sorry for him. That is until he tells me he had the reef and beef, mushroom sauce, entrée after entrée, drowned himself in a few far-from-homemade beers and made the most of it. His workmate is said to have mentioned, with awe, the incredible size of his meals. Trevor seemed to have lost his inhibitions about spending money and pulled out all stops. He says you may as well be hung for a sheep as a lamb.

Meanwhile, I've biked to school and spent the first money too. I've handed over $15 for Caleb's school textbook, photocopying and Queensland Arts Show fee. It felt very odd, even though it is a necessity. Queensland Education is not yet into barter.

11 February

We have so many peanuts ready to harvest and I'm going through them very slowly. I pull up a few plants each day, allowing them to dry before giving them a quick squish with the back of the wooden spoon, and then peeling off the shell. The skin on one thumb is getting dangerously thin. Trev helped out yesterday and made a pan full of roasted, hot chilli peanuts. So hot I gave myself third-degree burns on just one. These are placed in a jar and have become Trev's sole property. They've been made inedible for anyone else by sheer Scoville power. Wilbur Scoville developed the rating scale of chilli heat known as the Scoville Organoleptic Test. The test used humans to detect 'heat' in a sugar–water solution. If, after a sample of chilli was diluted in 3000 cups of the sugared solution, the masochistic testers could no longer detect a sting, the Scoville rating was 3000. While the rating numbers have been changed, and the testing methods aligned to laboratory standards, the ratings are still called Scoville units, 10 being the hottest.

CHILLI	SCOVILLE UNITS	CHILLI	SCOVILLE UNITS
Anaheim	2–3	Manzano	6–8
Bell peppers/		Pequin	8
capsicum	0	Poblano	3
Cayenne	8	Serrano	7
Cherry	1	Tabasco	8–9
Habanero	10	Thai	9–10
Jalepeno	5.5	Yellow wax	6–7

If you haven't discovered why it is that people consume a food that induces huge amounts of pain (both on entry and exit), it's because of the euphoria-inducing endorphins that are released in order to deal with it. I have an urge to start a rumour that greater degrees of pain can be achieved by rubbing the chilli in your eyes instead. You never know with addicts, they might prefer it; and chillies, due to the morphine-like endorphins, are mildly addictive. Trevor, who has an addictive personality, certainly is.

If you've taken on too great a chilli pain load, it can be eased, not by water, but by milk or yoghurt, as the fat-soluble capsaicin oils do not disperse in water.

I have a story about chillies that Trevor will hate to hear repeated. (I repeat it often.) It goes like this. There I am, loyal to his tastebuds, having harvested a 10-litre bucket full of sweet bell peppers. I proceed to de-seed them by hand. The pain, after a while, becomes so intense that I immerse my hands in water frequently, assuming that once I've finished the pain will soon dissipate. The pain sets my teeth on edge, and then continues on till it's whole face rictus, but I persevere until finally the seeds are all separated from the flesh. I assume the pain will start to dissipate but, no, it keeps on. Three hours later I cannot keep my hands out of iced water for longer than a few seconds. Caleb, who was still in nappies at the time, is oblivious. Trevor, after a hard day's work in the recycling centre (then known as the dog box), is also.

I end up, in desperation, ringing the hospital for advice — is there something I can put on it to counteract the chilli?

'You've chemically burnt yourself, come in and we'll do something for you.'

Trevor announces from his horizontal position on the couch, where he is drinking beer and watching one of those ridiculous man sports where they run around earnestly, persecuting some hapless ball, 'When I lie down, I stay down'.

I try and change Caleb's nappy before I go, but have to do it in stages as the pain gets so great I have to run back for the ice.

At the hospital a nurse runs out and hands me a bowl of cold water. Grateful I plunge them in. She tells me about chemical burns and how instead of destroying the nerves, they remain intact and continue to send signals of pain, so it can be more painful than when physical heat has burnt away tissue. My hands are an angry red, but there are no blisters. They start smearing on goop and go to wind bandages around my hands.

'Hang on,' I say, 'I won't be able to drive home if you do that'.

They look surprised, 'You drove here?'

I nod. They make me up a package to take home with me so I can dress my hands there. They add to it a pair of disposable gloves. 'Next time, wear these', they smile.

When I get home Trev is still on the couch, and has no idea that, four years on, he will still be the butt end of this story. A story, mind you, that he denies — at least anything to do with his part in it. Having said that, I've probably told enough people now. It's been told a final time.

We had 9 millimetres of rain overnight. Not much, and certainly not enough. Soil moisture is being rapidly depleted.

12 February

'Well Mum, if we start to starve we can always eat Soil Beans.'

Caleb points to the big jars of soybeans at the top of the shelf.

'Yes, and we could always go outside and find ourselves some nice dirt burgers.' I grin.

It's time to make tofu. It's so nice cubed, lightly fried and served with steamed vegies, covered in a thick, spicy satay sauce.

Tofu

Tofu is made from soybeans, water and nigari. Available in health shops, nigari is what remains of salt water once the water and salt are extracted.

500 grams soybeans (Daizu)

20 grams nigari

Soak the soybeans in water overnight. Ensure the beans are covered the entire time so they can double in size. Drain off the water and blend a small number of beans at a time, using enough fresh water to cover the beans in the blender. Pour the bean mixture into a pot and add enough water to double the volume. Bring to a simmer and skim off any foam that collects on top. Continue stirring and skimming for 20–30 minutes.

Meanwhile, dissolve the nigari in a small amount of water. Then, using a cheesecloth-lined colander placed over a bowl, drain the contents of the pot. The liquid is soymilk and the remaining material in the pot is called okara (we use it to make veggie patties or feed to the chooks).

When the soymilk cools to 70 degrees pour in the nigari and stir gently. The tofu will start to coagulate almost immediately. Leave for five minutes.

Pour the mixture into a cheesecloth-lined mould (cheese-making moulds are ideal but you can make do with a 'holey' container). Place a 1-kilogram weight on the tofu for half an hour, then remove from the mould, place in water and refrigerate.

'You know who Dad looks like?'

'No, who does Dad look like?'

'The Grim Reeker.'

'What, does he smell bad?'

He looks confused. 'No, he's up the top mowing the lawn with his reeker.'

'Ah, you mean he's using the scythe and he looks like the Grim Reaper.'

I go up to see how it's going and end up grabbing hold of the push-mower and following in his footsteps to get a nice even length happening. I've let it get away on me lately, and the longer grass chokes the pushie. I chase Caleb with the mower for a while to get him laughing. I realise that, to the neighbours, we must look like loons. Needless to say, that thought is unlikely to stop us. Our neighbours are not environmentalists; we don't live in a secluded community of like-minded people. Our neighbours are indulgent about our wackiness; we're grateful that they don't complain about the crowing rooster, the bellowing goat, the unruly jungle. We barter small amounts of food with one neighbour, usually eggs. Most of our barter is with people outside our immediate area, which is a pity. Elsie is our mainstay. She likes her egg yolks orange; she loves our fetta cheese.

Trev and I put the sunflowers through the 'flail', one of Trev's ingenious inventions using an old spin-dryer, a length of water pipe and some bicycle-tyre tube cut into strips. Powered by an electric drill, it works beautifully. So quick and easy, my thumb skin is ecstatic. Then in go the sorghum heads — poor, half-eaten, not quite ripe heads — harvested early because we want to have at least something to show for all our work before the parrots get them. We still manage a good whack. The separated grain goes in the goat food bin. The chaff gets thrown to the chooks to pick through.

We move the chook pen. The five chooks, temporarily released, make beelines for mulched areas. We think it would be nice for them to have a day free-range. We cover up a vulnerable area of onions. There is only one other susceptible area, full of seedlings, but the chooks are heading in the opposite direction. We risk it. We regret risking it. We promise not to do it again. When we return, following a trail of chook poops, the seedlings have been demolished. I fish through the mulch and try to recover some. I find six cucumber seedlings out of the twelve. The rest is a war zone with the dead torn asunder. The chooks are returned to their pen, the door is firmly closed. A few words are muttered under our breaths as we bend to try to resurrect the dead. Words like 'axe' and 'fox' and 'chicken soup'. It's our own fault.

Five kilos of assorted tomatoes, galangal roots, apple crystal cucumbers, a pumpkin, zucchini, squash, sweet potato, carrots, potato and four eggs — today's pickings. A further two eggs have no doubt been laid in the jungle and are likely only to be found by the sharp-eyed crows. The crows were, at one stage, the source of much consternation. Eggs were going missing. I'd put them down on the ground to retrieve later and, on return, some or all of the eggs would be gone. The trees are so high that even from the verandah it's hard to see what is happening a short distance away. It had us perplexed for a few weeks until Caleb and I bought a fake egg. We laid it on the ground, walked back to the house, donned the binoculars and watched from the verandah. Within minutes a crow landed beside it, looked around, cocked his head to the side and pushed the egg into the mulch. Then he picked up more mulch and buried the egg. Another quick look to see who was watching and he disappeared. Caleb and I went down to inspect the crow's handiwork. It took us a while to find it, even though we knew where it was. An hour later, it was gone.

'I hope he broke all his teeth on that one, Mum.'

Caleb found a very old and stale packet of seaweed rice crackers at the back of the cupboard.

'Can I have cheese on these?' he asks.

'Fetta or cream cheese?'

'No, cheddar.'

'Goat's cheddar?'

'Is there any cow's booby milk cheese?'

'Nope.'

'OK, goat then.'

I cut him some and he eats it, saying words like 'yum' and 'this is great'. Pumpkin last night and goat's cheese tonight — my child's tastebuds are evolving. He will not starve.

13 February

Caleb presents us with a tooth so tiny I wonder if the rest is still somewhere in his gums but, no, that's all there is to it. He practises words like rabbit, rhinoceros and amphibious platypus to see how the loss has affected his speech. He's as proud as punch. Five dollars is the smallest denomination the toothfairy has. She may have to be generous with this tooth. Please don't let it burn a hole in his pocket.

Trev grinds up two cups of wheat to make flour for chapattis. He chops up garlic chives and puts them in the mix. He uses the last of the sunflower oil to cook them, and serves them with a cream cheese and garlic dip he made for last night's dinner, along with tomatoes and cucumber. They are delicious. We each drink a cup of coffee and ponder the few beans that remain. Our coffee bushes are loaded this year. Though the berries are getting big, they still have a long way to go. Plus, we've never processed them before and everyone who has says it's difficult.

While Trev grinds, I go down with the wheelbarrow and chop down a 3-metre-square area of sorghum plants, pile them in the barrow and bring them back to the house where the heads (mostly eaten) are removed and the rest put through the chaffcutter. The resulting mulch is caught in a canvas sheet and put into the wheelbarrow to take down to use as mulch on the area I just stripped it from. Trev offers to help, but last week he discovered he has an allergy to sorghum and developed huge welts around his waist and chest.

Possum is bellowing her hardest, by way of a gentle reminder. 'Hey, I'm here, I'm lonely, I might even be hungry, feed me.'

If ignored it soon escalates to, 'Get here now, you dozy bitch. Feed me, now! Get that? I said, NOW!'

We have reassured the neighbours that, while we love her milk, the cheese, the access to large amounts of drinking yoghurt, the time has come when we have to accept she is not a backyard animal. While she was pregnant, she entered a phase of tranquillity we all enjoyed. However, once the kids were born it was back to the demands of the termagant.

14 February

Big day in the garden. I harvest all the peanuts and spread them out in a large shallow tray in the sun to dry before shelling. The greenery is stacked to one side. I'll feed Possum some today, more tomorrow and wait till the enzymes in her rumen become accustomed to the new food before loading her up to the gills with it. Too much too soon and we could have a very sick goat. I cut down another bed of sorghum and take it up to the house where I pass it through the chaffcutter, turn it into mulch and then take it down again. It takes three loads to do, and navigating our block is a nightmare of wheelbarrow-snagging sharp turns. I hate wheelbarrows. Then I dig over the peanut bed and plant potatoes, greenskin zucchini, San Marzano tomatoes and Hong Kong broccoli. I sift through the goat pen for broken-down poo and scatter it over the line of potatoes. Then it's back to watering and navigating the 40-metre length of hose around as many sharp corners as the wheelbarrow. I hate hoses. This one usually pops off at the 15-metre join. Mostly because I, in my haste and unwillingness to show any form of patience with the uncooperative length of plastic, usually pull on it so hard it gives. I hate to imagine how many hundreds of litres have been wasted while I find the gushing end, fold it over and try to mend the line without turning off the hose. We won't talk about kinks, snags, leaks, or turning on the hose and getting to the other end to realise I've turned on the goat water hose and it's overflowed her bucket, requiring a sprint up the hill to turn it off and the required hose on. The neighbours have yet to complain about the level of verbal hose abuse going on around the yard. Today, I admit, an explosion of gushing water was met with an explosion of gushing invective emitted at high frequency and involving lots of words that have only recently been included in the Oxford Dictionary.

16 February

We pull out of the street at 7.30 am. There is an air of festivity in the car. We have, with much debate, decided that today is the 'free dress' day of the stomach. We will buy food while in Brisbane. We're already stressed enough without having to walk past chocolate bars with a hungry six-year-old. We stop an hour down the track; I tell Caleb he can choose to buy something to eat. He chooses an over-packaged fresh fruit salad. Faced with a range of greaseables, I choose an egg and lettuce sandwich (the white bread did it). I buy Trev a Chiko roll and, on impulse, a bucket of hot chips. We meet back at the car. Trev has disappeared in another direction and has bought back his own stash — soft drinks and a block of chocolate. We pull out at 8.30 am giggling like naughty school children. The egg sandwich was stale and stodgy and it wasn't long before I designated it chook food. Trev mentions, gently, that he's always loathed Chiko rolls; it too is consigned to the chook bucket. Caleb rocks his way through the fruit salad, exclaiming, 'Mandarin!' from the back seat, while we settle for salt-encrusted hot chips, most of which also go to the back seat.

Trevor pulls out the chocolate. I say, gently, 'You know how you feel about Chiko rolls?'

'Ahuh.'

'That's how I feel about Snack chocolate.' He's bought the *only* bar of chocolate that I dislike. I manage one piece and shake my head. The centres are sickly. It's no good. I can't even force myself. Here we are, all set to splurge, and it's failed miserably.

We occupy ourselves with a ridiculous conversation about 'self'. Trev has taken me to task for saying 'self-unaware'. Self-aware is a word, Trev tells me, but really 'self-unaware' is just ridiculous. I should say, 'he is unaware of' but all those extra syllables, I protest, and we sit there counting them. Self-honest, he thinks that's ridiculous too. How's it any different to just plain honest? Self-discipline, I assert, is an underrated virtue, which we do not, as a culture, value highly enough. Trev agrees on that one.

Without enough discipline we have a society that suffers from large credit card debt (currently $19.4 billion[3]), obesity (1 in 6 adults and 1 in 4 children[4]), linked of course to the trend towards lack of exercise and a daily television-watching habit of three hours and 23 minutes.[5]

I toy with the concept of self-denialists as a militant form of self-discipline, while slugging on a Vanilla Coke and rattling the empty chip bucket in hope of more. Difficult to drink with your tongue in your cheek.

We spend almost three hours at the hospital. Caleb, being the centre of attention, finds himself playing the role of an incredibly spoilt, misbehaving, whinging brat. He even says to one nurse, cheekily, 'You think I'm a brat, don't you?'

She comes back at him quickly with, 'You said that, I never said that, they were your words'.

The doctor has been very patient. Caleb is supposed to lie still but instead squirms and theatricates, lifts his legs and farts loudly, and then suffers from excruciating bladder pressure, so the doctor is forced to stop while we find him a loo, and return (stern warnings and dire threats are ignored) for further embarrassment. The outcome: he has a bicuspid aortic valve, which is also mildly regurgitative. He has a congenital heart defect. We take him down to another part of the hospital where he is fitted with a Holter, which will take a 24-hour electrocardiogram (ECG) — he wears it around his waist in a bum bag, five electrodes stuck to his chest. As soon as we leave the hospital his behaviour reverts to normal. This is a new slant on white-coat syndrome. Next time we'll take a gag. On our way out I decide to make use of the public toilets myself, thinking, 'Aha, toilet paper, this will be a new experience', only to find upon completion that there is none available. I try not to mutter too loudly. We discuss going to the Megaplex for some lunch but decide the temptation to walk into bookshops and toyshops would be too great. We head out of Brisbane and for home. Our stomachs are rumbling. We debate further whether we should stop and eat. Caleb is half asleep in the back seat after having mumbled on about hunger pains for several minutes. He looks very vulnerable there with his cords dangling from his chest. We pull over at Caboolture Travel Centre where we wake him with enticing words.

'Junk food, Caleb, would you like some?'

He's awake, and he's in there. We splurge, we eat, I find that I'm full very quickly and I'm annoyed. I haven't eaten anywhere near as much as I'm used to, or that I'd like to. I rest a little, then force myself to eat more. Trev returns from a foray into the eating world. Hunter-gatherer, he has steak sandwich and nachos in his arms, with cinnamon scrolls and some other unidentified pastry.

'There's gourmet ice-cream down there.' He points.

Caleb has finished over-consuming and is in the McDonald's playground, lifting his shirt to anyone looking in his direction and displaying his electrodes — he's 'Robo Boy'. I nod, make a dash of my own, and order a mega-sized cone full of vanilla bean (with seed) ice-cream. Trev and I discuss the possibility of eating so much you can't physically breath. Caleb, on return, sees the ice-cream and wants one of his own. Rainbow-coloured. It's been a big eating day. We waddle back to the car, I'm repletely replete.

Self-discipline has been murdered.

None of us feel like dinner.

17 February

Last night was uncomfortable, having to contend with 'leaky valve' from all the greasy stomach-stretching food. Caleb has done well and slept with the bum bag on without pulling off any electrodes.

The microwave no longer works. Trev blew it up poaching an egg yesterday. I find myself going to put things in it and then staring at it reproachfully. No longer can I quickly zap fruit fly riddled fruit, or a quick hot chocolate for Caleb, or a swift defrost of frozen bread. While it is still under warranty, we can't actually return it to where we purchased it, because it's 100 kilometres away. We realise that this is one of those things we will have to grin and bear. But the corollary is higher power use to heat things with the stove or oven.

The ongoing heat and lack of rain is cause for concern. Our one day away from home ended life on this Earth for several hundred onions, which were fried before their time without me there to water them two to three times daily. Perhaps 50 or so survived. They are on luxury amounts of water as they recoup. The beans at the top are looking thirsty and some of their lower leaves are browning off. Again, luxury amounts of my water, comfrey and poo fertiliser bucketed up, to my back's detriment. Some of the watermelons are suffering from what looks like blossom-end rot. So far they have been the healthiest plants on the block. I've watered in handfuls of dolomite around the root zone and hope this helps add calcium to the soil. But I'm no soil scientist and, right now, with everything in stages of droop except for a proliferation of weeds, I feel like not much of a gardener either. Trevor's latest mantra is, 'One day I am going to have a garden and use luxury amounts of chemical fertiliser, and every kind of garden poison they make'.

I make barely audible comments along the line of 'over my dead body'. However, the charms of organic gardening in this climate are few. We have bean fly, stem rot (maggots) in the pumpkin and cucumber fly killing off around 50 per cent of them before they set. One of my jobs is to pick off the yellowing fruit and 'nuke' it daily to try to keep the pest numbers down. But the pumpkin vines are so thick and so pervasive that I no doubt miss some. Fruit fly are in the capsicums, the tomatoes, the mangoes, the rockmelons, the zucchini and the squash. Everything has to be monitored for their presence and eradiated in the microwave ... ah, correction ... bucket of hot water, before being returned to the chook pens as a pulpy slop that some of them are brave enough to eat. My mantra: 'Let's move to Tasmania'.

Caleb and I bike to school as per usual. He has his bum bag on and electrodes attached. Caleb is quick to do his latest flashing routine and show the class his belly. It raises a stir. Just before lunch I return to school to remove them and post them back to Brisbane. When I arrive he is still showing off, this time in a teacher-approved impromptu show and tell. The kids are keen to see his electrodes removed, but I take him outside where he makes no attempt to muffle his yelps as I whip off the firmly adhering plasters. He is completely unconcerned about the ramifications of a heart defect. He thinks, and rightly so, that we will take care of it for him.

We are out of flour and oil. We drained the oil from a bottle of semi-dried tomatoes we'd made earlier and use that to fry vegetable fritters, which have a small amount of hand-ground wheat from the goat's food bin added to thicken them. It's hard to think of a recipe that doesn't require oil, even if only to fry onions. Caleb has begun to take the whole food thing a lot more seriously.

'Are there any onions in tonight's dinner?' he asks.

'No', I lie.

'Oh. I was hoping to try out my new adult tastebuds on them.'

'I'll see if I can manage some. How about caramelised onions?' I say, trying to make them sound as appetising as possible.

He eats them.

18 February

Trev barters fetta cheese for sunflower oil. I barter goat's milk for flour. We are both cheered by the appearance of such food in the pantry. Suddenly our hunger flares for something that combines both.

'Donuts!' we shout in unison.

'Jinxies!' says Caleb.

I haven't made donuts since I was a teenager. I miscalculate and make a huge batch of very fluffy, golden-brown donut balls, made with white flour and encrusted with raw sugar. Trev and I devour them with Homer Simpson-like drools, while Caleb looks at them with distrust and pushes the plate away. He has just tucked away a whole plate of ratatouille that I have blended into a pulp so as to make the eggplant indistinguishable from the tomato, with grated homemade parmesan cheese. He's eaten all but a few mouthfuls. I congratulate him on his adult toothbuds.

'Tastebuds, Mum!'

'Oh, sorry, your adult toothpaste.'

'Muuuum!'

'Oh, sorry, your adult tastepaste.'

'Oh Mummmmm!'

We lie on the bed and I pretend to have a brain short-circuit. He giggles so hard he almost falls off the bed. I go in for the big cuddle, and can't help but lay my head on his chest and listen to his heartbeat.

19 *February*

Trev fixes the microwave. On the back it says very clearly, 'No user-serviceable parts. Do not remove cover'. Trev sneaks it away and takes the back off. Within minutes he locates a blown fuse and replaces it. The microwave works again. We mumble on about how we live in a society with the motto 'replace rather than repair'.

THE WASTE-REDUCTION PYRAMID

The model above represents best sustainable practice; however, the inverse model is what our culture currently subscribes to.

Reducing our use of consumer goods keeps waste out of the waste stream. **Reusing or repairing** goods keeps them out of the system longer than **recycling**, which has variable results – most products have a limited ability to be repeatedly recycled, and still require significant amounts of energy and resources to do so. **Disposing** of one-time use items is, of course, the least favourable method of waste management, but it is also the most common. Rethink every purchase. Do you really need it? Choose not to buy products that require batteries, especially children's toys. What lifespan does the item have? Can it be repaired? Can it eventually be recycled?

Imagine trying to stem the flow of blood from someone with seven severed arteries using a single bandaid. That's pretty much what our recycling efforts could be considered as. Often people feel they are doing their bit by recycling plastic bags, glass jars and aluminium cans. There is a false sense of 'doing your bit' towards the environment, when it will never staunch the flow, only marginally slow it.

Recycling is an important part of becoming sustainable, but it cannot replace the far greater necessity of reducing our use.

Take action
- Use your own bags and containers when shopping.
- As soon as you've emptied the bags, put them at the front door to remind you to take them with you next time you leave.
- Shop at local markets, butchers, bakers, candlestick-makers. You are more likely to be able to use your own containers or cloth bags.
- Buy products that have reusable packaging, like glass jars or tumblers.
- When there is more than one option, for example sultanas, think about 'least packaging' when making your choice.
- If your favourite item is over-packaged, send the packaging back to the manufacturer and let them know what's wrong with it.
- Recycle *clean* glass, metal, paper and appropriate plastics. Contaminated containers will not be recycled and slow down the process.
- Buy products in bulk, or as concentrates, which will reduce the total use of packaging.
- Compost food and garden waste.

Plastic bags epitomise our throwaway mentality, our 'use once and move on' approach. The huge investment of media time and environmental pressure, and their sudden presence everywhere, has made green bags the new 'fashion accessory'. The great thing about the advent of the green bag is that it shows we can accept changes in domestic practice.

What about batteries, those horrid little bullets of heavy metals that require 50 times more energy to make than they store. A large majority end up leaching in landfill. In most cases they are 'economically' unrecyclable. Using rechargeable batteries is a good start in reducing the turnover, but more pressure needs to be exerted to provide, if nothing else, safer means of disposal.

Oil is another horrendous waste material. Thirty grams of used motor oil can create an oil slick big enough to cover an acre. It contains cadmium, lead, benzene and polyaromatic hydrocarbons and it's hard to dispose in an environmentally friendly way. Burnt, it gives off toxic fumes, while if dumped in containers it has an unhealthy future as soil, sea and groundwater pollution.

One of the best solutions is to drop used oil off at a collection facility that will re-refine the oil. You only need 1.6 litres of used oil to create 1 litre of oil right to go again; to get the same litre from crude, you need 67 litres. Your local council should be able to tell you where there is a drop-off point in your area, and if there isn't the facility, it's a good opportunity to request one.

So what's next? Downsizing the amount we can put in a wheelie bin? Apparently there is an inverse law of rubbish that means the bigger the bin, the more we find to put in.

In Australia we dump 21 million tonnes of solid waste in landfills each year[6] – around 1.146 tonnes per person or 3.14 kilograms a day. All up it's equivalent to stacking 3 million African elephants in a 9000-kilometre-high pile each year. (There's a real knack to keeping them balanced …)

We are now the second largest waste creator next to the United States.

The DUMP Awards

The DUMP (Damaging and Useless Materials from Packaging) Awards are sponsored by Environment Victoria, the Australian Conservation Foundation and the Total Environment Centre. They aim to draw attention to products with excessive packaging and to inspire consumers to be more aware of what they purchase.

And the winner for 2004 is:

EXCESSIVE USE OF MATERIAL IN A PACKAGE:
Dove Cleansing Pillows – Vanity case plus refill pack (Unilever)

LARGE RATIO OF PACKAGING TO PRODUCT:
Friskies Heartworm and Allwormer tablets for large dogs (Nestlé)

POORLY DESIGNED FOR RECYCLING:
Kellogg's cereals in 2 x 30g bowl packs.

MISLEADING LABELLING FOR WASTE MANAGEMENT:
Epi degradable plastic bags

REGRESSIVE DEVELOPMENT IN PACKAGING:
M&M's Snap N' Share (Masterfoods)

LIKELY TO BE LITTERED:
Mr Mallow marshmallows (imported by Mike & Jack P/L)

GOLD DUMP AWARD (FOR MULTIPLE TRANSGRESSIONS):
Schick 'Intuition' lady's shaver (Pfizer/Energizer)

Trev and I work in the garden all day. I harvest sorghum and sunflowers, pulling up the sunflower stalks and laying them out to be turned into chaff. Watering takes the usual hour or so while also feeding the goat, who is going through a quiet phase. The chooks are too, with only two eggs out of the possible nine.

I get my period, which wouldn't normally be reportable news material, apart from the fact that I don't use pads or tampons, or any of those, god forbid, rewashable nightmares. I use a small rubber cup called the Keeper. As women use an estimated 10,000 menstrual sanitary items during their lifetime, it makes sense to find the method with the least environmental impact. The Keeper is a great compromise; it's cheap (around $65), lasts 10 years, is convenient, comfortable and clean, and is made from a natural product. I started using it a year or so ago. It took me a while to get the hang of it (but then so did tampons). A collapsible rubber cup, it is fitted inside the vagina, where it can remain for up to 10 hours. The cup is then washed with soapy warm water and reinserted. There are others on the market made of silicone. Sanitary cups are also popular with bushwalkers who can't leave rubbish. It works well when swimming, is less likely to suffer from leaks, and hasn't caused any known cases of Toxic Shock Syndrome.

WOMEN'S SANITARY PRODUCTS

There are a huge number of euphemisms for menstruation and menstruation products, from 'I could cure the plague' (which comes from the 14th century when people would drink menstrual blood to try to cure themselves of bubonic plague), to 'using Dracula's tea-bag' and having your 'full stop'.

Whatever your name for it is, it's a sanitary item waste issue. Most options use bleach, cotton, plastic, wood, dioxins and other equally unsustainable things in unsustainable numbers. During the average woman's lifetime she will use 10,000 sanitary items, many billions of which find their way into sewage outfalls and landfill.

So, what are the options?

Sea sponges

These are small sponges that can be inserted into the vagina. They are purported to be comfortable and not inclined to leakage. They require rinsing out and regular boiling for 8 to 10 minutes to eliminate bacteria. They last for around six months. As long as they are sustainably harvested they are a good option because they use no bleaches, dioxins or synthetic fibres.

Rewashable pads

There are a number of commercially made, brightly patterned pads designed to be washed after each use. They come in varying sizes and shapes and are soaked in cold water then washed after use.

Menstrual cups

These types of menstrual cups are about the size and shape of a small egg cup. They are inserted into the vagina and can be safely left for up to 10 hours. When removed they are washed in warm soapy water and reinserted, or, if in public toilets, emptied into the toilet bowl, wiped with a tissue and reinserted. They usually come in two sizes, one for women who have given birth and one for those who haven't. They are around $45 to $65 and last approximately 10 years – a significant financial saving. They are clean, comfortable and less likely to leak compared with traditional materials.

For dinner we have Caleb's favourite meal: Nothing.

We go for another round of donuts; this time I convince Caleb to eat them. My device is to make odd-shaped donuts with little protuberances and call them 'dead dog donuts' — it's surprising how many of them do look like badly tortured dogs. The idea appeals, and he eats them, giving me a grotesque running commentary: 'I'm chewing off his head, I'm splitting him open and tearing out his flesh, I'm eating his intestines, his poo bag, his wee bag, his bottom hole'. I think we'll give donuts in all their various shapes and sizes a miss for a while.

20 *February*

I'm stung by a bee. I've been stung before with very little effect, apart from a sting and a smart that lasts an hour or too and then an annoying itch as it heals. Not so this bee. He was dark-bodied and Trev called him the Queensland bee. My arm swells, my wrist is difficult to bend, my fingers hard to extend. I can't bear to touch it or bump it or let it hang at my side. This makes my day difficult. I'd been in the swing of things, moving chook pens, harvesting tomatoes, pulling out weeds and peanuts, feeding the goat and more of that interminable hose business. But this puts an end to it. The more I try to do, the worse it gets. I give in after helping prepare and flail sunflowers and sorghum. We get a nice 5- or 6-kilo mix for not a lot of work. We try the peanuts in the flail, but they are shattered too easily. They must be shelled by hand. Caleb comes down and helps us out. He's bored. He has no one to play with and feels isolated and lonely. Trev and I are always busy and, of course, we never go anywhere. Nowhere, that is, but school. His teacher told me last week that he is very solitary, preferring his own company, which seemed at odds with the naturally gregarious Caleb we know. She said he is often in his own world, and resists the pull of his peers. I asked him what he thinks about when he's at school.

'Escape', he says. He tells me that at lunchtime he sits and reads a book.

'Please, Mum, can I please stay at home. Can't I do home school with you?' I wonder if our lifestyle is at fault. We do not venture far, and remain quite insular. Is this having an effect? Are we creating a little introvert? But then, as a child I hated school with a passion and spent most of my time reading books, preferring to stay at home and find time to myself if I could. I realise that Caleb would be better off if he had a similarly aged brother or sister. But as Trev has already 'replaced' himself with Ehren and with another child, Leela, then Caleb, as my replacement, is our limit. We take our population control concept quite seriously. In a traditional family group, it would be mum and dad and the two kids but, in this fragmented and probably more normal family, this has not happened. No more nappies for me.

THE TRUTH ABOUT DISPOSABLE NAPPIES

There are more than 800 million disposable nappies used in Australia each year. Each child will generate around 845 kilos of nappy waste before being toilet trained. Disposable nappies can take up to 500 years to decompose. The difference between cloth and disposable nappies is shown in the table below with regards to the energy used in producing the nappies, the solid waste and waste water generated and the materials consumed. The last column shows the environmental impact of disposable nappies compared with cloth nappies.

Environmental impact of nappies per child per year[7]

IMPACT	CLOTH	DISPOSABLE	IMPACT DIFFERENCE
Energy	2532 MJ*	8900 MJ	3.5 x
Waste water	12.4 m3	28 m3	2.3 x
Raw materials: non renewable	25 kg	208 kg	8.3 x
Raw materials: renewable	4 kg	361 kg	90 x
Domestic solid waste	4 kg	240 kg	60 x

* Megajoules

Currently we are overstocked with humans — the issue of population is huge. We have an economic system based on growth, one that does not factor in the limitations of our environment. More people are being born, and they're compounding the problem by living longer. Tim Flannery estimates that an Australian population of 6 million to 12 million would be more sustainable;[8] others estimate that we would need to reduce our individual resource use by 70 per cent to maintain our current population.

> *I have often thought that at the end of the day, we would have saved more wildlife if we had spent all World Wildlife Fund's money on buying condoms.*
> SIR PETER SCOTT, FOUNDER OF THE WORLD WILDLIFE FUND (WWF)

Conversely, in some less-developed countries the residents could bear to increase their resource use by the same amount to bring them out of a state of poverty and starvation. It brings to mind a photo I saw of two women cutting down the last tree in a devastated landscape; despite its rarity they are forced to as they have no other way to cook food. Both ends of the spectrum are environmentally hazardous.

But what can be done? On one hand we have a small proportion of the world's population who, used to a life of affluence, are unwilling to voluntarily reduce their use by the considerable amount required. On the other hand, there is the larger proportion who, in their state of poverty, are virtually powerless to make significant change. As Albert A Bartlett said, 'Starving people do not care about sustainability. If sustainability is to be achieved, the necessary leadership and resources must be supplied by people who are not starving'.[9]

In what form should this leadership and these resources come? We have two major limits: environmental and human. One can't bend too far without breaking (nature) and the other refuses to, even when it skites about how flexible, how adaptable, it can be.

Humans need more than just reassurance that they are doing the right thing. They need financial, social and personal goals to be fulfilled at the same time. Without these they will judge the endeavour too difficult or not worth their time or financial investment. We want things; we don't want to know consequences. We don't want to be the first to make the move. It's like when we were school kids and it took the first brave soul to volunteer before there would be a forest of hands prepared to do the same. We judge this to be a government issue rather than a personal one. We want technology to solve it, when it's been technology that has, to a large degree, brought us to this point. It seems there are so many avoidance strategies. As a world society we need to own the issue of our environment on a person by person basis.

HOW MANY PEOPLE HAVE EVER LIVED ON EARTH?[10]

YEAR	POPULATION
50,000 BC	2
8,000 BC	5,000,000
1 AD	300,000,000
1200	450,000,000
1650	500,000,000
1750	795,000,000
1850	1,265,000,000
1900	1,650,000,000
1950	2,516,000,000
1995	5,760,000,000
2002	6,215,000,000
Number who have ever been born	106,456,367,669
Percentage of those ever born who are living in 2002	5.8

Instead of controlling the environment for the benefit of the population, maybe we should control the population to ensure the survival of our environment.
SIR DAVID ATTENBOROUGH [11]

I make pancakes for dinner with a hot salsa and cheese and onion sauce with a liberal sprinkle of chopped parsley. Plain, simple, easy and nutritious. I get halfway through the dishes and give up. My arm is throbbing. Trev, who has dug over garden beds and carted around wheelbarrows of soil, is stuffed. He sighs, but finishes them while Caleb and I lie on the bed and play silly buggers.

During the day I have redesigned the garden, at least in my head. As we had never really started with any clear idea of what we intended to do, we began by plonking trees around higgledy piggledy and, when we needed more room we extended to the bottom slope, adding 5-square-metre garden beds wherever. Now it's a nightmare to navigate (read hose and wheelbarrow dramas). What we should have done was fence off the bottom third of the block, making it part of the existing goat pen, and plant it out with pigeon pea, lab lab and other high-protein legumes. The chooks could free range there. On the left-hand side of the goat pen would be the entire main vegie beds laid out at close range to the tap, with a watering system set up. On the opposite side, where the greywater outlet is, all the orchard trees should grow, watered by greywater, the whole area mulched. This would be wiser, with less time spent watering and less time feeding the goat, who could have a friend and not think I'm her best pal (and yell at me to come play all the time). The garden beds could be more intensively planted, with all the best resources piled into them rather than spread thinly over a larger area. I talk it over with Trev. He agrees. When this is all over, we will remodel the place to make it more productive. This is something we would have liked to have realised earlier. Gardening is all about learning, experimenting, changing things, adapting, being observant and open to new ideas. I am not an expert gardener, and probably never will be. We've made mistakes; this has made the experiment harder. It's too late to make changes. We decide to review the situation in July. Either that or move to Tasmania.

22 February

Yesterday's scheduled fortnightly barter did not go ahead, but was postponed until today and now possibly till next week. It makes life difficult. I use every scrap of flour we have to make bread, pasties, biscuits, custard tarts, mini-loaves and lemon meringue pie. I need a few 'instant' things for lunches, as I've had enough of preparing things each day. It's nice to just reach in and grab one I prepared earlier. The swelling in my arm is still an issue. Biking to school is a series of painful jars. I step cautiously through the pumpkin flowers today, wary of bees like I've never been before. I thank God we didn't end up buying a beehive. Give me 10 or so bites like this and I'd be hospitalised. Trev and I are both feeling low. He's starting work at 5.45 am, carting around and planting trees in field experiments, and he's hot, tired and suffering bouts of AF, ones that leave him weak and dizzy. He physically can't drink enough water to replace what he loses. He's a worry, and so is the garden, which cannot seem to replace the water it transpires, and it steadfastly refuses to rain. February's total is close to being an all-time low. So far it is the fifth-lowest February rain-fall since records began. We have heaps of water in the tank, but not knowing what the next few months will bring makes it difficult to use it as freely in the garden as we need to. I keep watering seedlings and around the root zone of fruiting plants, but the potatoes are going thirsty. The pigeon pea, arrowroot and lab lab are slowing down. The regrowth is hardly enough to sustain Possum. Being in the garden at the moment is a depressing experience; it was lush just a month ago but it's changing to bedraggled and dry. I know from repeated and bitter experience that, just when you decide it will never rain again, it does. For some plants it will be too late, and our succession planting is already in jeopardy. We have missed out on beans and the army of onions have suffered major losses. There's a gap in the carrots and in my sleep patterns.

23 February

The arm is back in action — I used it to hold the hose while I watered for three hours this morning. I walked gingerly past the rainwater tank trying to be oblivious to its falling level. We received the rates notice and we owe $16 for water used during the last year. We'd used 36 kilolitres. The previous year and a half we used no town water at all. Hopefully we won't experience another five-month drought like we had last year.

I went to pick a watermelon, only to find it had rotted on the inside and only its shell remained to be picked. Not impressed. I immediately went around and picked a few of the 'already ripe but wait till we need to eat it before we pick it' watermelons to try to avoid a repeat of that experience. A good chook turnout today — one chook was so keen she laid one and a half eggs; the second one was less than an inch long and without a yolk. Caleb is amused.

The first two macadamias were found under the tree. I'm looking forward to seeing if the corn kerneller will rip off the outer husk. We've transferred the Colonel onto the verandah to get it out of Trev's workspace and to use as a conversation piece.

Carted around buckets of comfrey, weed and poo gloop, watering the beans, cucumbers and rockmelons. The cucumbers are really suffering in the heat and dry, and are not setting. I glanced into the herb garden today and got an instant impression of bare and grey. Everything is struggling. I could empty both tanks onto the garden and it still wouldn't be enough.

We made peanut butter. The three of us sat around talking while we shelled peanuts and took pot shots at the bowl. There is something pleasant about sitting around doing something as monotonous as peanut shelling with a group of people. Your hands are busy, but your mind is free to wander and your mouth to converse. It's very relaxing. We salted and roasted a huge pan-full. Trev ground them with the hand-grinder, and then further blended them with the blending stick, adding a little sunflower oil to get things going. It tasted great. Caleb has never been a peanut butter eater but, after having had a hand in making it, he was keen to have some smeared on bread for lunch.

Caleb made a bow and arrow. I'm guilty of not yet making a hand-sewn quiver. After dismantling half a tree, Caleb found a flexible stick to use as a bow. Trev tied on twine and provided him with pink drinking straws as makeshift arrows until they find time to make 'real' ones. The effect is more like Cupid than Tolkien's Legolas.

I embarrassed him badly on the way to school. Most of my clothes no longer fit and I'm finding myself opting for the 1970s poo pants look (as we called the dropped crutch fashion when we were kids), mostly out of necessity. I hitch them up repeatedly, and have even discovered that some can be removed without undoing any buttons or flies. Today I wore a wrap-around skirt that is similarly loose, so I improvised with a small gold safety pin. Said pin made it down two hills and around two corners before popping open. I felt it flap in the breeze and then heard Caleb's horrified yell: 'Mum! Your bum is showing!', and sure enough the skirt was on its way to the ground. I whipped it back on, but not in time to avoid giving a few passers-by a shock. The safety pin, secured again, popped 5 metres further down the track. This scenario is repeated at least 10 more times.

'Geez, Caleb, would it be so bad if I just took it off and walked in my knickers?' He's laughing, but looks worried.

I swivel the skirt around and quickly sit on it so it can't wind its way off and we bike the rest of the way to school. Only last week I had to ask him to walk a bit slower, as my knickers were falling down. My usual forceful gait became more akin to someone needing a hip replacement. I wonder if I'm up to taking in my knickers on the sewing machine. I'm not going to be in the market for new ones for another four months.

Along with the weight loss has come a new sense of athleticism. When I walk, I feel a spring that used to be a slog. Sometimes I have an urge to do something drastic, like run. When I lift, carry, haul things around, I know I'm doing it with a leaner, fitter body and it feels great. Trev has been losing weight too, and has had the joy of rediscovering his wardrobe and saying things like, 'I haven't worn this since the 70s'.

So the world's most elaborate diet is working. Through increased exercise and a diet based on vegetables, fruit, grains and nuts we look and feel better and there have even been a few tigers growling around the place when Trev and I eye off each other's new bodies. Caleb's weight remains steady.

Home-grown peanut butter

Grow peanuts in the garden using bought raw peanuts (shelled) as seed. Plant those that still have their skin intact into damp ground. After about 3 to 4 months of keeping them well watered, you'll have a low-growing plant featuring small yellow flowers with 'pegs' that burrow into the ground. At the end of those are your peanuts. Crack open a few to see if they have matured. They'll look like the bought variety, though a shade or two paler until they have dried completely. Dig or pull up the whole plant and leave upside down in the sun or in a sheltered area to dry for a few days. (Never eat or cook mouldy peanuts – they are poisonous.)

Gently roast shelled peanuts in a warm oven or dry pan, stirring frequently. They are ready when the peanut smell becomes strong. Allow them to cool and then place in a food processor with a small amount of oil. Blend them thoroughly. If too dry, you may need to add more oil. Add salt to taste. Spoon into a sterilised jar. Then store in the fridge or spread directly onto bread.

24 February

A nice overcast day — how I love them. I've pulled weeds, harvested the next lot of peanuts, watered for more hours than usual, planted tomatoes, tended chooks and goats and tested soil moisture with a small probe, making regular heartfelt sighs as I do. I've also said g'day to my elderly neighbour whose orchard is full of over-ripe cherry tomatoes and rotting fruit. I ask for a bag and pick what's useful and give it back to her, and haul away the rotten stuff. It's not that I'm a particularly nice person, more that it's one of the methods I use to reduce the local fruit fly population.

I've put out the wheelie bin for the first time in five weeks, mostly because Trev cleaned out his workshop and there are things even he can't recycle. The neighbours have commented on how we have been 'forgetting' to put it out. It feels good to know that we no longer fill it with plastic packaging, pizza boxes and junk. We'd like to get it down to zero. We reuse the empty flour packets till they disintegrate; plastic bags are washed out and reused till they go the same way. Glass bottles and jars are filled with pasta sauces, jams, cordials, chillies and preserves of all kinds. There are no milk containers; there is no flimsy plastic packaging. The inside rubbish bins now sit at the front door. I'd probably only throw something small in them once a day and when our neighbour Shane comes down once a week or so with a six pack to share with Trev (as he always has) he contributes the lion's share to the recycling bin. People often ask how can they possibly do without plastic bags to line their bins. Maybe I'm just not as fussy, but I'm happy to place all wet scraps, generally food, into chook or compost bins, or wrap anything non-chook/compost, but still wet, in a few sheets of newspaper before tossing it in the rubbish bin. Everything else is dry and therefore leaves it relatively clean. A quick wash-out with the hose and it's back in the house. Who needs a plastic bag?

CONTENTS OF DOMESTIC GARBAGE 2002 [12]

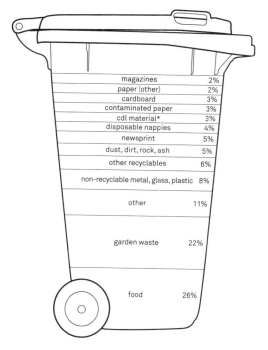

magazines	2%
paper (other)	2%
cardboard	3%
contaminated paper	3%
cdl material*	3%
disposable nappies	4%
newsprint	5%
dust, dirt, rock, ash	5%
other recyclables	6%
non-recyclable metal, glass, plastic	8%
other	11%
garden waste	22%
food	26%

* Container Deposit Legislation material, SA only

THE 2004 TOP 10 CLEAN UP AUSTRALIA DAY RUBBISH ITEMS[13]

(accounting for 53 per cent of total rubbish)

1	Cigarette butts	15%
2	Plastic chips & confectionary bags	13%
3	Plastic bottle caps/lids	10%
4	Glass alcoholic beverage bottles	10%
5	Glass pieces	9%
6	Small paper pieces	7%
7	Plastic water/soft drink bottles	7%
8	Metal/aluminium alcoholic beverage containers	5%
9	Plastic packaging	5%
10	Plastic straws	5%

27 *February*

I have the flu, the type that comes with three kinds of sore throat, a runny nose, headache, sinus and a gamut of aching bones. I have this vague idea I should lie in and read all day, but it doesn't happen. I sweep the floor (no vacuums used here). I wonder what kind of sadistic family would renounce all the wonderful excesses of our time, even if only for six months. Why can't we just do like everyone else does and go with the flow? Why fight against the current, the one that wants to sweep me closer to a consoling bar of blackforest chocolate. This denial really sucks. I suck on homemade peanut brittle, which isn't bad, but no real alternative. I potter, watering for the usual number of hours, trying to capture some of the bearded dragons on video for Caleb's next show and tell. During the week, the biggest one accepted a grasshopper from the end of my secateurs, chewing it down while he kept a watchful eye on me. We try to replicate this for the camera, but fail.

I harvest ginger. Trev immediately turns it into a carboy full of ginger beer. In a few more batches the ginger will be finished. I'm looking forward to experimenting with galangal and lemongrass beer. A fair amount of the sugar we barter goes into making alcohol. While I'm a complete wowser, Trev would suffer without something at least a little bit hard to drink after a hard day's work.

Trev digs over garden beds that are dry as a bone while the wind whips away any last bit of moisture. We discuss options and decide that, no matter what, we will make it through the six months, and that might mean having to buy in some food for Possum or even, at worst, use town water.

We've concocted a plan with our friend Marguerite. She will sell some of our pumpkins at work and the money can go to buying a commercial grain mix for the animals. While Possum is not suffering on the diet of wheat, sorghum, sunflowers and pigeon pea seeds, the chooks are not keen on it; picking through for the good bits, they turn their noses up at the rest. They are still not fully on the lay and we need the extra eggs. Plus we have so many pumpkins it's ridiculous. Some are still setting fruit, while others, having fruited, are dying back. They take up a lot of room as they scramble over garden beds and must be pulled back time and again with remonstrations at their disobedience.

I pull up a bed of potatoes, which are stunted from lack of water. They go towards dinner and, as I dig the bed over, I find thousands of worms about 10 centimetres below the surface. I know the soil is good. It seems such a shame that the weather doesn't want to be in on the act. Trev and Shane discuss the tendency towards having dry Februarys followed by flooding Marchs. The ants are going berserk in the kitchen, always a good sign of rain. Yet the forecast is for more sun, more wind, and the possible showers they predict always fall somewhere else. While we only have our pride at stake, pioneers would have had their livelihoods, and lives, at risk. While they would have hauled water by hand, I complain about the hose. While they cooked over smoky fires, I have most of the mod cons, and enough power to do most things at the flick of a switch. We have it easy. But, typically, this will in no way inhibit the desire to complain.

I convulse with sneezes, give up and trail up to the house to contemplate lying down. I don't. I pot up plants and go back down to milk the goat.

Ginger beer

Step one

2 teaspoons dried yeast

4 teaspoons sugar

1 cup warm water

Step two

4 cups sugar

2 teaspoons grated lemon zest

2 tablespoons ground ginger, or 4 tablespoons fresh grated

2 teaspoons tartaric acid

4 litres hot water

4 litres cold water

Stir the step one ingredients together in a glass and leave them in a warm place.

Put the first four ingredients from step two into a large clean bucket, add the hot water and stir until the sugar has dissolved. Then add the cold water. When the liquid has cooled to only just warm add the yeast mixture from step one. Cover the bucket and leave for 1–2 days then strain into bottles. Fill each to within 3 centimetres of the top. Add 1 teaspoon of sugar to each bottle, cap and shake well to dissolve the sugar. Place in a warm spot for 1–5 days. The liquid will expand in the bottles over that time. Refrigerate for several hours before drinking. Open cautiously – they can be very fizzy. Drink sooner rather than later; set yourself a goal of a month.

Makes around 10 litres.

28 February

Last day of the second month. Caleb and I bike to school, and make the observation that all the suburban chariots — supposedly off-road vehicles, but which have only a 5 per cent chance of ever leaving the bitumen — make up for it by only ever being half on the road. We bike far across in the gravel on the right side of the road, where we feel it's safest. They come around the worst curve, dangling a metre over the white line. We are forced against the railing, teetering over a long drop into a creek bed. I have a whole repertoire of angry comments to make should one of them ever stop to listen. Mostly I'd point out that while they think they are keeping their family 'safe' by driving in a tank, they are in fact jeopardising their future by polluting it — every 1 litre of petrol is 10,400 litres of polluted air. Then I'd advise them to 'Get a life!', though Caleb insists the term is 'Take a life'. I worry that one of those families trying to keep themselves safe will.

All up February has been a trying month. Perhaps during the next we might get to see some decent rain. It will go a long way towards restoring our circadian rhythms as well as the growth patterns of various plants.

Trev's rave

I keep asking myself how I got into this. After all, it's not like I don't have form. I can say, with that insouciant flick of the wrist so beloved of the jet-setting cognoscenti, 'been there done that'. But the triumph of hope over experience and the persuasive powers of a determined, capable woman are not to be underestimated. Because, in a desperate, slapdash sort of way, I have attempted something like this before.

During the late 1970s, it was the big hippie dream to bust out of the city, buy some land, be part of a commune (man) and forget the rat race. Since I was an undoubtedly big hippie, that is what I did (with about a million mates and assorted hangers-on). Or, more accurately, attempted to do.

We were living in the heart of Melbourne, young, bored, disgruntled, smoking enough dope to fuel another Woodstock, when one of the gang noticed an ad in the paper for cheap land in Queensland. There were nine of us living in the house; twelve and a half grand for 160 acres wasn't a lot, even then. We sent a small scouting party to check it out and before you could say 'pack a cone', we were adding Esquire to our names.

There are usually good reasons for land being cheap. It may be of marginal fertility or in a low rainfall area. It may be covered in noxious weeds. The soil may be hard setting, or prone to all forms of erosion known to agri-science, and then some. The soil pH may be so low it causes aluminium toxicity. It may be hotter than the devil's pitchfork in summer, which may happen to be almost all year round. Electricity may be many kilometres and many more thousands of dollars away. Yes, I think that almost covers it. There were probably other reasons but as these were the business of the vendor, and may be libellous if printed here . . . well, I'll leave it there.

We (it'll be we for a while yet – the number of semi-permanents and frequent visitors was still in the low thousands) didn't know any of this until it was far too late, although I think, given the rate of bailouts over the next few months, that there were sneaking suspicions among more than a few that a Garden of Eden situation was going to take more doing than any of us poor hippies, fresh from the big smoke, could ever imagine.

You may have gathered by now that we were lotus-eaters, adherents of a diverse and motley crew of gurus, teachers and assorted charlatans. The less generous would say we were useless layabouts; today it would be ferals. So, what does a bloke raised on a diet of Neil Young and Lobsang Rampa decide to build as his first dwelling? A log cabin. This is all very well, I daresay, in the cool mists of North America, using nice, friendly softwoods, straight as a die from butt to crown. Using Aussie hardwood, with a small axe as my only tool and absolutely no idea how to use it, it's a lot harder than it sounds. A lot. I had 40 blisters on my hands after the first week, seven on one finger alone.

The log cabin did get built. About the size of your average hall cupboard, it had huge gaps between the logs which were filled, after a fashion, with crushed ant bed. It had a dirt floor and a bark roof, which leaked like a sieve. During the first wet season we discovered, to our horror, that the lovely creek bank site we'd chosen went under water; we knew we were in trouble when the first yabby crawled through the door seeking shelter. During the subsequent dry season (lasting about five years, from memory), the site burnt to the ground.

These were the outcast years. We put the council offside by standing in front of the bulldozers they sent to clear trees from the side of the road. The police raided us about every six months.

'We're Joh's boys', they'd say, as they swaggered in, turned everything upside down, found nothing and left. The annual dob-in-a-druggie campaign invariably resulted in a plethora of calls pointing the police in our direction. For all I know, there were even sermons preached from the pulpit denouncing us. Eventually, the novelty wore off and the respectable community largely learned to ignore us, especially the council, who from the time of the 'protest' onwards refused to grade the road outside our place, lifting the grader at our property line and laying it back down once past.

By this time, many people had decided the bush was not for them and had returned to the city, leaving the hard core of us determined to make a go of it. We, along with others who had moved onto the surrounding properties, formed a solid community of like-minded people, many of whom became lifelong friends, and got down to the serious business of having kids and building altogether more substantial houses.

My then partner and I went the whole hog and started work on a two-storey post and beam mud-brick house, which, 15 years later, was still not quite finished. Mud brick and stone were the popular building materials, and there were some truly magnificent efforts. It's one of the ironies of life that by the time I'd finished (I use the term loosely) building the house, I felt I knew what I was doing, and should probably have bulldozed the joint and started again, this time without the mistakes. I didn't have the energy, or inclination.

The house was, after all, serviceable. It had a rudimentary 12-volt power system, which ran the lights, stereo and black-and-white TV (there was only the ABC then anyway), a rainwater tank for drinking water and another, on a high stand, for the shower. We had two dams and a generator, which had to be started every time I wanted to drill a hole or use a power saw. I became proficient in the use of hand tools. It was close to being a sustainable house, although this is probably making a virtue out of necessity. At that stage in my life, if I could have afforded things like power and a four-wheel drive, I would have had them.

The garden was another story. The soil was only good for holding up the plant. This could be improved, but the local fauna, especially the possums, ate everything we planted. Nothing short of a cage keeps possums out of a garden, and it's not practical to build a fence, complete with roof and concrete footings, over everything you plant. The other option was to bulldoze their habitat, clear the dry sclerophyll forest that surrounded us. To cut a long story short, the possums stayed and the garden, excepting a few citrus trees, went.

But it was a great place for the kids. By the late 1980s, the community as a whole, occupying a total area of about 1000 acres, had produced a fairly hefty tribe. They ran wild in the bush, swam in the dams, took the bus to school and gained an appreciation for the natural world. They revelled in natural phenomena such as floods and violent storms and learned to respect, but not fear, the bush. We lived in close contact with kangaroos, wallabies and any number of smaller marsupials, a veritable Noah's Ark of reptiles and insect species of astonishing variety. I lived there for 20 years, and saw insects I'd never seen before on an almost-daily basis.

But all things must pass, as the cliché runs, and by the mid-1990s it was, for various reasons, time for a change. I had met Linda by this time and was regularly staying at her (rented) place in town. I was becoming enamoured of the white tile bathroom that didn't have a resident python (pythons are OK in themselves, but you don't want them crapping on you when you're in the bath); the lights that worked without the worry of flat batteries; the kitchen appliances; the computer. And there was no way Linda was going to move into my 'tree house' in the bush. This impossibility is probably best epitomised by the story of how one night, just as we were about to hop into bed, she pointed to the wall and remarked on the uncommon size of the spider she'd seen there enjoying a snack (probably a small bird). At this stage in our relationship, we knew each other in the biblical rather than the literal sense and I failed to detect the note of horror in her voice. I smiled, said something offhand and continued to get into bed. She made it clear that this was not good enough and it began to dawn on me that I actually had to remove the monster from her sight. I tried to explain that, were I to remove every spider in the house, there would be little sleep got that night, or indeed, that week. We reached a compromise. My house in the bush was not part of it.

We bought our own place in town, Caleb was born, and the events that led to this madness ... I mean adventure ... were in place. This time we have fruit fly instead of possums, but the soil is better; the infrastructure and planning infinitely better; the skills and determination in place; the motivation clear. This time we're doing it properly.

march

1 March

Trev and I spent a few hours last night creating an Excel rainfall sheet. We now have all the rainfall totals for the area from 1870 onwards — it will be interesting to see if there has been any noticeable times of drought that follow the pattern of those we are experiencing now. Is global warming having a noticeable effect? A few more hours of data entry to go yet before we can start crunching numbers. Amateur climatology at its worst. (See Appendix 1, page 266, for our results.)

 Global warming changes climate in jerks, during which climate patterns jump from one stable state to another. Because of the atmosphere's telekinetic nature, these changes can manifest themselves instantaneously across the globe. The best analogy is perhaps that of a finger on a light switch. Nothing happens for a while, but if you slowly increase the pressure a certain point is reached, a sudden change occurs, and conditions swiftly alter from one state to another.
TIM FLANNERY[1]

Dinner was fried rice with ginger, capsicum, parsley, squash, leek, carrot and egg. Dessert was passionfruit custard with sliced bananas. We bartered fetta for bananas and most of them are already soft so we are going hard trying to eat them all. Drying is a good way to store them, but Trev is the only one who has them.

7 March

'Mum, I'm not wasting my breakfast.'

'Well, that's good. I'm very pleased to hear it.' I have my back to Caleb in the kitchen while I wash dishes.

I've fed him poached egg, hot chocolate and a slice of warm pan-scone smeared with peanut butter.

'Yes,' he continues, 'the ants seem to like it'.

I whirl around and see he has found a trail of ants and placed the scone in their path.

I whip it out of their path and read him the riot act. Rah, rah, rah, I go. I can hear myself and there are little fragments of my conscience jumping on my shoulders going rah, rah, rah at me too. I shake as many ants off the scone as possible and put it in the fridge, thinking of the day I let him throw bread dough on the ceiling beam and had let it pass with barely a mention. Ah, the days of plenty, not so long ago.

'The ants have to eat too', he mumbles from the couch.

I make him pancakes and offer them in apology.

'Caleb, food is a bit hard at the moment.' Can I hear myself? Am I really saying this?

'We need to be careful with what we have and not waste it. Feeding it to ants is a waste when they are just as happy to eat dead cockroaches.'

THE LAND OF THE LOST LEFTOVERS

Approximately 3.3 million tonnes of food are thrown away each year in Australia. (That's equivalent to 470,000 elephants.)

Planet Ark calculates that the waste represents one quarter of our food supply in Australia, and is almost half the amount distributed in 2004 to 825 million of the world's starving people.

The Australia Institute stated that Australians spend $5.3 billion every year on food they do not eat.[2]

Last night's dinner was an event. I made a pumpkin and tomato stew with soybeans and coriander, sprinkled with chopped, salted, roasted nuts, plus a swirl of yoghurt, topped with fresh herbs, beans and asparagus. Good stuff. Trev's and mine had a flotilla of roughly chopped onions fried in curry paste. Caleb refused to eat it. By 8 o'clock he had spent time in his bedroom with it, been bribed and had his pumpkin aversion, which is directly connected to his gag reflex, psychologically analysed. I 'did a deal'. I turned the stew into fritters and served him two. He needed to take 20 bites of it to qualify for a chocolate pancake dessert. He managed 10 before the gag reflex jeopardised the ones he'd already swallowed to such a point I gave in.

If it was just Trev and myself, we would be able to haul ourselves, and our appetites, through the pumpkin patch. We have an army of them lying out there; the vines are dying back, leaving them golden and ripe on the dry ground.

I make repeated and monotonous lists of what is growing: radishes, pumpkin, squash, zucchini, a few less than turgid carrots, eggplants, daikon, parsley, chives, basil, coriander, rainbow chard, Ceylonese spinach, leeks, arrowroot tubers, Jerusalem artichokes, capsicums, chillies, a few potatoes, sweet potatoes, peanuts, tomatoes, passionfruit, lemons, limes, watermelons, rockmelons, a few beans (soon to be many more), water chestnuts, paw paws, macadamias, mandarins and oranges, with bananas coming on. I'm forced to say that while the list looks good, the reality is that each zucchini is hard won at the moment. The garden is barren, full of fruit fly and wilting plants. There is no water to plant more and while some garden beds are watered intensively, the rest go without. The moveable chook pen is placed over an area, and then moved on, leaving empty sunflower heads and a few chook feathers behind. It all adds to the look of desolation.

In a futile attempt to be positive, I will mention that as the weeds and grass no longer grow, less time is required removing them, or reducing their length.

The only promise of rainfall in weeks has passed without a drop. To both of us it had been a point of hope, and that has faded fast. So, if there is a low point in this strange little battle of ours, it's now. We've spent the day making the garden look tidy — pulling up, chaffing and mulching the parrot-blighted sorghum plants — and watering, sighing deeply and promising each other that we will not allow anyone else into the garden, and that we will seriously think about moving somewhere with regular rainfall.

On cue the wind pops up, and forces plants to transpire all the harder, whirling piles of dust in circles and driving Trevor to moments of rage. Caleb, hearing this, goes upstairs and comes back down with a glass of water.

'Daddy, you'll feel better if you drink this.'

I laid sleepless in bed last night and pretended not to notice that Trev was too. If we spoke it would only be about one thing and, as we'd spent the day 'miseralising' about the state of drought and discussing various plans of action, anything we said would revolve around the harsh sounds of compromise. I couldn't bear a continuation in that vein. Instead I continue it in my head, through one hour and out the next. I recall having mentioned on our website the question, 'will it be a marginal existence?' It hasn't taken me six months to realise that it is very likely to be a dribble out to the end rather than a blazing trail of success. We resolve not to give up. We know that an all-expenses-paid trip to a shopping mall would be ashes in our mouths.

It's getting to the point that no amount of rainfall will be sufficient to pull us out of this hole. Now should be the time of plenty, of preserving excess ahead of the slimmer pickin's of May and June when rainfall would normally drop off and the growing season slows down a pace or two.

We look up 2004's rainfall and, from our notes, read that Kidd Bridge was underwater this time last year and we were contemplating flood measures. Now the creek no longer flows and the river is a brown sluggish thing showing its bones. After the flood we had a drought – 59 millimetres of rainfall over five months in what was a new record low – and now, five months later, we are recording more lowest lows. It seems very much like a case of global warming and yet when we look at our Excel sheet, there have been worse years than these. The 1870s, 1902 and 1957 were shockers. This, of course, doesn't take into account that you might get the majority of your year's rainfall in one week and spend the rest of it in drought. Last year didn't even make the 15 worst years, despite the record dry spell – though 2000, 2001, 2002 did.

GLOBAL WARMING

Global warming is caused by an increase in greenhouse gases in the Earth's atmosphere. The main greenhouse gases are water vapour, carbon dioxide, methane and nitrous oxide, as well as some manufactured gases such as chlorofluorocarbons (CFCs) and some of their replacements.

Reducing the amount of greenhouse gases produced by human activities – particularly the burning of fossil fuels and land clearing – is increasingly being recognised as an important issue by governments, industry and the community.

Australian households generate almost one-fifth of Australia's greenhouse gases – about 15 tonnes per household each year – through everyday activities such as transport, household energy use and the decay of household waste in landfills.[3]

Warming to global issues

Whether global warming is happening or not is beside the point. So many people waste time debating: is it happening? If it is, is it really our fault? The ambiguity around global warming has caused vacillation. We can see smoke. Is the house on fire or not? Shall we grab a bucket? Should we just stand and wait till it bursts into flames and do something then? By the time it's conclusive it's too late. If it turns out to be wrong, then reducing our environmental impact by lowering CO_2 emissions, stopping land clearing, using resources sustainably and so on can only be positive in regards to biodiversity and other environmental issues. Don't get stuck in the freeze-frame of doubts surrounding scientific prophesies – they always contradict each other – and no one really knows what or how it will happen. We do know that the world's wild lands are being cleared at a rate of 1.6 acres per second at the same time as we're emitting 708 tonnes of CO_2, with 2.8 more people added to the world every second (taking into account births and deaths) to help us increase the rate – things cannot go on as they are indefinitely.

There are thousands of species in the world who would agree if they weren't already dead. The World Conservation Union (IUCN) has estimated that over 5500 species of animals, birds, fish, reptiles and invertebrates are being threatened by extinction, along with 6700 species of plants. And they are dying out at a rate between 50–150 species per day. Apocalypse? It's happening now.

Facing extinction are:
- close to 1100 species of mammals (about 24 per cent of the total number of mammal species)
- over 1100 bird species (around 12 per cent of known species)
- over 750 species of fish (49 per cent of total surveyed)
- around 290 species of reptiles (62 per cent of total number surveyed)
- an estimated 157 species of amphibians (39 per cent of total number surveyed).[4]

And the environment is suffering too:
- More than 50 per cent of the world's wetlands have been drained.
- Since 1950 some 3 billion hectares of forest cover – nearly half of the world's total – have been lost. Each year a further 16 million hectares of forest are destroyed.
- Between 50 and 80 per cent of mangrove ecosystems have been destroyed.
- Roughly one-third of the world's coral reef systems has been destroyed or highly degraded.
- One-fourth of the planet's topsoil has been lost.
- Sixty-nine per cent of the world's major fish stocks are fully exploited, over-fished, depleted or slowly recovering from over-fishing, and productivity has fallen in all but four of the 15 most important fishing regions.
- Nearly 2 billion hectares of crop and grazing land are suffering from moderate to severe soil degradation.[5]

About the only proactive thing we can do at the moment is perform rain dances. Over the years, Caleb has evolved his own peculiar custom. He stands out on the verandah and abuses the rain, tells it off, exhorts it to leave, urges it to precipitate elsewhere, but in language his own size. He believes, and sometimes it seems as though it's true, that the rain is listening, for the louder he tells it to go, the harder it seems to pour. He tells me, proudly, that he believes his reverse psychology is working.

For us the lack of rain is an inconvenience, a possible blow to our pride should we fail to complete what we have set out to. It is depressing to look out our window, but our livelihoods are not at stake. This is not the case for a lot of rural families, who do not have a six-month limitation on stress, but will rely on seasonal rainfall year in and year out, and will often have to face long periods of rainlessness. With rural areas suffering from higher rates of suicide it makes me wonder if they peak when the Earth is showing its blistered back?

Trev and I have a fair understanding of depression and suicide, as we met due to both. When I arrived in Gympie in late 1995, Trevor was unknown to me, and it was unknown to him that he was about to lose his partner, Louise. She suicided on New Year's Eve. Trevor and his 11-year-old son, Ehren, found her the next morning. Several months later I heard about the incident — two years before, my partner had died in very similar circumstances and I was only just beginning to surface from my loss. I felt compelled to make contact with Trevor and offer my support. For months we spent hours on the phone talking about life and, when he could bear it, about death. I recall getting off the phone one day and realising that it was only because I had been through what I had that I was able to help this, in some ways, anonymous person. In a funny way I thanked Carl, my partner, for putting me in a position to do so. It was the first time I'd found something positive in the experience.

Eventually Trev suggested we meet in person. I wasn't so keen; I enjoyed our phone calls and wanted to keep it at that, but I could find no good reason to refuse. We met one Saturday morning. I had always envisioned him as an old (he was 37 — I was 26), tall, skinny, bearded hippie. He wasn't. He was tall and muscular with long, dark, curly hair — a hippie with the word 'spunk' (metaphorically) tattooed across his forehead. It was quite disconcerting trying to talk to him about his grief while hiding my attraction. He had a reputation with women that had me on my guard, but, though it was some time before we would consider ourselves on romantic terms, from then on it really was all history.

8 March

The television stopped, would no longer respond; no heartbeat could be detected. It happened halfway through the half-hour, four-nights-a-week thrill of *Doctor Who*. Trev and Caleb are mouths dropped, grief-stricken, and I'm overwhelmed with gratitude. I hate the thing. Caleb and I are always constructing 'deals' about how much TV he can watch. Often when I'm in the garden for a period of time I return to find it unexpectedly on and Caleb's brains long since dribbled out his ears.

9 March

'Come on, Possum. Move over!' Possum has me wedged between her flank and the fence and is resting on me. I'm in the process of giving her a midday milk. This is something new. As we had her 'serviced' five months prior to September 2004 in anticipation of starting then, and because we didn't till January, she is already past her peak. Recently, her milk flow has been reducing despite her bulging sides. The midday milk is a brain wake-up tactic. 'Hey brain, I'm always empty, my babies need more milk, produce more.' This is only the second day, and there is no discernable increase. I'll keep this particular experiment going for a week to see if it does any good. When I finish I drop great handfuls of parsley, which is supposedly a galactagogue (increases milk supply), into her food trough and she scoffs it up.

Milking Possum over the last few years has been a giant learning curve. We were quick to realise that Possum was a mistake. First, she had two large horns, two very small teats, and she came with two kids, Earthworm Jim and Hallelujah. Possum arrived stressed, and refused to feed the pair, who bleated pathetically and tried their hardest, even though Possum used those two large horns to defend her two very small teats.

I learnt the limitations of reading. My whole life has been about becoming interested in something, and immediately devouring every book I can find on the subject. Usually, during that process, I find something else of interest as interests intersect with other interests to form a giant ball of research that never really amounts to anything other than entertaining stories. Buying books about goats did not assist when buying goats.

It wasn't until later I learnt that first fresheners give less milk and are typically less broken in to milking, that small teats which you can get only one finger around are not ideal (by week four we had managed to milk all of 20 millilitres), and that Toggenburg and Anglo Nubians are two of the noisiest breeds, something Possum, a cross between both, takes very seriously.

We tried to do what Possum's former owner advised: separate Possum from the kids overnight then milk her in the morning, so at least we get one milk out of her a day. In theory it sounded easy. For one full hour we listened to the clamour of three distraught goats and felt unbearably cruel. We liberated the goats in the yard and gave the neighbours a dozen eggs each.

We were not going to give in. We tried again, this time during daylight hours. We tied Earthworm and Hallelujah to the outside of the pen and they managed to stay there a whole day before losing their voices. I ran down every 10 minutes to check that the horrible gargle coming out of Hallelujah wasn't the sound of a strangulation in process.

Possum seemed to enjoy the day's respite, but their noise must have bothered her too, and she threw them around when they got back inside as if to reprimand them for their tiresome behaviour. Still we failed to milk her. By this stage we were completely under cow and the goat knew it. All pretence at cooperation was dropped as she refused outright to stand still and be milked.

Hallelujah had an infected foot on arrival and it never managed to heal, mostly because she was incredibly skittish, and went into a frenzy of small horns and hooves every time we attempted to apply curative to the hoof. She was 'given away' to some nice people who will look after her and let her live unencumbered by requirements such as birth or producing milk. They will pet her regularly, and feed her ice-cream three times a week.

Her departure signalled a turning point in our goat-keeping phase. We gave up. Stressed by Hallelujah's disappearance, Possum fretted and summarily dismissed Earthworm from all 'booby feeding' as Caleb called it. Several days later, her udders were huge and distended. She wouldn't let us touch her. We couldn't milk her. We hung out a 'to give away' sign and decided to call the vet. We were resigned to letting her dry up when Shane dropped around for an early morning visit. He's an ex-dairy farmer and was in the process of asking Trev for a favour when I quickly dropped in a request of my own. Sure, he'd take a look at her. Two minutes later she was being successfully milked for the first time, streams of it. He made it look easy. She fought, but knew she'd met her match and eventually submitted to the indignity. It was a week before we managed to do it with anywhere near the assurance he had.

Possum would struggle, turn this way and that, lift her hooves and aim for the jug. One of us would straddle her neck and suffer the twist and shove of horn in thigh (Trev) or stomach (me) while the other milked, though, on one memorable occasion, she took off so unexpectedly I was unable to get either foot to the ground in time and managed to do a lap of the goat pen on her back. Caleb thought it was hilarious.

'Do it again, Mum, do it again!'

With my dignity dragged through the small black balls of goat poo, I got back to milking.

'Why can't goats just piss milk into a bucket and leave it for me to retrieve, like chooks leave eggs?' I grizzle. 'Why can't they be like plants and just grow where you put them?'

First, we had to drop all our preconceived notions of how to milk a goat, throw out all the textbook images. We had to strip her: roll our thumb and forefinger very firmly down the teat, and we saw lovely jets of white milk land in our milking jugs. We used milk as lubricant but found it wasn't that great, so we tried small amounts of olive oil. It worked. The first few jugs were rendered undrinkable by the addition of hoof, but we were away. My textbooks (I referred to them by the hour those first few months) said it was not wise to use stripping as a method of milking, but Shane shrugged and said it would do no harm. I'm still doing it. Compared with Earthworm Jim's technique of milk extraction – winceable – ours seemed mild.

Earthworm Jim was a delight with his scrambling, tumbling falls and graceful leaps: 'Did you see him? He clicked his heels in mid-flight!' He was the first to enjoy a bit of human interaction. Caleb quickly dubbed him 'his' and enjoyed climbing over the railing to play with him. Then Earthworm grew hormones. His general rambunctiousness, his amusing cavorting, became dangerous. Caleb learnt the hard way how hard a goat's head is when it hits yours. He left the pen swearing at Earthworm all the way to the house.

'I hate you, you "fucknin", you're not my friend!'

Earthworm began to pick on Possum too. Every time she tried to eat, he pushed her out of the way, shoved his head under hers and tossed his horns into her neck. She was getting skinnier while he was often seen bulging at the sides until he looked like one more bite would bring him to stage pop. She got sick of him. When he got his head stuck under the fence and had to be 'surgically removed', she tossed him around for five minutes as if to say, 'Don't bother doing that again, you little idiot'. Then he mysteriously managed to jump onto the shadecloth sail that covers their pen and motored around head first, pushing himself along with his back legs until he fell off. She shook her head in dismay and looked away. He used a tree stump to hijack her, jumping on her back if she walked past. They were often seen in various stages of entanglement, he underneath, his head wearing a pair of painfully large udders as he attempted to walk uphill and she down. He became noisier and more demanding, 'yelling' out all day for 'more food, more food'.

If I tried to give Possum a brush, which she loves, Earthworm would shove himself under the brush so he got it instead. He began to head-butt in earnest. We vowed he would go, and our squeamishness over his demise lessened as his painful behaviour increased.

I hung up a give-away sign. But no one wants a castrated male kid with a bad attitude.

Ehren was our saviour. He arrived in his shiny white ute, loaded Earthworm on board and took him down to the meatworks where he was turned into chops of various sizes and dog bones. Ehren arrived home and I asked him in a whisper how it had gone.

'Wow!' he said, 'I got there, they came outside, stunned him and cut his throat right there and then'.

'Shhhh!' I said, but the kids heard and all the stories of ice-cream three times a week came to naught.

Trev ate Earthworm, but then we always knew he would.

All that is over now, and we've become very fond of Possum. When in the garden she follows our progress, and enjoys the titbits we feed her. She nibbles us gently with her lips, grabbing hold of any piece of clothing she can, and tugging ever so softly. She is mild and patient, though quick to respond to any change in routine — negatively.

Each morning at 6 am I bend over Possum's rear (from the road it must look disturbingly bestial). With my left hand, I hold the jug; my right does the milking. Trev is crouched to the left, as he industriously milks the other udder. My udder is always more fruitful, and it's a race to see who finishes first. Trev and I discuss the garden, the lack of rain, Possum, the number of flies, the lack of rain, our plans for the day, the lack of rain. It's become our morning and evening ritual, bending over the back of a goat, expressing milk from reluctant udders, and waxing pessimistic over drought cycles. Trev and I have also added to our routine. Once we've milked her we stand up, stretch our backs and give each other a quick morning cuddle. I laugh about how romantic it is standing there, covered in goat hair, amid the little black balls of poo, with Light Orange the deranged chook giving our feet a good peck to check for food content, and having an opportunistic snuggle.

The milk is then filtered, measured and chilled. Unless I'm making ricotta, yoghurt or cheese, I don't pasteurise the milk.

We've been keeping notes and records on Possum's behaviour and milk production. The most she has produced is 4.2 litres in a day; the least, 1.1.

Goat's milk isn't an acquired taste if it's fresh. It's certainly sweeter. Caleb developed an aversion to the idea of goat's milk and requested a glass of cow's booby milk, please. I resorted to subterfuge, telling him the glass he was handed contained cow's milk when it didn't. He consumed every drop, declaring it far superior to that goat stuff. He wasn't impressed with my smirk and explanation as to the origin of his own milky grin.

From then on he was happy to drink it. His daily drink is goat's milk, raw egg, vanilla and a banana blended up and gulped down.

Caleb became interested in mastering the art of milking. Possum isn't keen on his ticklish fingers, but he does manage to express 5 millilitres or so of milk before she forces him to desist. One night, when I believed he had completed his 5-millilitre exercise, I saw him bend down and quickly express milk in one well-aimed shot into his mouth. He came up grinning and I wondered what had happened to his former squeamishness about the origins of his glass of milk.

We freeze the surplus milk and, when we have 10 litres (usually three or four days), it is thawed overnight and turned into fetta, which is either left in brine or soaked in combinations of olive oil and spices. Alternatively, we can make other traditional goat's milk cheeses, like Chevrotin or Saint Maure. I've tried bocconcini and mozzarella, which I've never managed to get to melt as they should but, when raw, were as plastic in texture as the real thing. Instant cheeses like ricotta and cream cheese are easy, but the hang-around-and-wait-two-months-before-you-get-to-taste-it cheddars and bries are more difficult. The fridge sports its own cheese shelf with red, wax-coated cheddars, jars of fetta in brine and bowls of ricotta.

Ricotta

10 litres milk
¹/₂ cup white vinegar
¹/₂ teaspoon salt

Heat the milk to 90°C then stir in the vinegar. The milk will quickly coagulate, dividing the curd from the whey. Allow it to sit for five minutes. Line a colander with cheesecloth. Pour in the curds and whey. Let drain for five minutes (retain the whey for the cat or dog, or goat or chook). Blend in the salt with a fork. Place the ricotta in a covered container and refrigerate.

Makes roughly 1 kilo.

Goat's cheeses that are ready to eat immediately are far more palatable than those that are aged. Caproic acid in goat's milk increases with time and this is what causes the goaty taste and smell. So we've learnt to stick to the cheeses that don't require extended ageing. When I first came to Australia it took me a while to adapt to the bitey dryness of the cheeses that Australians prefer, as I was used to moist and mild Colby's. But getting used to them was far easier than adapting to cheeses that are white and tangy, and refuse to melt at any temperature. Trev is doing his job, consuming everything in range and then some. Caleb and I initially hung back, reluctant. Every now and then a block of yellow cheese would turn up in the fridge, plastic-wrapped and ready to eat, and Caleb and I would hoe in. Now we're finally integrated, goat's cheese pizzas are fantastic!

Without having to feed Possum, the job of creating enough food would be a lot easier. However, the variety of foods would lessen considerably. Where would we be without chocolate custard, if only to bribe Caleb to eat his dinner? We have thought about eliminating dairy products from our diet, as humans are the only animals who insist on drinking milk throughout their lives. After the age of two the human body begins to produce less of the enzyme lactase, and the less lactase the body creates the poorer its ability is to break down the lactose or milk sugar. The symptoms of lactose intolerance are cramps, bloating, gas, diarrhoea and nausea, the onset of which can occur anywhere from 30 minutes to two hours after eating dairy food, the severity depending on the degree of lactase secretion.

Some people are more susceptible to lactose intolerance than others: 75 per cent of American Indians and African Americans, and 90 per cent of Asians are lactose intolerant.

As dairy products are such a high source of calcium you'd think that those races would suffer higher rates of osteoporosis. Yet amazingly Asian cultures have the lowest incidence of osteoporosis. The reason given is that Asians tend to eat more calcium-rich leafy greens, and exercise more than the western world with its high-calcium, high-fat diet and sedentary lifestyle.

It takes a lot of energy, water and land to produce animal products for our consumption. How much food is grown to feed animals so we can eat their products and drink their milk? How much land would become available if this usage was cut? How much water?

MEAT COMES AT A PRICE

Around the world 38 per cent of grain is fed to animals, who are only 30–40 per cent efficient at turning an already high-protein food into meat. It takes 7 kilos of grain to produce a kilo of beef, 4 kilos for a kilo of pork, and 2.5 kilos for a kilo of chicken.

Water efficiency is also a factor: it takes between 50 and 100 times more water to produce a kilo of feedlot beef than a kilo of wheat. It takes up a great deal of cleared land to grow grain to feed Australia's 26 million cattle and 120 million sheep. The United States Union of Concerned Scientists has concluded that halving the average household's meat consumption would reduce agricultural land use by 30 per cent and water pollution by 24 per cent.

If you choose not to eat meat, not only would the environment benefit, but we would also be able to supply the world's hungry with the excess grain.

How much meat do we eat?[6]

	MEAT EATEN KG/PERSON/YEAR	CAL/PERSON/YEAR
Australia	110	3,224,000
Developed world	77	3,240,000
Developing world	26	2,650,000

Agriculture and grazing have a serious impact on Australia's levels of salinity. Australia was once ocean floor and as such has substantial amounts of salt stored underground. Human practices such as land clearing result in changes in drainage and groundwater levels. Rising groundwater brings salt to the surface and creates salinity, which can degrade water and soil quality and affect the health of river ecosystems.

Dryland salinity

When native vegetation is removed and replaced by crops with shallow root systems, such as pasture, grains and vegetables, these crops cannot utilise soil moisture, causing the water table to rise, bringing with it the salts stored below. Grazing exacerbates this effect as it decreases the grass's ability to use and transpire moisture.

Dryland salinity affects more than 2.5 million hectares of land in Australia.[7]

Irrigated salinity

Excessive irrigation and poor drainage result in water-logged soils. The unused water seeps down into the groundwater, raising the water table and bringing salts to the surface.

Around 40 per cent of irrigated land in Australia (600,000 hectares) has a water table less than the safe level of 2 metres below the surface.[8]

Around 70–80 per cent of irrigated land in New South Wales is threatened by rising water tables and associated salinity problems.[9]

Urban salinity

Sewerage (septic and drainage systems), garden watering, clearing of native vegetation, and buildings, roads and other infrastructure can all change drainage patterns that affect the water table and cause salinity issues.

Each day I climb up into Caleb's cubby house, lean out and chop down more of the golden rain tree for Possum to eat. The large ice-cream bean trees out the front were to be part of her diet too. When she first arrived she seemed to relish the branches, but she decided, on introduction to much tastier foods, that they aren't worth eating. We'll offer her tender new growth; she will go hungry for days, but won't give in. Having her in our backyard means we grow fodder trees that also increase the nitrogen in the soil, and tap deep into the Earth to bring nutrients to the surface. She also enriches the soil with her own high-nitrogen additive. Because no transport factors need to be added to the energy equation, we are drinking milk at a lower environmental cost than most. However, now we're bartering for her grain, we have to add this huge land area, water use and transport cost into the equation. This makes her space in the backyard unsustainable.

Incidentally, the television has risen from the dead. Elation for some.

10 March

After yesterday's goat talk, we walked down this morning to milk her and found her in distress, pawing the ground, stretching, obviously straining and, though passing lots of healthy looking black marbles, no wee. She did not meet us at the gate trying to push her nose into the grain bucket. Instead we had to lead her out of her pen and it became obvious all was not as it should be. We milked her, she turned her nose up at the grain; we debated what to do, then hit the books, which were soon tossed to one side, and resorted to the Internet. The most serious possibility is urinary calculi, which is caused by too little calcium in the diet compared with phosphorus, the result of poor diet-management on behalf of the owner. I hyperventilate. It is something I've always worried about. Now that her diet is limited to fewer leguminous feeds, which are calcium-rich, and is increasingly higher in phosphorous-rich grains (because she refuses to eat what's available), it seems to make sense. I call the vet. This is a first for us; apart from having difficulty milking her through our own ineptness, Possum has been healthy. The vet cannot get here for an hour — it turns out to be two. I'm rushing down every five minutes tearing my hair out and abusing myself for putting the poor thing through our experiment. Good lord, I can't even remember asking for her permission. And if she dies ... oh no! I've seen people go spare over their animals and I've always found it sickening, but here I am spinning out over Possum in the worst animal-owner style. The vet arrives. She's very young, very confident and handles both animal and me beautifully. Her verdict is nowhere near as dramatic as mine. Possum has colic, her bladder isn't huge, her stomach is making weird noises, she isn't anaemic and she looks otherwise healthy. I hold Possum while the vet pushes a long tube down her throat and pumps half a bucket of water and a litre of paraffin oil into her. We decide 'medicinal' amounts of lucerne hay would be good.

Possum seems suddenly quite content to eat. She squats and has a small yellow pee, another good sign. It's been the change in diet from a staple of her favourite pigeon pea to foods not so favoured that has made her ill. I sigh heavily, gratefully, and then zip off to the school to give a cheese-making demonstration to a class of six- and seven-year olds. Then, using the car, with airconditioning on full bore, I do more zipping until I arrive at the feed store and, for the first time in months, buy her two bales of lucerne to keep her going till the rain comes. She eats it, with relish. While this has been an abnormally difficult season, at this point I would have to say that having a backyard goat, while better than buying milk at the store, is not sustainable. But I can't imagine living without her.

11 *March*

Caleb calls it quits.

'I've had enough now, can't we just quit the six months?'

It takes me 10 minutes to talk him around. Last time it took five.

I know what the issue is — the last two nights' uneaten dinners. Tonight it is rice balls full of grated carrot, chopped zucchini and squash, peanuts, steamed asparagus, capsicum, onion and egg. They taste great, but Caleb is not having any of it. He picks off a few grains of rice and chews on those as we discuss last night's dinner, the omelette pancake with basil, parsley and garlic chives, smeared with a thick tomato sauce (Trev's and mine full of chilli), then folded in half, and folded again so it resembles a triangular stack, garnished with fresh basil leaves. It went untouched, and the next morning he doused it in cold water rather than have to eat it. He is going through a food stage. Caleb is good at those, and we usually let him starve his way out of it. But I'm getting exasperated; my food fuse is getting shorter. I made him coconut macaroons as a special lunch treat. Trev and I guzzle ours; Caleb brings his home. He used to love vanilla custards with fruit for his lunch; they come home too. He asks for two poached eggs in his lunch and gets them; they come home, still chilled from his freezer packs, and undeniably whole. Kumara chips, salty and yum — nup. Even dead dog donuts have had their day. His friend Elliott came over after school and I made a batch, and he loved them. I packed up the rest for Elliott to take home, because there was no way Caleb would soil his lips with one. The week before, I made the boys hot salted, roasted peanuts; Caleb's friend downed them with accolades, Caleb was immune. Right now he only wants kebabs, but it wasn't that long ago they were condemned as dirt too. What he really wants is potato chips in a crinkly bag or KFC, along with a toy, or anything that is not made at home. And Vegemite of course. We are winding ourselves up for a Vegemite barter to try to keep him from death's door.

14 March

An invasion of ants, a sudden population explosion of flies, kookaburras churning up the silence with their raucous laughter, a few black cockies alerting us to their presence with their harsh cries — these are the precursors to rain. The sky remains leaden and grey, the wind howls, and occasionally the sky spits on us, but that is all.

I've planted out wong bok; savoy cabbages; lemon cucumbers; squash; English spinach; three colours of onions — red, brown and white; and peas — telephone, Massey early and greenfeast. I've covered all the beds with hessian and water in an effort to keep the wind and the sun from whipping away the moisture. I've decided to plant in the expectation of a worthwhile rain event. One that looks increasingly unlikely to arrive. I've always hated late-arriving guests. It's rude.

I'm making cheese, failing to motivate myself for something really strenuous like going down into the garden and piling the wheelbarrow with pumpkins and bringing them up under the house, which was the plan, and then chaffing up all the sorghum plants that Trev pulled out over the weekend. My excuse is that it's windy, but really I'm feeling lazy. I'd love to coat my tongue in chocolate and lie in bed with a book.

Caleb crawled into bed with us this morning and whispered, 'I dreamt that I've got a little bit of magic in me. Love magic, and there was some stuff that was hope too. And I released it'.

'Where did it go?'

'I don't know, it just came out of me.'

He's told me of an out of body experience (without knowing what one is) and often comes out with 'enlightened' concepts, none of which he would have learnt from me. Grin.

We bartered limes, lemons and dried bananas over the weekend for 2 kilos of apples and fresh bananas. Caleb is devouring the apples and leaving cores around the house for the ants to congregate at. They will not last long.

16 March

Trev is eating monster fruit, which is what we call the oblong, scaled fruits of the monsteria. He is the only one who does not, upon setting teeth into them, run gagging, spitting and howling to the bathroom trying to rid himself of what feels like a mouthful of acid, which they are fairly close to being. Caleb is scoffing apples and bottled plum puree. At the moment the figs are finished, and the passionfruit and paw paws are coming in waves, none of which are breaking on our shore right now. The bananas are almost there; mandarins and oranges are blushing shyly. The limes and lemons are on in earnest but we mainly drink those in cordials. There is not a lot of 'edible' fruit to be had.

I made a batch of ginger beer, which is usually the province of Trev, but I decided to give it a go. Very simple, very low alcohol, but full of fizz and glorious ginger.

The garden productivity is at an all-time low, but strangely we always seem to have enough for a healthy meal. Tonight's is a bit of a cheat — there's been a can of coconut milk in the back of the cupboard that I've been ignoring, plus half a packet of vermicelli noodles, so it will be steamed beans, squash and zucchini with gently fried, cubed sweet potato on a bed of fried vermicelli noodles. Served with boiled eggs, halved, and smothered in satay sauce. We enjoyed it, but felt sick all night from all the saturated fats our livers are no longer used to.

The power bill arrived. It's a moment we've been dreading; we are behind. We owe them (what is for us) a massive amount — we used an extra 180 kWh more than we produced. This has been our worst quarter yet. There have been so many overcast days (and yet still no precipitation). Our idea of the worst possible day: low power creation and no rain. We have to settle with knowing that in the next three months we should be able to offset the deficit with lower temps meaning more power creation and less power use.

We also have to remind ourselves that we are, comparatively speaking, doing very well in the power stakes. It's been a long and interesting journey to getting it this low.

MEASURING ELECTRICITY

A kilowatt (kW) is the basic unit of electrical power and equals 1000 watts. A kilowatt-hour (kWh) is a unit of electrical energy equal to 1000 watt-hours, or 1 kilowatt of power used for one hour, so a 100-watt light bulb switched on for 10 hours uses 1 kilowatt-hour. Kilowatt-hours are the standard measure of the amount of electricity sold and used.

How much power are you using?

Not many people know how much power they use, but many can tell you how much it costs.

We all have a convenient metering system on the side of the house. A week's or month's monitoring will give you a good idea of how much you use. Seasonal changes may make a marked change (your power usage will be higher if you use an electrical heating system in winter or cooling system in summer).

There are a number of different metering systems. The ones that make it simple are those that give you an easy-to-read five-digit numbering system. Slightly more complex are the five dials as per below. Until a number has been reached, always read the lower number: for example, while it sits between the numbers 1 and 2, the reading is 1. Have a go at reading the meter below.

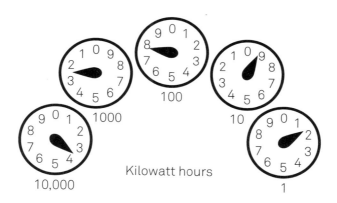

Kilowatt hours

The reading is 3 – 2 – 7 – 9 – 1. Keep track of your own power usage by filling in a table like the one below. Each week, divide the power used by seven to work out your daily usage.

WEEK	1ST READING (BEGINNING OF THE WEEK)	2ND READING (END OF WEEK)	POWER USED
Week 1			
Week 2			
Week 3			
Week 4			
TOTAL			

This year Trev's birthday present was a digital clock that runs on water. Around 20–30 millilitres are added to a vial, and the slight acidity of the water acts like a battery to power the display. When we used its alarm clock feature, it was only able to emit three feeble beeps before it drew so much power the display faded out. But, other than the alarm, it has operated without a hitch. Caleb will attest to the fact that I have not left him waiting in the schoolyard for half an hour while I hunt around trying to find a watch, as I did once. (He has forgiven me, but not forgotten.) Its predecessor ran on limes, but it eroded and after a year we could no longer bludgeon it to work.

A digital clock sounds like one of the last places you'd go in order to reduce power use — the average digital clock only uses 10 watts an hour. It seems insignificant, and yet, as the clock is in 24-hour use, it adds up.

Ten watts an hour, 24 hours a day, is 240 watts a day. Over a year that's 87.6 kWh of coal-based power, which produces 87.6 kilos of CO_2 (1 kilo of CO_2 is enough to fill the average family fridge). So it's a significant amount of air that is being polluted just so we can glance, once or twice a day, at the bedside table. They'd be in far less use if we had to put the coal directly in them and they sat and puffed away, turning our walls lovely shades of black. That's the problem with electricity: it seems clean, but it isn't. It's also shamefully cheap. Australia has huge reserves of coal, so the incentives to move into more sustainable power sources are less than for countries that don't and need to have coal shipped in. Very few countries, apart from those in the third world, rely primarily on coal. Another good reason to move to Tasmania where the power is hydroelectric. Not perfect, but closer than coal.

GREENPOWER

In Australia 91 per cent of our electricity is derived from fossil fuels; only 9 per cent comes from renewable energy sources.[10] Globally 63 per cent of electricity is generated from fossil fuels, 21 per cent from renewable sources and 16 per cent from nuclear sources.[11] Australia is certainly not leading the way in terms of renewable energy. As a developed nation it relies primarily on coal-based power due to an abundance of it. Our power plants are 19th-century technology in a 21st-century world. The average household's annual use of coal-fuelled electricity creates around 8 tonnes of greenhouse gas.[12] Before you rush out and buy big blue gadgets for your rooftop there is something you can easily do about reducing your tonnage.

If you're prepared to pay an additional $3 to $4 per week, you can purchase Greenpower. Your energy supplier puts your money towards energy derived from renewable sources, such as solar, wind, biomass and hydro power rather than coal-based power. No special equipment or appliances are required.

This program has been set up with strict environmental and reporting standards so purchasers can feel assured that their extra contribution is going where it should.

Over 100,000 households and businesses across Australia have joined the program since 1997. The additional funds have resulted in the installation of over 150 approved renewable energy projects including the largest solar farm in the Southern Hemisphere in Singleton, New South Wales, and numerous wind farms.

For information or to join Greenpower, visit www.greenpower.com.au.

This is one of the reasons we are doing what we are. One day I was idly wondering about how much coal is burnt to fuel our house. I got out the power bill, connected to the net and half an hour later I was so horrified by what I had found that it toppled the first domino in what has become our experiment.

We used to use around 22 kWh a day — just over 8000 kWh annually — requiring the burning of 8 tonnes of coal.

How come I didn't know this? How come we just switch on a switch and think of it no further than whether we will have a higher than normal power bill? Slowly this evolution of thinking about things in terms of energy rather than dollars meant we questioned every aspect of our lives. We had been using money to gauge everything and, while that was still part of the equation, it wasn't the only possible answer.

... over each year of our industrial age, humans have required several centuries' worth of ancient sunlight to keep the economy going. The figure for 1997 — around 422 years of fossil sunlight — was typical. Four hundred and twenty-two years' worth of blazing light from a Carboniferous Sun — and we have burned it in a single year.

TIM FLANNERY[13]

GHOST POWER

Ghost power, or standby power usage, can account for anywhere from 8 to 25 per cent of your household electricity bill. If you turn off your lights at night and then see a nocturnal community of small red and green lights, it's a good indication that you can start saving power and reducing CO_2 emissions considerably.

While not in use, a microwave with a display could be drawing 3 watts or more. Not much, but consider it over a year: you may be paying only $3.20 extra on your power bill, but you will be using an extra 26 kWh, making an extra 26 kilos of CO_2.

Big users of standby power are TVs, videos, stereos, mobile phone chargers and computers.

Turn everything off at the wall when not in use. At an average of 10 per cent of your power bill, the average home could be saving around $100 a year in bills and 800 kilograms of CO_2.

Approximate ghost power in different appliances[14]

SOURCE	WATTS USED PER HOUR
Radio	0.6
Mobile phone charger	0.3–1.5
Desktop computer	1.5–10
Answering machine	2.3
Cordless phone	3.0
Microwave oven	3.0
Compact stereo	3.1
Clock radio	3.2–10
Laptop	6.2–10
Television	6.4–10
Monitor	6.9
Modem	7.0
Video	12.0

I started looking under electrical appliances to see how much power they used per hour and how often we used them, and then rationalised them out of the house in garage sales. Two desktop computers, usually on, became one laptop, turned off when not in use. A vacuum cleaner, which I was addicted to, was renounced for a glorified broom. We have wooden floors, so a vacuum cleaner really isn't necessary. It took me a while to get used to the broom, but it's quieter, gloriously cordless, just as effective and a great deal more power-efficient (it takes up less space in the hall cupboard too). My three-times-a-day habit is guilt-free.

We thought about ghost power, which is the power used by appliances that are left on at the wall but turned off at the appliance (think of stereos, TVs and videos). They can use up to 25 per cent of their in-use power when 'off'. Now we turn them off at the wall. We outlawed heaters in winter, and used heavy jumpers and ceiling insulation. Air-cooling is limited to fans on at night during the hottest weather. Even the microwave was chosen because it did not have a permanent display.

Installing solar hot-water instantly halved our power usage. Most years we only need to boost once or twice to keep the water hot. It seems bizarre looking back that we could even think of using electricity, which is inefficiently produced by burning coal and then even more inefficiently transported to us via lines that 'leak' power over distance, when the sun was right there and ready to transform cold water into hot with relatively no conversion inefficiencies, and for free. The system we bought, with added assistance from the government rebate program, has already paid for itself. If there's any one thing a family can do to reduce their impact on the environment, solar hot-water would have to be it.

Gradually we reduced our power usage to a level where it could be conceivable that we could cover our usage by installing solar panels. In February 2003 we did just that and have since created 3673 kWh of power and used 3891 – a gap of only 218 kWh, and most of those in the last three months!

WATER HEATING

Electric hot-water heating uses around 40 per cent of household power. Converting to alternative water heating is the most cost-effective way of reducing your ecological footprint. It's also an excellent financial proposition. On average, solar hot-water systems pay for themselves within two to five years, depending on state rebate schemes, the chosen system and the local climate. After this period they continue to save you money, ranging from $250 to $400 per year, depending again on the system and local climate. Only one in 10 Australian homes has a solar hot-water system installed.

Grab a few bills and you will probably see the hot-water component in your electricity usage, as water heating is typically on a different tariff.

Each of the states has an estimated percentage of how much solar hot-water systems will contribute to heating water. In our area the suggestion is 75 per cent; some years we would put it closer to 90–95 per cent. Last year we only needed to boost twice. We did, however, put up with lukewarm showers on occasion. This year, it's been closer to 75 per cent. The more southern states have lower, but still significant, expectations of around 60–70 per cent. Solar hot water is considered a valid and cost-effective method of heating water in London.

The various hot-water systems don't require a great deal of maintenance. Ours has been limited to hopping onto the roof to give the panels a quick clean with a squeegee once or twice a year.

Choosing a system can be confusing, as there are more options available than ever. The guide below is not exhaustive, and cannot adequately cater for the differences in rebates from state to state. Check with a supplier or your state government.

Thermosiphon systems

These are the most common systems: both the tank and the panels form one unit mounted on the roof. Warm water rises (the thermosiphon effect), circulating the water through the system until it reaches its maximum possible temperature. This negates the need for a pump.

A gas or electric booster is required for overcast days when the sun fails to heat the water to suitable temperatures. A gas booster produces less annual CO_2 emissions than an electric one.

Pumped solar hot-water systems

Some houses may not have sufficient structural roof strength to allow for the considerable weight of a 300-litre (or more) tank, or owners may prefer the aesthetics of having only the panels mounted on the roof and the cylinder or tank at a lower level. These systems require the water to be electrically pumped into the panels.

Heat pumps

These are up to 65–70 per cent more energy-efficient than conventional hot-water systems. They require electricity to run an evaporative compressor. Heat pumps work the same way a fridge does, except in reverse – heating, not cooling, the water by extracting heat from the atmosphere. They are typically one unit with the cylinder, although there are solar-boosted heat pumps where the panels are mounted on the roof separately from the cylinder, taking advantage of solar radiation to increase their efficiency. These systems can be mounted with an existing hot-water cylinder.

Costs and rebates

The size of the system, including the number of panels and the estimated reduction in greenhouse gases, affects the amount of rebate you can claim, as well as the initial system cost. A rough estimate of costs and savings, based on an average initial costing, is:

- Cost, including installation, before rebate $2600
- Renewable Energy Certificates (RECs) rebate $700 (average, all states)
- Additional state government rebate (if applicable) $700–1200
- **Total cost of going solar**   **$700–1200**
- **Total cost in states without additional rebate**   **$1900**
- **Savings on your power bill per year**   **$400**

These kinds of savings will see the system paid off in two to five years.

If you are replacing an existing electric hot-water service you will be eligible for Renewable Energy Certificates (RECs), regardless of which state you live in. These are worth around $30 per REC depending on how much greenhouse gas a heat pump or solar hot-water system will save. You may receive anywhere from 10 to 64 RECs, worth $300 to $1920. These are bought from you by energy suppliers or assigned to an agent such as the supplier of the heat pump or solar hot-water service.

For further information on RECs visit the Office of the Renewable Energy Regulator's website, www.orer.gov.au.

Rebates are different state by state and subject to change. Ask for assistance from a local supplier or visit the appropriate website:

ACT   www.environment.act.gov.au

NSW   www.environment.nsw.gov.au
(No additional rebate available at time of printing.)

NT   www.ipe.nt.gov.au
(No additional rebate available at time of printing.)

Qld   www.epa.qld.gov.au

SA   www.sustainable.energy.sa.gov.au

Tas.   www.dier.tas.gov.au
(No additional rebate available at time of printing.)

Vic.   www.sustainability.vic.gov.au

WA   www1.sedo.energy.wa.gov.au

Reducing your water-heating requirements

Hot-water systems can waste a lot of power through heat loss. Up to 60 per cent of heat loss occurs through poor cylinder insulation and large lengths of pipe between the cylinder and taps. An Australian Greenhouse Office study in 2000 estimated that 32 per cent of the energy used by smaller electric water heaters and 20 per cent used by larger heaters was lost. These heat losses equated to 1115 gigawatt-hours, with 1.15 megatonnes of CO_2 needlessly created. The cost to the consumer came in at $134 million dollars.[15]

Electrically heated water creates a kilogram of CO_2 for every 13 litres of water. Annual greenhouse emissions from a conventional electric water heater equal the emissions from an average car travelling 14,000 kilometres each year, so it's worth trying to reduce your water-heating needs. Here are some ideas on how dredged up between Trev and I, plus a few filched from the Australian Greenhouse Office:[16]

- Insulate your hot-water storage tank or cylinder or, in cooler areas, keep the cylinder inside and reuse the lost heat for drying. There are foil-backed insulation blankets available to reduce heat loss from the cylinder.
- Use at least 10-millimetre-thick insulation around external hot-water pipes to reduce heat loss, especially the first few metres from the cylinder.
- If you're building a house, design so that the cylinder and pipes are only a small distance from high hot-water use areas, such as the bathroom and kitchen, to eliminate heat loss.
- Showers are the biggest household users of hot water. Install a low-flow showerhead and limit the time spent in the shower. (Try singing in the car instead.)
- Turn off your electric or gas hot-water system when you go on holiday.
- Install a system that is the right size for your family: too small and you may run out of water; too large and you are unnecessarily heating water you don't need.
- Set the temperature of your hot-water storage system to 50°C, high enough to eliminate harmful bacteria without using power unnecessarily. It also reduces the possibility of scalds.
- Keep any system maintained to the manufacturer's standards.
- When using a solar hot-water system, install or use a manual switch for the booster, rather than have it pre-empt your solar hot-water needs, and always keep the panels clean.

18 March

Spent the day in my outdoor gymnasium. Crawling under the lime tree to retrieve the 20 pumpkins that fell out of the wheelbarrow when I lost control charging it up a steep hill — cardiac fitness. Followed by an hour 'on the wheel', turning the chaffcutter and creating in situ mulch with a huge pile of sorghum Trev pulled up last week — arm and upper body strength and I can feel my abdominals already. I swept large areas of paving, watered large areas of seedlings with my recalcitrant hose, which can snag itself on a dandelion when it wants to (lots of muscular activity between brows and vocal cord extensions), then an energetic scrape-out of animal housing for chook and goat poo and placing the produce in a large bucket to soak and age before becoming a nice high-nitrogen brew for the garden. Usually there'd be more weeds and comfrey to add more nutrient to the mix, but they've all died back. Then back to the house to make yeast. Cross a few things off my list, and then limber up my fingers on the keyboard, one key of which has developed a neurological disorder — it no 'onger registers the 'L' key, unless used with great force. It will undoubtedly stop for good before the end of the six months, and I will be signing myself off as 'inda' forever. Soon I will grab the bike and head off for the 2-kilometre ride to school to retrieve Caleb and then another 2 kilometres home again. I feel fantastic. I often notice how my breathing feels different, as though I have more lung capacity, and maybe I do — it just feels easier, the air isn't as sticky. When I walk I feel limber and strong, and I've taken to admiring my own biceps in the mirror, for they've taken on definition and shape. But I'm not alone; Trev is behind me and gloating too.

EXERCISE IS THE KEY

Our increased levels of activity and exercise have helped our weight loss and general wellbeing incredibly. Once you choose to give up your addiction to the car, you will use more energy. Consider the following comparison:

CALORIES USED WHILE STROLLING

Body weight	10 mins	20 mins	30 mins
20 kg	10	20	30
40 kg	20	40	60
60 kg	30	60	91
80 kg	40	81	121

CALORIES USED WHILE BICYCLING

Body weight	10 mins	20 mins	30 mins
20 kg	10	20	30
40 kg	20	40	60
60 kg	30	60	91
80 kg	40	81	121

CALORIES USED WHILE SITTING IN THE CAR

Body weight	10 mins	20 mins	30 mins
20 kg	3	7	10
40 kg	7	14	21
60 kg	10	21	31
80 kg	14	27	41

20 *March*

Productive weekend. A big bake-off, with plum puree scrolls for Caleb, curried pumpkin and green bean bread pasties for Trev, and five small tureens of lemon meringue pie, ostensibly for everyone, but three of them have my name written on them. Six loaves of bread, 16 rolls and a cheesy plait. I spend most of the day kneading bread.

Yeast

1 potato
1 tablespoon hops
¹/₂ cup water
1 tablespoon sugar
1 tablespoon plain flour
2 raisins

Wash and quarter, but do not peel, the potato. Plonk it in a pot, along with the hops and enough water to simmer it in (around half a cup). Simmer until the potato is cooked, then drain off any surplus water, retaining it for later use. Mash the potato and hops mixture with the sugar and flour. Add the reserved potato water and mix. Place in a glass jar with the raisins. Seal and leave in a warm place to ferment (usually takes between 3 and 5 days depending on the temperature). Strain and use the liquid in your dough.[17]

Trev does the washing, and starts work on a portable chook house. We are dividing chooks up again. The latest two are not yet laying. My theory is that the two more established chooks are bullying them off it. Trev's miracle of recycling takes place and an old metal slide is disassembled, along with odd bits and pieces of fibro and an off-cut of corrugated iron, and reassembled into the neatest looking chook house in town.

Trev is keeping his lighters alive hopping off his bike and retrieving those discarded on the roadside. He filches a flint from this one, a bit of lighter fluid from another; a body of one made to look like a cigarette is found and keeps him entertained. He also decides to remodel the goat's feed hopper so she doesn't keep pushing the food off the edge and then yelling at me to retrieve it for her. Less wastage, we hope, though goats are masters of it. I haul up the rest of the sorghum in wheelbarrow loads and work my way through it with the chaffcutter. It makes the worn-out top beds look renewed, though they are still bare. In between I make another three fetta cheeses, two of which will be bartered — one lot for sugar, the other for apples as Caleb mowed through the last lot, and he is sick of bananas, though watermelon is still on the not-to-miss list.

While we work in the garden, Caleb practises dangerous trampoline manoeuvres and, when tired of that, comes inside to draw pictures of castles and knights.

'What's happening in your castle, Caleb?' I ask, picking up a pencil and joining him.

'Oh, everyone is getting killed. They're pouring hot oil out the windows right now, and there is "blod" everywhere, and there are piles of the "ded". What's happening in yours?'

'Oh, we're having a carnival, all our friends are arriving and we're throwing lollies and balloons and flowers out the windows as they approach.'

'Doesn't sound very interesting. My enemies are getting decapitated.'

I stop in from time to time and have a game of Ludo with him on my great, great auntie's board — it must be a hundred years old. The dice appear to be made of bone and are gnarled and yellow. Caleb does not mind in the least and now he knows his six plus threes and his five plus fours.

We're using town water in the lower garden today. It was a big decision. But we have to start rationing the rest in order to save it for the house and nearby garden beds. At this rate we may have to top up the tanks too.

I head outside to see how the chooks are taking to their new house. Having chooks around makes the whole place seem more like a farmhouse than just owning a goat does. They're certainly a whole lot lower in maintenance than a goat. Around the time that Caleb was starting to walk we bought four Seabright bantams. We chose bantams solely because they were cute. The cuties grew and became masters at digging up or burying seedlings and removing mulch from around trees. Their chosen roost was the front door step and, if the door was left open they liked to scuttle around inside and peck at Caleb's droppings — that is, what he'd dropped from his breakfast, lunch and dinner. One ended up claiming a space behind a chest of drawers. We didn't discover this until 10 days and 10 eggs later. She would saunter in every morning, disappear into the bedroom, reappear not long after, watch us while we scuttled around trying to clean up our own nest, and leave. None were ever named, but were all referred to as 'chookie'. It was an affectionate term. We felt they were fairly well integrated into the family and we were on good terms, until two of them grew spurs, combs, wattles and an arrogant swagger.

We resisted building a permanent chook house, preferring to round them up in the evening and move them into a no-fox box. But gradually this became an activity based on terror. The dominant bantam (let's call him Dead) began to chase me more than I chased him. I didn't dare turn my back on him at risk of having him rake his spurs down my calves. I became very good at walking backwards. Trev encouraged me to get the upper hand with Dead, to show him who's boss, so I retaliated a few times, which really only upped the violence and his ferocity.

Once, while changing their water, Dead attacked. I dropped the water tray directly on top of him (and admit to grinding it in a little). He emerged, fell over a couple of times, shook his head with confusion, and staggered around for a few minutes. He was back to calf raking minutes later.

It got so bad I was frightened to go into the garden. I didn't know where my cute little feathered friend had borrowed his attitude from, but I wanted him to give it back. I developed a phobia — alektorophobia, a fear of chickens.

One day Dead signed his own death certificate. Caleb and I were sitting in the sun — I was reading, he was playing in the dirt. The mob came around the corner, Dead in the lead. He sidled up, a worm-eating, menacing mafia boss. I tried to meet his eye; he ignored me. He seemed intent on removing invisible-to-the-eye seeds from a few feet away. Caleb remained oblivious to the approach, cramming dirt into the back of a toy dump truck. I was wary: I knew this chook and he was 20 centimetres of hell on legs. He managed to look bored, preoccupied; I wasn't convinced. But before I could react he made an agile leap at Caleb's face and scored a line from the inside of his eye to his chin.

That afternoon there was a solemn ceremony at the now jailed bird's pen. Dead, an axe and a nice solid block of wood. Me, the vengeful onlooker, and Trev, who promptly removed the little bastard's head and tied his legs to a nearby eucalypt, where he dripped and twisted for minutes more while the horrified chooks watched on.

I stood on the steps and crowed, 'Let that be a warning to you, you shalt not touch my child and live!'

The second rooster (shall we call him Gone), who had seemed comparatively mild, rapidly took over Dead's role and came to just as rapid an end. I was away at the time. I received a call from Trev, who sighed heavily as he told me, 'Gone is dead' (which does sound confusing I'll admit).

'How? What happened?'

'He got out of the chook pen at 4 am this morning and sat under the bedroom window and crowed non-stop, till I stopped him — with the axe.'

Trev then cooked and ate him.

I don't miss them. I'm glad Dead and Gone are exactly that.

We bought a pair of Aracuana hens, but it didn't take one of them long to grow spurs, a comb, wattle and a good imitation of a crow. He was big, glossy black-green and docile; he is with us still.

The original chook pen Trev built didn't move. As I became more involved with permaculture I saw that as a problem. At irregular intervals we were climbing in, digging out the high-nitrogen soil and carting it around to the garden beds. All that hard work really wasn't the done thing. We needed a moveable chook pen (one that wasn't an eyesore), which meant that the chooks could eat insect pests, weed and seed, and dig and poo onsite, even lay eggs if they were up to it. Intrepid Trev tackled the job with vigour and we now have a 2.5 x 2.5-metre almost-moveable chook pen called Mark I, which we have shifted ourselves on several occasions. On one I managed to get myself pinned underneath and the other time Trev put his back out. So it became a waiting game: wait till we have visitors. Before offering them tea or coffee you suggest a quick trip down to the chook pen for the communal lift — any children present enjoy shooing chooks back in (Caleb has required a further explanation of 'shoeing', our version was spelt differently from his).

We aren't particularly sociable people; in fact we're happy to call ourselves hermits. Sometimes the wait between moving jobs was getting too long. So I tackled the job of Mark II. It cost $75 to make, a fraction of Mark I. Trev welded and we covered it in chook wire and a plastic tarp. It was light — I could almost lift it with one finger — which is why a neighbour rang me a while back to ask me if I knew where my chook pen was. Nonplussed, I looked out the window at the now-vacant spot where it should have been.

'It's on the road', he explained.

Cordless phone in hand, I went to investigate and indeed it was. It had flown 20 metres, which puts a new slant on flying the coop. Modern-day aeronautical engineers might find the design of interest, but its days as a chook pen were over. It was cannibalised for all things reuseable. So all my gloating over creating a 'moveable' versus 'almost moveable' chook pen came to naught.

Trev came to an ingenious rescue and made the roof of Mark I removable. With the reduced weight we could manoeuvre it around the block without personal damage.

But the chook pen trials were far from over. It took him four years to do it, but finally the fox found a way into the chook pen. It was 3 am and I woke to a kafuffle in the pen (not uncommon as we have an early layer and they all like to make a fuss about having to give birth on a daily basis). But this went on too long and involved more than one kafuffler. Torch in hand, I ran down in time to catch a fox in the act of removing himself from the hole he had dug under the pen. We stared at each other, only 10 metres apart: he was long, red and completely malevolent. He took off and I watched him disappear down the culvert. In the chook pen were five pairs of chooky legs pointing at the sky — he'd killed them all in a frenzy without feast.

Only two remained: the Aracuana hen and rooster. I've never seen two more traumatised chooks. Neither of them were injured, but both went into a serious decline. We removed the dead and shifted the pen away from the scene of the crime. That next night we realised we couldn't leave them in the pen, because the fox had figured out how to get in. We did something that I'll always regret — we transferred them to the top immoveable pen, which housed half a dozen brown Lowman hens. Feathers went flying as the pecking order process began. The rooster seemed completely out of it; he retired to the back of the pen where he literally stuck his head under a rock. We pulled him out a couple of times but he crawled straight back under. The Aracuana hen was being chased around relentlessly and, though I sympathised, it seemed a better fate than fox sport. The Lowmans had always been hens with attitude; they considered me a part of their pecking order and were keen to work things out on my toes. I assumed it would sort itself out soon. The next morning I left for work before 6 am and Trev not long after. I stayed away overnight, Trev didn't get home till after dark, and left the next day before dawn. I arrived home in the afternoon and went straight down to see how the survivors had fared. The rooster still had his head under a rock and the hen was crouched beside him, a 10-centimetre-square area of flesh bared almost to the bone — I could see her parson's nose. The culprits, six brown Lowmans with a taste for blood, were in the process of eating her alive.

The evil egg-layers were unceremoniously swung from the pen. I ruffled feathers and swore at them, calling them lurid names, most beginning with 'f'. I found it hard to believe that members of the same species could do that to each other, then had to admit that, as a human, I didn't have a great deal of standing room in my disgust.

I devised a great revenge. The rooster and hen were put into their own pen until they healed and had gained some confidence, then I reintroduced the Lowman hens, one at a time. We sat and watched with pleasure as the first Lowman was chased around the pen, chastised and demoted to the bottom of the pecking order. Once she was sufficiently demoralised, another was added to the mix, until they were all together and my wee Aracuana reigned supreme.

Two chooks are dedicated goat penners, there to keep the flies down. Natural biological control, plus a bit of company for Possum. They also make best use of the grain and food she decides she's not going to condescend to eat. We often see them roosting on her back, between her horns, or sharing the same feed trough. Occasionally we have to remove the evidence of their roosting from her sides.

Three, including the rooster, live in the first-built immoveable pen with luxury ensuite and laying boxes. Two of the newest and yet to lay chooks have been relocated to the 'paddock' — the area currently struggling to grow lab lab and now featuring Trev's latest recycled masterpiece.

Five live in the almost moveable pen, which has been adapted so a door can be secured each night. It's the job of whomever is most prepared to go down in the dark and shut it each night. It's usually me, though I have a repertoire of excuses, from feigned sleep; exhaustion (never feigned); I can't find my shoes (usually true); to 'Hell, I've undressed, I'm in bed, I've just remembered.

Oh, it's OK, you're still clothed', followed by an appreciative smile (pulling a swiftie).

Altogether we have nine egg layers and our now one-eyed rooster, who either lost it to the evil ones or the fox.

We've tried feeding them all sorts of things. Apart from the staple of table scraps, they've tried the by-product of tofu — after 1 kilo of it, one of them laid an egg so large I rushed around to see if she had survived the process. Snails, which after a while were ignored, lots of delicious maggots (mostly fruit fly), and clabbered milk, a traditional chook food made from unpasteurised milk left a day or so to sour (pasteurised milk spoils). They are also fed with whey, which is high in protein. Lately we've had a large number of very big brown grasshoppers, and it's a team effort to catch them. I spot, Trevor catches, though I'm getting good with the secateurs. We then throw them in the chook pens where pandemonium breaks loose as chooks grapple — a great spectator sport and source of protein. One thing the chooks and goat have taught me is an appreciation of protein, and I often find myself thinking of insects in these terms.

We don't eat our chooks as a rule, and it's just as much of an environmental as a sentimental decision. I'm sure they appreciate it too. I've let Trev know that I'll do my best to raise meat chooks, but he will have to be the one to kill them. He's not happy with meat chooks, he believes it's cruel to breed them so large. We've heard of occasions where their bones have broken under the strain of their own weight, and that most of their body weight is fat. If necessary, he will chop the head off any young roosters. The older Trev gets, the less inclined he is towards such slaughter. He decided he'd rather go vegetarian although he considers kangaroo, an unfarmed and native animal growing in large numbers, 'fair game'. I wonder how many more vegetarians there would be in the world if we had to kill and dissect a pig before we had bacon with our breakfast, or personally kill and prepare the 92 sheep, 17 beef cattle, 15 pigs, 1171 chickens and innumerable fish the average Australian eats in their lifetime.[18]

The ABS estimates that in 2000–2001 around 400 million birds were raised and killed at between six to eight weeks of age for human consumption in Australia. The consumption of chicken has increased by 38 per cent in the last 10 years — currently the average Aussie eats 23.7 kilos of chicken a year.[19]

Eggs are a useful commodity for barter. Currently, we are getting half a dozen a day — nice, large, brown organic eggs.

Caleb refused his baked beans for dinner, they had a different texture than he expected, as they were from our own soybeans and tomato sauce. The gag reflex stepped in and the masticated results lay on the table as verification of its inedibility. Trev relented and poached him an egg in a star-shaped cookie cutter.

21 March

I cheated. I pulled the cover off the car, set it in motion and went and bought two big bags of chook and goat food, plus two more bales of lucerne. I had bartering worth nowhere near the amount of money required.

I couldn't find a way to get around the problem of transporting 40-kilogram bags on our bikes, so the car was bought into the equation. Rather than make numerous trips it made sense to go once and buy up big. Second, we are no longer attempting to grow enough grain for the animals. We simply don't have enough water, and with the added parrot population it was always going to be impossible. We concede defeat — we can't feed them all. We're compromising our integrity even further by then bartering their products (value added) for staples.

To further add to this horrid list of compromised dealings, I stopped by at the closest place that sold Easter eggs, walked, blinkered, through the store and bought foil-covered chocolate bunnies and then, shuddering, chose two themed bundles with enough packaging to stretch to the moon and back. By the time I walked to the car I was so overcome with guilt I almost returned them. I had considered making something, but Caleb would spot the amateurish attempt and, with his keen intellect, figure out that the Easter Bunny was dead and that I had tried to 'fudge' the chocolate-covered festivities. They didn't even have any bilbies. However, I know my politically incorrect offerings will be a lip-smacking success.

I've started thinking of all the things we no longer buy with packaging compared with a list of things we barter that do — we have seriously reduced our packaging waste. In a perfect shopping world every product would have a rating — for example, from 1 to 10. The highest ratings would be awarded to products that:

- are grown or manufactured using water-efficient techniques
- are water-efficient/power-efficient when in use
- are not grown or produced using techniques that cause erosion or other land degradation
- are organic
- are grown in Australia (for energy efficiency in transport)
- if coming from overseas because no local alternative was available, are grown or produced sustainably by farmers who are dealt with ethically
- use only a minimum of packaging, and are recyclable
- do not incorporate any genetically modified foods
- do not involve animal cruelty such as testing, housing in small pens or limited movement
- do not use hormones or antibiotics
- do not use any phosphates, optical brighteners or other water and soil pollutants
- offer refillable container stations or used-product return and recycle facilities (for example, for batteries) or other ingenious waste-management strategies
- allocate money towards research/charity/environmental organisations.

There are probably more things to write in this list, but the idea is simple. It's easy to see when you go shopping, from a shopper's point of view, that every aisle is a minefield of unexploded options, and we can't, as consumers, keep up with who is producing healthy, sustainable and ethical foods or products. If we were to try to, I can envision aisles full of paralysed people as they contemplate the 60 or more types of shampoo on the market. Instead we buy the ones that promise the most, are packaged the prettiest or are in our price range.

Greenpeace came out with the *True Food Guide*, which was a fantastic initiative to assist shoppers in buying foods that were not genetically engineered. I familiarised myself with it, but I know things change and it's hard to keep up. Visit www.greenpeace.org.au/truefood/guide2.html to find out more.

Since 1964 people in Germany have been able to refer to an online consumer magazine called *Stiftung Warentest*. (Not hard to remember — Stiff tongue Warren test.) It compares products on a variety of environmental and quality levels and generates a rating, which is published online each month. When consumers are thinking of buying anything from a car battery to a television, they can easily obtain comparative results and make an informed purchase. It has been hailed as a success, with poorly rated products dropping in market value until such time as the manufacturer/producer changes the ingredients, efficiency or materials and it is re-tested and gains a higher ranking. I think there are a lot of products in Australia that could be given a stiff tongue test by Warren.

In 2005 the big names in chicken — Steggles, Inghams and Baiada, who produce 80 per cent of Australia's chicken and import around 150,000 tonnes of genetically engineered (GE) chook feed a year — backed down under consumer pressure and will now source GE-free chook feed, which is fantastic. It's also a great sign that we, as consumers, aren't as powerless as we might have thought.

Rather than fighting each new issue as individuals, we could have an organisation that does the research, providing easy to understand information on every product (the producers/manufacturers could have an appeals process if they feel their products have been unfairly rated). The organisation could make the information readily available. The consumer has the power of choice and, instead of buying on the basis of 'how many extra features does it have?' or the price, we would know that the product, for example, contains cadmium and could be a potential hazard, as well as the overall quality of its manufacture and its environmental standing. Transparent purchasing power. *Choice* magazine in Australia comes close; it campaigns for clear food labelling and raises concerns on GM food. But we can get environmentally closer to the mark yet.

25 March

Over the last couple of days the weather forecast has been for storms. Thunderclouds loom, it spits a bit, even struggles to bring forth a five-minute burst of something similar to rain, lots of loud banging, a few close lightning strikes, even a few stones of pea-sized hail. Then it passes us by. Thirty kilometres away it removes 18 roofs, and pelts the place with hailstones, this time cannon-ball sized. All up we receive 10 millimetres in the two storms. The first few millimetres of each were used to flush the roof clean; they barely settle dust.

27 March

The Easter Bunny arrives! Caleb meets up with us in bed to share the news of his booty. He plays a dangerous game of eating chocolate right under my nose and loses some. He thinks it's hilarious and continues to taunt me at his own loss. I can feel every little grain of chocolate on my tongue. It's exquisite. I am so glad the Easter Bunny came.

28 March

Trev goes fishing. Friends, Pete and Marguerite, pick him up around six o'clock.

'Expect us around six or seven tonight. We come to shore on dark, it takes us half an hour there, then half an hour back. Don't worry.'

I am — and I'm sure you've probably gleaned this — a certified worrier. I try hard to make the O in worrier an A. I decide I will not worry. Caleb and I do the usual things: I make food, he refuses to eat it. This continues on till 8.30 pm when Trev is still not home and Caleb's dinner plate is alive with a thick border of congregating ants. I put him to bed. I call Trev on the mobile, there is no answer. I'm still not hugely worried. I call Pete's place to see if they are back there. No answer. I call Marguerite, her daughters answer. They are worried. We promise to inform each other if we hear anything. We hear nothing. By 9.30 pm another of the daughters has rung me to say that Marguerite was meant to pick her up from her trip up from Melbourne over three hours ago (she made her own way home instead). They are worried. Very worried. Perhaps it's time to call the police? At 9.45 pm, I do. I'm not sure how much it will achieve, but there is nothing else I can do. While I'm giving them the details I hear another police call in the background. Someone is reporting a one-vehicle accident on Fosters Lane — this is a remote, back road that Pete lives on and to which they were heading. The accident involves a white ute. Pete drives a white ute. I interrupt to say, 'I think that's them!'

'Were they towing a boat?' he asks. My knees give way.

'Yes', I say.

'I'll give you a call back shortly', he says and hangs up.

For 10 of the longest minutes I arrange funerals, drive over and inform Marguerite's daughters that their mother is dead. I dress Trev's body in his purple shirt, black pants and trench coat. I wonder how I can possibly tell

Caleb his father is dead or, better, that he's in a helicopter heading for Nambour with head injuries. I wonder which neighbour I will ring to stay in the house while I go to identify bodies. I tell myself that I've had a fair bit of practice at this; I should be able to handle it. My first love, Andrew, died when he was 23; Carl, my second, died at 30.

The phone rings. It's the police: not to worry, it wasn't them.

I put the phone down, I call the daughters. I put the phone down, it rings. It's Trev, whose first disbelieving words are, 'You called the police?'

By the time he is home, in a jovial mood, at 11, I have killed eight cockroaches with a fly swat and read the same paragraph of a book 93 times. I don't give him a hard time, he gives me one. Apparently my whole demeanour is screaming accusations. I refute this. I'm finally in bed. It's been a long night. For god's sake, let me go to sleep. He has three fish. Two small bream and a flathead. I can only hope he thinks they were worth it.

29 March

Trev weighs himself. Fantastic, first time under 90 kilograms in many years. He looks great. My turn — yes, seem to be settling in between 63 and 64 kilos, not bad. Caleb, how about you? Hearts sink, he has lost weight. He started off at 25 kilograms, now he appears to be 23.5. This is significant. We know it is not lack of food that is causing the problem, rather Caleb's lack of inclination to eat it. He is also burning off more energy with his two-to-three-hours-a-day trampoline habit.

Trev and I retreat to the goat pen where we milk Possum, and change the topic from unseasonably dry weather to whether or not we should call a halt to the experiment. Caleb's health is a higher priority. We go inside and try to entice Caleb with vegemite on toast, minus the butter. We've not had any for three months. Then we try hot chocolates and apples, with poached eggs that Trev cooks in the star-shaped cookie cutter for extra nutritional value. The value being it means he might just eat it.

I disappear into the garden, which I contemplate while feeding the chooks. It's like a desert with small oases of green, well-watered garden beds. I work out here every day. I don't want to work out here today. I consider escape. I've been few places other than to school and back over the last three months. I could do with a day out. Trev's home on an extended Easter break, so should

I nick off on his electric bike? The last crop of sunflowers are bobbing their heads enthusiastically. Where can I go? The local library would be good. It means venturing over Normanby Bridge, which hasn't got a footbridge and is a thoroughfare for some very large trucks and tankers and the usual assortment of four-wheel drives. It would be great to take Caleb, but the fear barriers start slamming up along all the corridors that might lead to making the decision to take him. I wander back inside and mention that I have made my escape plan.

Trev instantly responds, 'Great idea, we should all go, Caleb could do with a trip out too!'

All the alarms along the corridors are triggered.

It's difficult to follow our conversation for all the noise, but I find the kill switch and accede that it would be good. An adventure. Trev agrees to take Caleb on the back of my bike. It is a logic-defying 10-kilometre round-trip and uphill both ways. Gympie is a mess of streets. After living here for eight or so years now I still become disoriented: there are 10 ways to get anywhere and all of them require 53 right-hand turns. Trev's theory is that 100 years ago roads were built along the pathways of drunken miners.

We pack our bags. We call Marguerite, who lives not far from the library, and announce our intention to visit. I consider amending my last will and testament, then throw caution to the wind and we set off. Trev and Caleb bike in front; I bike a discreet distance behind, offering my body as sacrifice to the inattentive driver. Bike riders are considered low priority and there is often nowhere else to bike but amid the traffic. We stop before the bridge, which is about 150 metres long. We time our sprint, racing across. I can see Caleb leering over the side at the long drop down. By the time we get to the other side we have been passed by three four-wheel drives.

'Wow,' says Caleb, 'I did well. I faced my fear!'

On the other side is a near-vertical hill. We don't get far before we are forced to get off and walk to the top. From there it is a constant array of choices — less traffic, but steep slopes, or a few pedestrian walkways we can use against downhill slopes. We get there. Trev is in a lather. I'm doing daisy-fresh. This electric bike thing is a lark.

Trev and Marguerite make conversation mostly revolving around how I don't understand the thrill of fishing, while I make conversation about what their thrills did to the rest of us expecting them home at 6.30 pm.

'Don't you agree, Grace?' I entice Marguerite's daughter into the conversation. 'Aren't these adults just so inconsiderate. You always have to worry about them. They never do what they say they will.'

We chuckle, drink coffee and make a dash for the library through frantic traffic.

Getting there is an achievement; we bask in the airconditioned climate and sort through books. Caleb finds the video section and selects five, then looks at books on the Middle Ages, Incas, Egyptians and Ancient Rome. I escape in the fiction section, then leaf through a fantastic book, *Sticks, stones, mud homes* by Nigel Noyes. It's full of alternative houses people have owner-built. Trev is cautious. He doesn't want to go there again. He built his own mud-brick house in a remote area only reached by matching mud roads; he started 25 years ago and laid his last brick 15 years later. It was dubbed the tree house, and featured a huge upstairs bedroom with open-air views. The house is set in the middle of a forest with a charming mud-brick outhouse. Ehren has fond memories of it. Growing up there was wild, both geographically and socially. For the first three years Trev cooked over an open fire, bath water was boiled up in a copper and nappies washed in a hand-turned Bamix. Trevor is a bona fide hippie, best known for turning up to parties wearing his sarong and leaving without it. I have no hippie credentials. My formative years were spent in the culturally defunct 1980s. Occasionally people have referred to our house as the hippie house, but I figure that – seeing as I'm not into tie-dying, recreational drugs and spacey kinds of spiritualism, instead seeing the world in terms of energy that we can quantify, in scientific principles that apply to realistic environmental limitations – there should be a new term for a new generation. Mind you, I do enjoy mung beans, ethnic foods and wearing dangly earrings, and occasionally I break out a deck of cards not used for playing things like poker, euchre or go fish.

The library session draws to a close, and we clamber back on our bikes, head up a hill, take the 23 right-hand turns, some of them with puzzled looks on our faces and questions as to where they eventually lead, before coming out at a supermarket. This is our secret mission. Caleb's weight loss has weighed heavily on us. We've agreed to compromise further and buy him chicken, butter and a bag of potatoes. Inside we walk up aisles in a daze. Caleb does not badger us, instead he disappears off to the toy section, knowing full well we will not be buying him any. Trev and I tuck in a big bag of grapes and a clove of garlic; the stuff in the garden is stunted from lack of water. We queue up quickly before we are enticed into buying more. My eyes skip over cheap Easter treats and I torment myself on two for the price of one potato chip deals.

My backpack is bulging with food, my bicycle basket with books. We set off on the last stint home. Miraculously we get there, no broken bones, only broken boundaries.

Dinner is fresh flathead nuggets for Caleb and his friend Bradley, a fillet for me, two bream fillets for Trev, all served with potato chips. Caleb downed his in record speed. The fish tasted great. Perhaps they were worth that fishing trip.

30 March

The day we fell off the wagon.

It's Bradley's birthday today — he's seven. The kids tell Caleb that they are going to McDonald's with a few friends and he's invited. We take this as a given, he disappears down the road; 10 minutes later I discover him lying on the trampoline crying. While the kids had invited him, Bradley's mother hadn't and she'd sent him home. Caleb is distraught. It's not often he has an outing like this dangled before him and then snatched out of reach. I try to think of ways to compensate him, and really there isn't anything remotely like party food to be had. Trev and I look over his head while he tells us the story. I'd love to take him there myself. But I don't say so. Then Trev mentions the possibility. I cave. Yes, bugger it all, we're halfway through, why not. I'd been planning to celebrate with a few sparklers, but a trip out to keep the oil in circulation (our mechanic advised us to drive the car at least once a month) and to the drive-through seemed as good a way as any to ease the burden of such a childhood hurt. So we did. Easter has been a litany of lapses.

Trevor tells me I should write 'The Book of Lapses'.

31 March

I bake, making the first biscuits in three months, chocolate. Caleb and his friend Sam make circuitous routes around the house and into the kitchen where they raise their eyebrows at me waiting for a reprimand that doesn't come, before stealing off with more. I make more lemon meringues and savoury muffins. It's not often I turn the oven on for such frivolous reasons.

It's raining, or trying to. I refuse to look out the window. To do so might result in it desisting. I'm beginning to understand pagan god worship, to question less any superstition involving control of the weather and to even consider the possibility that Feng Shui isn't complete bullpucky. No, no, I don't think I can go quite that far. Even so, I count on it stopping, and remain purposely surprised when it continues to alternate between light drizzle and light rain.

Any rain falling now will be recorded on 1 April. We have a new record rainfall low for February/March. Trev announces this morning that there is a 60–70 per cent chance of higher than average rainfall in the next two months, which will be welcome, but perhaps already too late. I'll keep up with the garden and hope we can continue to eat out of it over that time.

If there is a key word for the first three months, it's 'compromise'.

Trev's rave

Halfway. Or, at least, it will be tomorrow. In this adventure's timescale, that's about 1.2 years. Let me explain. January lasted, in your time, one month. In our time, it was more like a year. Likewise February, which for us lasted 18 months or so; March nearly four years (it's an exponential relationship); and it's been calculated that April could go on for as long as six or seven years. By the time six months is up, you will have hardly noticed it – we will have aged horribly.

At this point some of you may be thinking that I'm not having much fun with the whole dollar-free thing and, to a certain extent, you'd be right. But not for any reasons other than those of self-indulgence and, more to the point, my seriously curtailed opportunity to that end.

After all, somebody's got to do the grizzling. If you only read what Linda has to say and swallow it whole, you'd be forgiven for thinking it's all 'wish you were here in paradise', and nothing but deep-fried lotus and great draughts of ambrosia on the menu. There needs to be some balance in the tale. It's a yin and yang thing.

This is not to say, as Linda sometimes assumes, that I think we in any way lack variety or quantity, or that what she provides is inferior to what could be obtained elsewhere. Far from it, although a beer would be good, and I'd just about chew your arm off for a lamb roast (although if I chewed your arm off,

I probably wouldn't need …) Anyway, the point is that the thing I find the hardest is the curtailment itself. I would never have stopped at KFC on the way home for a bucket of chips but, now I'm not allowed, I want to. And there's a whole range of similar temptations, things I would never ordinarily do or want, like bungee jumping or synchronised swimming, that now, because I can't indulge … well, you get the picture. A gilded cage is still a cage. (I was joking about the synchronised swimming.)

All of which should probably tell me a lot about myself, like I'm a selfish, resource-hungry, grizzling bastard who's never satisfied and complains all the time. But I already know that. Maybe I should get Linda to tell me; she's harder to ignore than my conscience.

Perhaps I shouldn't give the impression that nothing about our holiday (as we so euphemistically like to call it) has been fun. Breaking the record for the driest February and March combination on record was a highlight, as was the time the goat got crook and we thought she was going to die. Or that the chooks have chosen this year to throw off the imperialistic 'yolk' and stop laying eggs. Ditto for half the fruit trees. (I know trees don't lay eggs, use your powers of assumption.) A real hoot.

But make no mistake. If I didn't believe that what we're doing is not only the right thing to do, but also may in some respects (for example, solar hot-water and water tanks) be something we will shortly be compelled to do by government, I wouldn't be doing it. I should say that if it were not for Linda's drive, integrity and vision, I would not be here. It's also wonderful with respect to the old cliché of 'the family that works together, stays together'. We work in the garden together, we discuss the pros and cons of the whole thing together (Caleb often speaks of how we 'don't want to fail our six months'). Two days ago the three of us biked the 10 kilometre or so round-trip to the library, with a social call at Marguerite's on the way, which was a lot of fun and not something we would do if we had the car.

Which leads me to another obvious advantage. I ride the bike to work every day (electric, granted, but you can choose how hard you pedal, and the nature of the beast seems to be the longer you ride it, the harder you choose to pedal), I eat little fat and drink no beer, all of which combines to make me lighter and fitter than I've been in many years.

I look upon the project as an adventure and, like any adventure, the satisfaction is not always in the journey, but the achievement. Ask an endurance adventurer, or a climber of Everest what they enjoyed – the hauling of the weary body up (and down) the bloody great mountain or the planting of the flag at the summit. I know what the answer is for me.

april

2 *April*

Trev digs garden beds, I plant them out. Telephone peas, Massey early, Chantenay carrots, Hong Kong broccoli, two types of non-hearting lettuces, sugarloaf cabbages, pak choi. The carrots and broccoli are planted in the frost zone, everything else hopefully out of it. The San Marzano tomatoes are starting to flower, the winged beans are vigorous but are yet to produce, the snake beans have an aphid problem and I spray them every other day in a soap, oil and pyrethrum mix as the chilli and garlic spray seemed to be without effect. We shift the chook pen with Ehren's help. We discover why one of the beds I despair over is dry. A mulberry tree has tapped into it and drawn all the moisture from it. My Ronde de Nice zucchinis failed miserably, no matter how much I watered them. They are pulled out. Trev hauls out the sticks from the goat pen. They accumulate so quickly. Possum strips them of their leaves, drags them through her feeder and drops them disdainfully on the ground. I rake up the mulch and moist black balls and draw them into a heap at the very bottom. Hopefully they will compost quickly there and I'll be able to shovel it into a fair few wheelbarrow loads and into nearby garden beds. The chooks love it, following the rake's progress eagerly as it uncovers the unwary worm or slater. We discuss the dilapidated state of the bananas, whose leaves have all been shredded during the windy weather. I count the potatoes that have sprouted, and steal or 'bandicoot' a few from around the root zone of more mature plants. Autumn is a wonderful season to be gardening in Queensland – a nice breeze, a temperature that it is possible to survive in, a general lack of body moisture – the only drawback this year is the general lack of soil moisture. I go count the next round of pumpkins to keep myself happy.

HOME GARDENING IN AUSTRALIA

In 2004 nearly 3 million households (46%) reported they grow fruit or vegetables in their garden. Most of these households (84%) reported that they used some form of fertilisers in this activity: 76 per cent stated they used manure or compost and 40 per cent used other fertilisers. Nearly 29 per cent of households use pesticide or weedkiller when growing fruit and vegetables in their gardens.[1]

Organic is the way to go. There are any number of reasons why, some of which can bear being elaborated on.

Great reasons to grow or buy organic vegies

- **Avoiding chemical fertilisers, herbicides and pesticides increases the diversity of plants, insects and birds.**

  A 2000 report comparing organic with conventional farms found organic farms have five times as many wild plants, including rare and threatened species. They also have around 1.5 times as many insects, close to three times as many butterflies and 40 per cent more birds.[2]

- **Growing organic food tends to be more water-efficient than conventional farming methods.**

  Anecdotal evidence from many growers, especially irrigation users, indicates that organic growers apply water less often than similar non-organic growers. This is largely due to increased soil moisture storage in organic soils, which are well supplied with organic matter, and to the use of simple practices on organic farms, such as soil mulching.[3]

- **It employs more people.**

  Organic farms are more labour-intensive and have a higher number of employees than equivalent conventional farms.

- **Organic food has lower embodied energy.**

  Most modern farming is energy intensive. On certified organic farms, labour-intensive techniques reduce fuel inputs, soils are not over cultivated, intensive housing and long periods of artificial light for animals are banned, and energy-expensive chemical pesticides are not used.[4]

- **Organic and straight out of your garden is better for you.**

  A study commissioned by the Organic Retailers and Growers Association of Australia (ORGAA) found that conventionally grown fruit and vegetables purchased in supermarkets and other commercial retail outlets had 10 times less mineral content than fruit and vegetables grown organically. For the study, tomatoes, beans, capsicums and silverbeet grown on a certified organic farm using soil-regenerative techniques were analysed for mineral elements. A similar range of vegetables grown conventionally and purchased from a supermarket was also analysed. A major flaw of the study, however, is that it compared fresh produce at the farm with produce in a supermarket. Thus, there could have been a difference in freshness, which could have affected the nutrients measured.[5]

We've been building up beds using the no-dig method (we have a fairly rocky clay soil) for six years now. We found that, with the high humus level that resulted from this, less water was required and soil moisture was retained to a greater extent.

We mulch heavily, which helps reduce soil moisture loss, regulates soil temperatures and also means weeds aren't popping up and transpiring precious water.

A while back I invested in a hand-held soil moisture meter that gives an indication of the water level in the soil. A probe is pushed into the soil around the area I think might be getting too dry, so I only water on an as-needed basis rather than as a calendar event.

I also purchased a number of water-saving devices, the best being a trigger hose adapter so I only water where I need and not everywhere else while I'm heading back to the tap to turn it off. I experimented with using recycling bottles and a water spike that delivered water to the root area of established plants and small trees, so I didn't have to needlessly waste water penetrating through the topsoil, which would rapidly evaporate anyway. This was effective, but required more time to oversee, though I did find it useful to add liquid fertilisers and fertilise at the same time.

We are on a slope and need to do all we can to reduce run-off. It's a big block, 2180 square metres in size; that's a potential 1,853,000 litres of rainfall annually, according to the local average. The huge amount of mulch that we used assisted in creating a trickle-down effect: the water soaked in at a much gentler rate and the water that penetrated remained there longer due to its protection. At the base of garden beds we used bales of sugar cane and hay mulch to reduce soil erosion and water run-off.

One garden bed, growing potatoes, was never watered during the whole season. When I dug them up the soil was still beautifully moist despite having gone four weeks without rain.

One of the first things we did in our quest to save water was to install rainwater tanks. Rainwater is softer than reticulated water. This means less harsh cleaning agents are required. We wash dishes with Sunlight soap and rainwater – they end up beautifully clean. Use mains water, however, and the result is oily and unsightly. We wash our hair with sunlight soap and rainwater – soft and silky, just like the ads. Try it with mains water and it's like exchanging your hair for a steel wool hat. Then there is the smell and the taste.

While mains water varies from region to region, most people who have drunk rainwater will turn their nose up at a glass of mains. I recall one man telling me he'd rather drink out of a muddy puddle.

> *Of the total water used by households in 2000–01, 96% (2,085,768 ML) was supplied by mains and 4% (95,512 ML) of water was from a self-extracted source (i.e. rainwater tanks and direct extraction from surface waterways or groundwater). South Australia has the highest proportion of rainwater tanks (48%) of any state or territory.*[6]

RAIN HARVESTING

If we all had rainwater tanks, there would be considerably less pressure on our water supplies. For example, a 10,000-litre rainwater tank in a typical Sydney house could reduce imported water demand by 48 per cent and stormwater run-off (from the roof) by 35 per cent.[7]

So, how much water could you reasonably expect to harvest from your roof?

- 80 per cent of Australia has annual rainfall of less than 600 millimetres.
- 50 per cent has less than 300 millimetres.
- The Australian average annual rainfall is only 472 millimetres.
- Some areas receive even less than this and other areas 10 times more. However, it is mostly the inhabited coastal areas rather than the arid areas that receive more, so most people will have an annual rainfall well in excess of the national average. (See the map in Appendix 2, page 267.)

Once you know your average annual rainfall, you'll need to identify the approximate area of your roof. Each square metre will collect a litre of water for every millimetre of rain that falls. For example:

100 square metres (roof area) x 850 millimetres (annual rainfall)
= 85,000 litres of water.

A small percentage will be lost due to evaporation and to the use of a water diverter, a recommended device that diverts the first flush of atmospheric- and roof-contaminated rainwater away from the tank.

If the average household uses 900 litres a day, that adds up to 328,500 litres per year. In an area that receives 850 millimetres a year, a roof area of 386 square metres would be required in order to obtain that amount of water. That's a very big roof.

Once you have determined how much water you could harvest, and you know your daily water use, you can either pat yourself on the back or try to reduce your use to get the two readings within closer range, and rely on town water for a top-up when required.

Council regulations require that no cross-connections be made between town and tank water. This prevents the possibility of tank water, which may be contaminated with Giardia, cryptosporidium or other waterborne bacteria, infecting the town water system. In most cases a town water hose can lead into the top of the tank and be used when required. A cock and ball system can automatically detect when the water drops to a certain level and top up the tank until it reaches the required level.

Check with your local council as to their regulations. Some councils are offering rainwater tank rebates, which are well worth looking into.

Rainwater is considered non-potable (not drinkable), and in most areas its use is limited to garden, toilet, shower and laundry use. However, households in non-reticulated water areas can drink rainwater. An inconsistency I've not managed to resolve.

Rainwater tanks require 'desludging' every 2–3 years to remove any build-up of organic material, mostly leaves and fallen debris that finds its way into the tank. This is why gutter guards are recommended, as well as leaf-excluding fittings and the trimming back of trees that are likely culprits.

The purchase and installation of low-flow showerheads and taps was the next step in our efforts to reduce water use. We scaled down the time we were in the shower and the strength the taps were turned on. Caleb rapidly learnt to half-fill a cup with water, do a pre-rinse of his toothbrush, apply toothpaste, brush, rinse with the water in the cup and spit, then rinse his toothbrush in what remained of the water and dump it down the sink. Seems a bit over the top? In a four-member household, the average water used to brush teeth is 5 litres per brush. Assuming they're brushing their teeth twice a day, that's 40 litres a day all up, 14,600 litres a year, just to brush teeth. This way, around 1000 litres.

Just being aware of the amount of water you're using is the first step in saving water.

Washing the dishes. Well, even we smile at our methods, so have a grin on us. First, we grow loofahs, a zucchini-like fruit, which we empty of seeds and dry. We then shove a small piece of sunlight soap into the loofah and use it to wash the dishes. We use a sink three-quarters full of solar hot-water and we do them only once a day. So 8 litres a day, 2920 litres a year.

In a week the average household uses 6300 litres of water, while we use 1400 litres. We've reduced our water usage to 22 per cent of the average water consumption and, except in drought conditions, it is 100 per cent rainwater.

HOUSEHOLD WATER USE

The use of water in the average household varies widely, changing by season, state, household infrastructure and the number and habits of its occupants. Most studies place it between 900 and 1100 litres per household per day, around 330,000 to 400,000 litres per year. For calculations within this book we'll stick to the lowest estimate of 900 litres.

In the average household, 43 per cent of water is used on the garden and outdoors, 13 per cent in the laundry, 18 per cent in the toilet and the remaining 26 per cent in the kitchen, bath and shower.[8]

How to read your water meter

Not many households are aware of their annual water use, though more will be able to tell you how much it costs. Using your water meter to keep track of your water use can be a great way to provide incentives to reduce household water, confirming the effect of any water-saving strategies in a calculable way.

Locate your water meter, usually in one of the most overgrown corners of your block. I used to worry I'd interrupt a brown snake snoozing in the grass till we cleared it all away, and began making our weekly meter check. Once located, lift the cover and take the reading.

Councils usually only read the first four numbers, but when taking your own records take note of all six.

| 2 | 6 | 8 | 9 | 2 | 5 |

This reading is 2689 kilolitres or 2,689,250 litres.

Old rates notices where water charges have been made (or for renters, water bills) will give you a history of your water use. You can also use the meter to check for leaks, by taking a reading last thing at night and checking it again first thing in the morning (ensure no one flushes).

Use the table on the following page to record your water readings. Aim to do it over at least six months so you get an idea of your water use across seasons. Include comments so you can record periods when you were away or when you had a house full of guests.

Your household's water use

WEEK	DATE	READING AT BEGINNING	READING AT END	WATER USE	COMMENTS
Week 1					
Week 2					
Week 3					
Week 4					
Week 5					
Week 6					
Week 7					
Week 8					
Week 9					
Week 10					
Week 11					
Week 12					
Week 13					
Week 14					
Week 15					
Week 16					
Week 17					
Week 18					
Week 19					
Week 20					
Week 21					
Week 22					
Week 23					
Week 24					
Week 25					
Week 26					
Total used over six months:					

The table below gives you an idea of how the average household uses water. There are simple, inexpensive things you can do to save water; tips are included below. It's also a great idea to make it a family project – get the kids excited about how much water they can save.

INDOOR WATER USE [9]		Average total water used	Annual savings and water-saving tips
Shower (average shower is 8 minutes)	Normal shower rose	120 litres per shower	Using a water-saver shower head saves 21,900 litres per person per year.
	Water saver rose	60 litres per shower	
Bath		50–150 litres per bath	Bucket out bath water and distribute to house plants.
Toilet	Single flush	120 litres per day	Using a dual flush saves 29,200 litres per year.
	Dual flush	40 litres per day	
Washing machine (figures based on 4 washes per week)	Twin tub	40 litres per wash	8320 litres total water use per year.
	Front loading	80 litres per wash	16,640 litres total water use per year.
	Top loading	170 litres per wash	35,360 litres total water use per year.
Dishwasher		18–50 litres per load	If you like to rinse dishes before loading, half-fill the sink rather than using a running tap. Full loads only.
Cooking, cleaning and drinking		150 litres per day	Wash vegetables in half a sink of water with a vegetable brush, rather than under a running tap.
Brushing teeth	With running water	5 litres per brush	Fill a glass with water instead.
OUTDOOR WATER USE			
Sprinkler or hand-held hose		1000 litres per hour	Use a trigger fitting so you can turn it off when moving around the garden.
Drip system		4 litres per hour	Saves time, and a great deal of water compared with hand-held methods.
Hosing paths		200 litres for 10 minutes	Oh, shucks, use a broom.
Swimming pools		Up to 55,000 litres	Use a pool covering, as a pool can evaporate its own weight in water each year.

Loofah sponges

Grow the loofah plant (*Luffa cylindrica*, a member of the cucurbit family, which includes pumpkins, cucumbers and melons) in summer months with plenty of water and over a trellis. It's a vigorous vine and it will sprawl all over the garden if left to its own devices. The fruits are similar to zucchini and can be eaten while young. Left to mature they will start to yellow and become spongy to the touch. Test one by putting your fingernail through the skin and ripping off an area. The sponge should be fully formed and without lots of white matted material.

Remove the skin. Take care not to get any of the soapy gel in your eyes as it contains saponins and is an irritant.

Remove the seeds by flicking the loofah down with force, but not striking anything. The seeds should be a dark olive green. These have been used to alleviate constipation, but they are better kept for next year's crop of kitchen sponges. Thoroughly wash the loofah and hang on the line to dry. Inside the loofah are three hollow chambers. We place small slivers of Sunlight soap inside and use it as a self-soaping sponge. When the dishes are done simply flick out remaining water and place in a dry area. Loofahs won't go mouldy or smelly and, when you've finished with it, you can toss it into the garden where it can decompose at its leisure.

4 April

I know Possum's noises and this one isn't normal. It sounds more like a gargling roar than her usual imperious bellow. I go down to investigate. I'd fed her a big pile of raw pumpkin 15 minutes earlier. I do this every day, chopping it up roughly with the machete. This time one of the pieces had lodged at the back of her throat. She was literally throwing herself to the ground, shaking her head from side to side trying to dislodge it. I walked around with her, trying to see if she could get it — she couldn't. She was half-choking and frantic. I looked around for a stick, then remembered that only yesterday Trev had picked them all up. There weren't any. I wondered if I could stick my fingers in her mouth. I grabbed hold of her beard, she wrenched her head away and backed off into her house, tossing herself around and hitting the walls. I could see a stick on the outside of the pen. I managed to squeeze my hand under and grab it. Stepping up into her house I eyed her as warily as she was eyeing me.

Using my hip I pushed her up hard against the wall. This left a hand free to grab a horn and hold her head relatively steady while I used the stick in the other to lever open her jaws and flick the pumpkin from where it was lodged. Once loosened she spat it out and staggered out the door, a brief wheeze and back to the rest of the pumpkin. I look at the offending piece; it is about 7 by 3 centimetres. Not huge. I vow to halve the size. It's all over in less than five minutes but makes me realise how practical I have become. Ten years ago my practical skills were limited to being able to change a tyre and a light bulb. Now there isn't too much I wouldn't have a go at. I'm often able to think of ingenious ways to get around practical problems, though either a lack of strength or an inclination towards idleness means Trev often gets to implement them. I try to think of a limit to what I would try and I realise snakes are way beyond me and always will be, although I can step aside whip snakes, blind snakes and legless lizards without too much horror. I did pick one up in a handful of mulch a while back and that resulted in some high-pitched noises. Only the other day a whip snake hunting a skink almost ran over my feet. As long as I know it's not fatally venomous I'm happy enough sharing my garden space with it. I've learnt so much in the past five years or so. I remember when we first bought Possum I was horrified by how big she was and how long, curved and wicked those horns of hers looked. Now I handle her with respect, but without fear.

I was on midwife duty while she had Chocolate and Vanilla. Trevor found himself mysteriously occupied with other things like other people's cars and engines. Possum was in pain but allowed me to remain with her when she settled into the straw in her house. When Chocolate was halfway out I pulled her the rest of the way and together we pulled away the membrane so she could breathe. Then Possum went into a frenzy. Chocolate was, by instinct, trying to stand and to feed, but Possum would have none of it. Vanilla was on the way and she was prepared to use her horns to keep Chocolate out of her space. Twice Chocolate was violently thrown against the side of the housing. I dragged her to safety while Possum birthed Vanilla. Caleb and his mate Bradley stood at the door, pale and gagging, while I waxed on about what a wonderful experience it all was. Within five minutes both Vanilla and Chocolate were standing and feeding. And Possum went from what seemed like a bad mother to a wonderful one. I retreated, also pale and at the point of gagging, while she ate up the afterbirth. If nothing else, it showed me clearly that goats deliver their own babies naturally, as women deliver theirs. Doctors are there as precautions only. Even if women don't understand what is happening, their bodies do. Caleb, who was born in the bath, came back from school one day puzzled as to why it was all the kids at school were born in a hospital.

'Was there something wrong with them?' he asked.

Humans are so good at creating complexity from simple things. The Industrial Revolution must have seemed like such a great idea, making machinery to save time. The only problem was, in order to purchase it we needed more money; to make more money we had to become bigger, use more land, and plant more intensively and beyond the capacity that natural systems could sustain. To become bigger we needed more time, and more machinery to save time, then more knowledge of how to use and repair the machinery. The extra time used doing these things meant we needed to find other ways to save time, so we invented more machinery to save time, and in order to purchase that machinery we needed more ... The paradox is that all our time-saving devices have led us into a world where people have less time for their families and themselves. As an experiment, the highly industrialised world has had its successes, but if we were to add up the pluses and minuses, we would have to conclude that our society is currently operating on an energy deficit and has failed to create the foundations on which we, as a species rather than a generation, can survive. We are supposedly a very adaptable and clever animal; we should, by rights, be able to understand the implications of our current mode of living and alter it to ensure our long-term survival. However, this is proving not to be the case, and our inability to consider changing our domestic, agricultural, industrial and environmental practices indicates that we are, perhaps, nowhere near as smart as we perceive ourselves to be.

Nowhere can this be more clearly seen than in the answer to one of the questions I love to put to people: 'Do you consider yourself to be an animal?' Most people, after careful consideration, declare that they are not. 'But you are a mammal. Does that not mean you share physical similarities to other mammals, like sheep, possums and cows?' However they look at it, they come to the same odd conclusion – they are not animal, they are something more than animal. By this thinking they exclude themselves from the animal world, remove themselves from the natural world that animals must live within, and create for themselves the illusion that for humans the rules of nature do not apply. We might be good with our hands, we might be very clever at utilising our environment and we might create complex systems of our own, but our base premise of how we 'fit' into our natural system is fundamentally flawed.

What would have happened if things had remained simpler? We would have had to work physically harder; we would therefore be fitter, leaner and healthier. We would have built personal and lasting relationships with our friends and neighbours in order to achieve those things we cannot achieve alone. No camaraderie around the plough when you own a noisy tractor. We would have been less lonely.

Technology is only one form of progress. I think we often overlook other ways in which we, as a human race, can evolve and change. Spiritual rather than material evolution. But then I guess I'm starting to sound like a hippie. A recent news item suggested that the human race has stopped evolving physically because our bodies no longer need to adapt to our environment — we have learnt to adapt the environment to us.

As things become more complex we seem to require further complexity to keep ourselves interested: for example, high-tech movies that require millions of dollars to create, and drag racing, which creates thousands of tonnes of CO_2 not just in the performance vehicles, but from all those who travel to watch it. Perhaps it also works in reverse: when we make our lives simpler, the simpler things in life take on added interest. I know I valued our bike trip to the library immensely; it stands out as one of our best family outings. When Caleb gets invited to a birthday party, it's sheer excitement for him. His grandmother in New Zealand has sent him two 'relief' parcels. He eagerly anticipated each arrival. In such a short time what would once have been humdrum has become anything but.

5 April

Recently we have made the decision to barter in exchange for money so we can go do our own shopping. We will be transporting it by bike, and therefore not incurring any further CO_2 emissions on our behalf. But mostly because it feels like Christmas when we contemplate spending the $20 or so we've accrued. We discuss priorities and debate each purchase. Will there be enough left over for another jar of Vegemite? That first one was devoured in a flash.

Yesterday Trev told me I was right, that something was eating the peanuts — straight out of the ground. Trev observed a peewee standing guard on the verandah. When Trev left the house it sounded the alarm. Trev was quick enough to see a magpie downstairs cracking the peanuts against a rock. On hearing the peewee's alarm, the maggie startled and flew off. Trev wants to know if the two are in cahoots and if the peewee gets his share. The incident was small, but fascinating. I love watching lizards, finding chook eggs in odd places, watering the garden and 'sensing' the plants detecting the moisture after rain, sucking it up and reinvigorating. It's absorbing watching the world change around me.

6 April

Caleb quits. We agree that his three months are over and that we will endeavour to provide him with a few extra benefits over the next three. We celebrate with the sparklers that I've had tucked away. At night we stand on the verandah and wave them around in circles, write our names and take photos. His benefits will still be meagre — things like a book from the school book club, butter, Vegemite, occasional chicken, extra fruit and the infrequent 'lolly'. Still no movies, Lego, trips into town, apart from on the back of the bike. He is happy enough with this arrangement. Our offer of $200 on completion of the six months is still valid. He is trying to augment this by doing 'chores', such as cleaning his bedroom and the Bionicle bed, and, last night when he insisted on doing more and I couldn't think of anything else, reading a non-fiction book about the Wild West, at 10 cents a page. He's built himself a money box out of Lego and can often be seen taking it out, counting and returning it and coming up with interesting questions such as, 'If I turn my $200 into 5 cent pieces, how much room will it take up?'

I try to describe how much and he decides he will ask for his $200 in 5 cent pieces and that he will drag it behind him in a sack when he goes on his end-of-jail-sentence shopping spree. I tell him every shop assistant will curse him and we will spend our whole time standing at the counter while they count it. He doesn't care.

'If I get it in $50 notes, that means I only get four notes', he muses. 'How many if it is in $20?'

We go through this and he decides $10 would be best as it's more money. We tangle ourselves hopelessly as I try to convince him that while it is physically more money it is of the same value as different combinations of different values. In the end I give up; he takes that as a win. I muse that one of the major points behind doing this experiment was to teach Caleb the importance of energy over currency. Not sure I'm winning there either.

7 April

Two unexpected eggs are found. The youngest chooks have started to lay. At the moment we get half a dozen a day, which is far lower than we had anticipated. Three of the older chooks never came back on the lay, the two newest have only just started — that's a loss of five eggs a day. We barter two to three dozen a fortnight, and never seem to have enough to cover our own usage. With an extra 28 a fortnight we hope to be swimming in them.

We lop off the heads of the sunflowers. They're not quite ready, although the cockatoos have decided they are. They are the last crop; no others were planted due to the lack of rainfall.

It has been drizzling on and off for most of this month. Overcast skies have meant little solar generation and lukewarm showers, and between 1.5 and 3 millimetres a day. Trev informs me that it is mizzling, a Scottish term for more than a mist, but less than a drizzle. Everything is surface damp, but there is little soil moisture below the top couple of centimetres. So while it is technically 'raining' I am still full of grist — not quite the full-scale grizzle.

8 April

It's cheese-making day and baking day, plus I had planned to take our accrued barter money and go squander it at the supermarket, this time on my ramshackle bike. Caleb begs me to leave it till after school so he can come too. Trev has already made noises about wanting to be in on the trip as well. I relent. I was going to get a few extra things for the big bake-off today, but figure that the family outing wins over a 500-gram block of butter. Because goat's milk doesn't lend itself well to butter-making, we have done without. It limits me when baking, and means anything you put onto a sandwich sinks into the bread and disappears. When we bought Caleb butter a while back he enjoyed it so much he requested butter sandwiches for a week. So it looks like we're going to have a joint family adventure across the urban wilderness. Up hill, down vale and into the great land of temptations. I suspect Caleb's Lego money box will be making an appearance.

9 April

It's overcast, but not raining. We're wearing sunnies not so much for the glare but to protect our eyes against the possibility of roadside projectiles. Bike seats are adjusted, helmets on, the final pump of air in tyres and we're off on our combined social, library and supermarket quest. We bump into friends we haven't seen in ages and chat. We visit the library, that great smorgasbord of books on every possible topic. Trev and I find it hard to limit ourselves. Caleb is inevitably drawn to the video and DVD section, and books about dragons and ancient cultures. Back on the bikes we head up what feel like never-ending steep slopes and eventually wind our way through the backstreets and to the supermarket. Another smorgasbord. Today it's busy. It doesn't take us long to become claustrophobic. Trev and I shuffle behind others and find ourselves looking into the depths of their shopping trolleys. We both agree it seems amazing to buy, without thought, what you need or want without any idea of where it came from, what it went through to get to the shelves and the ramifications of the whole process. We make jokes at our own expense. We try hard, with some success, not to be judgemental.

We have Trev's calculator and we're going through justifying each purchase. We agree that Caleb's treats are Vegemite, a packet of noodles and a small bag of plain chips. All up, around $5 extra. He has his Lego money box with him (he's already dropped it twice) and he's deliberating over toys. We talk him out of it and tell him to keep saving and then we'll bike to Toyworld in the next fortnight and he can spend it then. We line up at the counter with our backpacks and trolleys and load 11 kilograms of sugar and flour into my backpack, along with 4 kilos of potatoes — the kilo of grapes is carried separately. We manage to load them onto my bike, along with the 10 kilos of books already in it. The trip home comes close to excruciating, and there's an impatient four-wheel drive idling behind me. (I'm envisioning a backpack explosion of flour and sugar as I peddle across the Normanby Bridge.) Seeing all the four-wheel drives out on the roads makes me realise how little people know about the environmental impact of these beasts. I try not to think about how little most of them care. We arrive out of breath and sweating. What a great way to spend a Saturday morning. Caleb talks Trev into taking him snailing with the spotlight tonight. We make an agreement that 50 snails equals $2, a clean bedroom another $1.

EMBODIED ENERGY OF VEHICLES

A vital (and often forgotten) component of the energy equation, embodied energy is 'the energy consumed by all of the processes associated with the production of a building [or vehicle], from the acquisition of natural resources to product delivery, including mining, manufacturing of materials and equipment, transport and administrative functions'.[10]

The embodied energy of a car is considerable: mining, extraction and smelting are very energy intensive, as is the production of plastics. The vast majority of the energy involved in the manufacture of a vehicle is fossil-fuel based. So, while we consider the fuel consumption important, so too is the embodied energy the vehicle represents, a four-wheel drive being far less efficient and, in some cases, meaning one vehicle is made at the energy expense of two. For example, the Nissan X-Trail weighs in at 2000 kilograms while the Honda Jazz tips the scales at 1010 kilograms, around half the weight.

But it doesn't end there. The average passenger vehicle tyre weighs 9 kilograms and requires approximately 105 kWh of energy to produce, from a mix of natural rubber and petroleum-based products. The average four-wheel drive tyre weighs 20 kilos and requires approximately 232 kWh. (The power used to manufacture one four-wheel drive tyre is what our household uses in electricity over 40 days.) A four-wheel drive will continue to command a higher rate of embodied energy in its maintenance.

By choosing retreads over new tyres, a saving of 23 litres of crude oil for materials and process energy can be made and, according to current standards, no loss of safety is incurred. This is one way you can have less environmental impact while still driving. Or you could walk.

Greenfleet

If you can't bike or walk, you can always offset your greenhouse emissions by using Greenfleet's emissions calculator and tree-planting service. Visit their website, www.greenfleet.com.au, to work out how many trees it would take to offset your vehicle's impact on the environment; you then pay Greenfleet to plant trees to reabsorb the CO_2 you have created.

Greenfleet is a non-profit organisation so the cost is minimal: for around $40 (tax deductible), Greenfleet plants 17 native trees on your behalf. These trees will help to create a forest and, as they grow, will absorb the greenhouse gases that your car produces in one year (based on 4.3 tonnes of CO_2 for the average car).

Research shows that 17 trees will not only absorb a car's greenhouse emissions, but also help to tackle salinity, improve water quality and provide essential habitat for native species.

Since 1997 Greenfleet has planted more than 2 million trees on behalf of Australian motorists and fleets. These forests will not be harvested and will create an investment in rural Australia for future generations.

10 April

While Trev has been thinking wistfully about eating steak, he has recently realised he can live without alcohol. I know I can. Nine months of abstinence broke me of the habit. Occasionally I'll have a glass of wine or a scotch and dry on a social occasion and that's pretty much it. But for Trev getting home equates to 'sit down, have a beer'. We haven't been able to make beer. While we have hops, we'd also need malt, yeast and sugar and we haven't a hope of growing or bartering sufficient to keep him in stock. Shane from down the road makes a habit of popping up with a six-pack at least once a fortnight. Trev appreciates the reprieve. Before the experiment began, I was aware of the extra challenge of going without C_2H_6O. We found recipes for elderflower champagne; we made passionfruit and strawberry wine during a glut. Trev drinks the strawberry wine watered down to cordial strength. Straight, it's too sweet, and it lasts longer this way.

Strawberry wine

4.5 kilos strawberries, sliced

2 kilos sugar

1 packet wine maker's yeast (7 grams)

Mix strawberries and 500 grams of sugar in a large steel pot. Cover with cheesecloth or another aerating, insect-proof material. Allow the mix to ferment for eight days. Stir and poke the 'cake' down every day.

Strain the juice into a carboy. Add the remaining sugar, yeast and enough water to make 9 litres of liquid in total. Leave to ferment until bubbling stops. Depending on temperature, this may take around a week. Bottle the wine in sterilised bottles and leave for six months.

Makes up to 9 litres of very sweet wine. For a drier wine add less sugar at the second fermentation.

Lemon cordial

1 litre lemon juice
2 litres water
1 kilo sugar

Bring the water to the boil. Add the sugar and stir until dissolved, then take off the heat. Allow liquid to cool a while, then add lemon juice. Pour into sterilised bottles. Store in the fridge. The cordial keeps for a week or two. We also use passionfruit juice when we have a glut. Delicious.

Elderflower champagne is fine, but low in the required alcohol. The ginger beer was good till I made a batch that tasted like popcorn. We can't figure out how I managed that. Gradually Trev has let it slide to the point where he has a go at the lemon cordial in the fridge and claims himself content. To some this might be a digression rather than the sound of progress. However, Trev has had an ambivalent relationship with alcohol over the years and to come to the point where he can say, 'It's not bothering me', seems like a major step.

Trev brought home a big bag of unhusked macadamias last week. One of his workmates has 140 trees but not enough time to harvest them all, let alone process them. Trev made a few adjustments to the Colonel and away I wound, Trev pouring them in, and lo and behold out came macadamias de-husked, most of them dropping through the holes, rolling down and dropping into the bucket at the bottom, just as they should. The rest had to be fished out from the hulls. Hours of work reduced to 10 minutes. Now the green husks are off, we have laid them out to dry. A few warm days and several adjustments away and the Colonel might remove the hulls as well.

I'm in the garden when I hear Caleb call my name. He doesn't sound aggrieved, he sounds triumphant. It takes a while to locate him. He's standing on the roof — we're changing the angle of the solar panels today. By the time I get there Caleb is back on the ground. I clamber up onto the roof and Trev and I grovel around under the panels dropping nuts and screws and having to grovel still further to retrieve them from the gutters so we can lower the panels, but it seems that changing the angle has little effect on solar production. We decide to leave them at the original angle all year round. The time it takes per year in maintaining the system is around two or three hours: giving them a squeegee clean, reading the meters once a week and keeping records of how much power we are creating against usage. By opting for a grid-connected system, we negated the need for batteries. This decision was based on a number of important factors. The cost was one — we saved approximately $6000 by avoiding batteries. It was also an environmental factor, as batteries are the weakest link. Their lifespan is around six years, after which they need replacing and become a disposal issue. Choosing a grid-connected system also means we would always be able to draw power regardless of inclement weather and would not be limited by what we could 'draw off' at any given time, so Trev can still weld and I can still use the oven and iron clothes, though I reserve the right not to.

11 April

The end of last month, which, as Trev prophesied, lasted four years, and the beginning of this one have been the hardest. Not on a material, day-to-day level, but rather on a personal energy level. We've been feeling lethargic, impatient to get it all over with, a readiness to compromise, a desire almost to give in. I realise that I need to reinvigorate, re-motivate and otherwise get myself off my proverbial bum. Strangely enough the motivation arrives in the form of a book found on the library shelves, *Voluntary simplicity* by Duane Elgin. It serves to bring further into consciousness what it is we are trying to achieve. For Trev it comes in a completely different form — work commitments mean two nights away in two weeks, staying in motels that just happen to supply various forms of meat.

Last month there was a theme of reflection, of looking at how we got here and what we learnt during that process. This month seems to be drawing in on itself as a time to contemplate what it is we are doing and why, and developing a consciousness of that.

Our motivations are manifold. We wanted to change our lifestyle to one that, while being easy on the environment, was also easier on us. We were unhappy with how things were; we had no time, for either ourselves or each other. Little peace of mind, often no money, and certainly no real meaning to what we were doing, just ever decreasing circles where Caleb was put into daycare for long days and days on end. The guilt was eating at us. We were either in a state of hyperactivity or lethargy. To say we were unsatisfied with our cycle of consumer dependence is an understatement.

For the first 18 months of Caleb's life I stayed at home studying and Trev brought home the bacon. We had little money, but what we had ... well, it seemed the obvious thing to do was console ourselves with it and spend. The pattern of instant gratification was set, and we were addicted to it: feel low, spend money, feel low, eat junk food or, in Trev's case, drink beer. We can both trace this pattern back to our first pay packets. Living with that sense of having nothing and needing more was something we didn't want to go back to. There had to be some way we could get off the treadmill without embracing poverty as the only alternative.

Money saved is money earned. The old adage. I thought about it a lot. After I started working we had a great combined income, yet we weren't saving. If we lived more simply, removed all the excess shopping trips and lived with what we had and ate what we could grow and supplemented the rest by buying staples, we might reduce our expenditure. Perhaps we could get rid of one car, only paying one rego. If one of us wasn't working that would save us $360 a fortnight for daycare. The car was all but paid off, and when that was ... why not? Thankfully the funding for the program I was working on dried up. Every time another contract had come up I'd sign it. How could I throw good money away? But every time I did, I signed myself up for at least two nights away each week, sometimes four or five. The more I thought about getting out of the cycle the more I enthused. Trev was ready to move away from the frenetic pace we had been living at. Caleb loved the idea of finally having his mum at home and no more daycare. We also agreed the environment would suffer less if we managed our lives this way.

As with any addiction, you have to replace it with a healthier one. So we swapped for a simpler lifestyle, one that had inherent points of gratification that were not consumption-based. It was time to do what we dreamed of: spend time with each other, eat healthy food, exercise, and live with a belief that the benefits of what we were doing extend beyond ourselves and affect our environment. These aren't always instantly gratifying — I sweated a great deal before I could stand on the scales and feel good. But the gratification is there, and it's longer term. A bar of chocolate is usually only appreciated around here for five minutes, but the joy of growing and eating our own food exists well beyond any given meal.

The fact that we made a conscious choice about how we live and were not forced into it by external influences is vital to the long-term success of what we are doing. I believe self-determination is the biggest single factor in happiness. If you are extremely poor, but feel you have control over your destiny, that you are able to implement changes in your life, then you are going to be happier than someone who lives in the same level of poverty but who has no control over how their life is run. Self-determination makes what could amount to six months of poverty into six months of choosing not to spend a dollar. There is little in the way of resentment or deprivation about our six months — we feel we are achieving something important, something that will stay with us for the rest of our lives. This comment seems contrary to some of Trev's frequent 'grists', yet if you asked him to be serious for a minute he'll admit to feeling that what we do is of lasting importance and, while he laments it's like living in prison, it has freed him as well.

Imagine walking through a warehouse full of TVs, cars, barbecues, software, books, clothes and more, and instead of having a dollar value it was instead magically converted into the hours you would need to work to pay for it. Imagine you make $15 an hour, after tax; some of that must go towards mortgage, insurances, medical expenses and other non-negotiable living expenses, so the hourly rate might be closer to $7.50. If you choose an item valued at $30, then you are going to need work four hours to pay for it. It is no longer worth $30 — it's worth four hours of your life. Do you really want that item, or would you prefer half a day off to do with as you'd like?

I'd choose no shirt — give me the time. You'll throw in a free tea-towel you say? No deal.

Our society exchanges time for money; this is a simple fact that we all acknowledge as a given. If you're employed in a particular sector you would expect to earn a particular hourly rate. This, if you are qualified for the position, is your worth within that industry. We've lost the personal connection to the value of time and the worth of our own lives, which we often exchange for baubles, instant feel-goods, that last for less time than it took to earn them. Living simply isn't about self-imposed poverty; it's about consciously deciding what is important in life and reducing our needs to those of greatest importance. The rest is extraneous, often requiring too high a time investment, both in the purchase and the subsequent upkeep. Jewellery, music, clothes, electronic paraphernalia and a snappy looking hairdo are not things I'm willing to lose time or sleep over. If this is how I feel about them, then their lack is of no great loss. Living simply is not about giving things up, forsaking them, frugality, denial, stinginess, deprivation or lack. It's about taking things up: self-determination, freedom, autonomy and abundant living.

There are two ways to get enough: one is to continue to accumulate more and more. The other is to desire less.
GK CHESTERTON (1874–1936)

People who take up what has been called Voluntary Simplicity might be accused of withdrawing from society, but surveys taken by Duane Elgin, who is believed to have coined the term in the 1980s, show that they are more likely to be involved in their community, politics and the environment, and use their extra time to further worthwhile causes. Living simply isn't a withdrawal from life, it's engaging in it more fully and with conscious meaning.

We may have gone cold turkey but, when the restraints have been removed, what will we return to?

If anyone has a problem with this, it's Trev. I guess it's been a great deal longer since his first pay packet and he has, at times in his life, lived on carrots, rice and onions for months on end because he was without choice in the matter. His example of, 'I would never have stopped at KFC for hot chips but, now I can't, I want to', seems indicative of this.

As 'Poor Trev' – 'Don't say that, I hate that. It's not true' – is still working full-time, you may be asking where his extra time comes into it? There are several ways. He no longer has anything much to do with cooking or cleaning during the week; he gets up, makes his own breakfast and lunch, helps milk the goat and leaves; he comes home, helps milk the goat again and, after that, his time is his. He is healthier, less stressed, and he may well be tacking additional years onto his life to enjoy as well. Which is putting long-term gratification to the real test.

Of course there is the poverty consciousness. Living simply or sustainably, whatever term you use, may mean that from the outside looking in, you may be labelled poor. This is a construct of our society, which builds its successful-person model on income, what products they choose to spend it on, how they 'wear' it, what house they live in (the more energy-inefficient the better it would seem) and what they drive (once again, seemingly the more energy-inefficient the better). I bike on the rustiest old curmudgeon of a bike around — it's a hideous shade of yellow and Trev has tacked on bits here and there with the welder, but I'm so proud of its $2-ness. In choosing to live simply we've chosen to live proudly too. I'm always boasting about how Trev can recycle the most mundane of rubbish items into things of great use, and repair things, like his thongs, which are repaired to the point that the brand name should be removed as it's the only thing still on them that's original. Where there could be shame, there is pride. It's all a matter of a mental rather than physical process.

I can't make society live sustainably, but I can refuse to judge others by society's bias. I can also choose to live the way I think is of most value and, in being proud to do so, weaken that same society's bias. When someone drives off to work, I can wave them goodbye from my place in the garden and mutter, 'You poor bastards' under my breath. I can afford to — I'm time-rich. There are nomadic tribes who pity those who possess large amounts, as they need to expend more time and energy to transport them. He who owns least is considered free.

 After a lifetime of study of the rise and fall of the world's civilizations, historian Arnold Toynbee concluded that the measure of a civilization's growth was not to be found in the conquest of other people or in the possession of land. Rather he described the essence of growth in what he called the Law of Progressive Simplification. *True growth, he said, is the ability of a society to transfer increasing amounts of energy and attention from the material side of life to the nonmaterial side and thereby to advance its culture, capacity for compassion, sense of community, and strength of democracy. We are now being pushed by necessity to discover freshly the meaning of 'true growth' by progressively simplifying the material side of our lives and enriching the nonmaterial.*
DUANE ELGIN [11]

Trev feels rewarded by his employment, but, should the day arise when he doesn't, we can arrange a change in roles. By living sustainably we are able to save around 50 per cent of Trev's income.

Currently our food and garden have a time investment of around 20 hours a week. That includes weeding, planting, mulching, harvesting, processing food, and bread- and cheese-making. The rest of the time I'm free to do as I wish. Only I've been sending myself mad in a pursuit of 'doing', of justifying myself, because to lie around and read a book or relax would be *bad* … inactivity equals guilt. I hereby resolve to lie around more often.

14 April

'I don't want to go to school, Mum. Pleassssseeee. I want to stay home and do school here.'

This is a frequent refrain, one repeated ever since Caleb first encountered the concept of home schooling, which was soon after he started school. I've looked into it, but Trev and I agreed that the social aspect of school is important. But we've been taking another look at the possibility. Caleb has a hearing difficulty and, while only slight, it means he finds being in a noisy classroom difficult. I often wonder how much he is getting out of each day. Over the last few days he's had numerous nosebleeds. He goes through stages with them. It's both hereditary and a result of some fairly strenuous nose rubbing. Last night he was up twice with them. When the usual refrain popped out of him, 'Mum, can't I stay home with you and have school here?', I surprised myself with an 'OK'.

He looked as surprised as I did.

'You'll have to do work though. And I'm going to make it hard.'

He was happy with that. That was four days ago. He and I rearranged his bedroom and we set up a classroom. We've used old exercise books from last year; we have oodles of pens, scissors, a calculator that is so bright and lolly-like it looks almost edible; and a bookshelf crammed with fiction and non-fiction books. Books for me have always been an obsession, one I've hoped to graft onto Caleb. In Year One his reading level was assessed as being that of an 11-year-old's, so I guess I have.

We've set up a star system, coded each day's work with what he can work through independently and what he requires help with. He's decided fractions are phenomenally cool, realising the number facts he's always stumbled on are, in fact, easy. He's wearing both a digital and an analogue watch and has almost got his head around both. He's hurdled verbs, managed to rearrange his reversed letters, can add two-digit numbers along with carrying them over, and is a happy little sausage.

It's been a rewarding week for both of us. He usually has everything finished by one o'clock and he spends the rest of his day doing what he wants with his time. This afternoon he has, after an hour on the trampoline and another in his Bionicle bed, requested paper and pencil so he can write a thank-you letter to his Uncle Roger, who sent him the analogue, learn-easy watch. I can't see why he too shouldn't receive the benefit of extra time in his life freed up from enforced restraints. I make a few calls to start off the bureaucracy to make this official. Trevor seems happy with the situation; he believes Caleb will receive a better education at home. But we still harbour doubts, not just on the social level, which I think we can overcome with making sure there are lots of social things happening (and remembering he was bombarded with full-time daycare from 18 months). The issue is more with whether we are turning ourselves so inward we are closing ourselves off from society. One of the questions posed by the experiment was are we are excluding ourselves from the world. So far I'd have said no. But now, I'm not so sure. I'm also careful to tell people that this decision isn't a statement regarding the worth of the state school system, nor is there any intention to comment on how other families deal with the issue of education; this is about our family trying to find ways to enrich each other's lives.

At this point it's all very much in test mode. Perhaps next week Caleb will decide he'd prefer to return to school. But I doubt it. I remember what it was like. No contest: home wins. I have the time to spend with him now that I didn't when he was younger. Perhaps there is an element of guilt alleviation going on too.

As for society as a whole, Caleb and I will find ways to immerse ourselves. Last year he and I went to a dry creek-bed, picked up six plastic bags in 30 seconds, took a photo and wrote an article, which was published in the local rag. I've shown a group of kids how to make cheese, given motivational speeches, spent the day at the local school talking to classes about writing and being a writer, and attended writers' evenings. Trev often finds himself inveigled into walking the streets with a badge, a bag and a request for money for one organisation or another. Yeah, we're a part of our community; we're not ready to turn our backs on it yet.

21 April

I have been thoroughly immersed in the primary school education system: I now know that there is a frog who can vomit out its own stomach, clean it off with its feet and swallow it again. Every bulimic's dream. I also know that the integumentary system (our skin) is the biggest organ in the body and Caleb is able to get under mine with ease whenever he decides an activity is not worth completing. A few small issues of 'I can't be bothered', but with those satisfactorily resolved he seems happy enough to hit the books in earnest and get the work done. When he decided a snail's length would be best described in kilometres, I stuck the pedometer on him and we went for a 1-kilometre walk and imagined how big the snail would have to be. Today is weights and volumes day, and we'll be making pikelets and trying to save some for when his mate comes around this afternoon for a play.

Yesterday we biked up to school and said goodbye to his friends. He seems unconcerned about the ending of an era. Or perhaps only a slight lapse, who knows. We've left it open as to whether he returns or not. He stood at the door and shook hands or hugged his classmates, or made strange hand connections with those initiated into the language of the Bionicle. We gathered up his books and emptied out his desk, exchanged phone numbers and biked back home again. I'm going to miss the bike ride, the opportunity to wear a few fat cells down and get the heart rate moving.

Today we'll be charting our heart beats before and after exercise, so at least we'll keep track of my fitness's demise.

23 April

Not sure which hug or handshake it was, but we managed to contract a good dose of the latest stomach bug. And just when we thought we'd escaped. Two days lying in bed groaning.

We've had rain: about 22 millimetres in two showers instead of 20. We've been promoted; we now share with 1996 the worst rainfall over the months of February, March and April in the last 135 years. An improvement I suppose. We have around 10,000 litres in the tank. I occasionally use town water in the garden to try to preserve what we have left. I'm keeping records on just how much, for the final environmental accounting in June. Ideally it would have been none at all.

Trev is a walking dictionary — ask him the meaning of nullibiquitous and he can tell you.

Trev is very resourceful — he can make anything out of anything and is very thorough.

Trev is a good family man — he isn't much into boozing, carousing and late nights out.

There, now I've said three nice things about Trev. Part of my 'Let's get over it' plan since we had a bit of a ruckus in the goat pen this morning. Trev was whinging about how I left the stalky bits that Possum doesn't eat and just plonked more food on top. Which is true. He then proceeds to pull perfectly good lucerne hay out of the feeder and sprinkles it on the damp ground as mulch.

'Why are you wasting it?' I ask, alarmed.

He doesn't answer my question. Instead he continues to repeat in ever louder tones, 'You know she won't eat it!'

'Why must you repeat yourself so bloody much?' I yell, ending in a yelp as a chunk of lucerne hits me square in the face and at close range. I choose a few expletives and fire them off at him and march out of the pen. Trev is close behind. I make it to the goat's booby washing water in time to turn around and throw it at his face. I miss. I keep on marching and refuse to speak or look at him. Inside I jump back in bed with Caleb, who has come in for a morning cuddle. Trev ducks down to give Caleb and me a goodbye kiss but finds himself flicked in the eye with a fingernail or two when he comes near my face. I refuse to fight in front of Caleb, but I'll be beggared if I'll kiss the bugger. He leaves the house and bikes to work and I fume my way through the dishes pulling stray bits of lucerne out of my hair. It's not often we tiff, and I'm not much good at maintaining rage for longer than half an hour. Hence trying to find three things good about Trevor. By the time I manage to think of three things I know I'm over it; when I'm not, I can't think of one.

24 April

Trev is enjoying the recent rainfall for the added snail harvest; he's gearing up for another rubbery meal this weekend. Caleb and I oblige on the snail-seeking sideline, but neither of us have, or will, succumb to the lures of a not-so-long-ago-just-a-shell-covered-ball-of-mucus meal.

Trev looked up recipes and came across lots of warnings about the possibility of contracting meningitis, but on closer reading it seems to be related to those who dare each other to eat them raw. It also depends on what the snails have eaten and only one person in Australia has died as a result of eating snails since 1971.

'Them be good odds', he says.

Raw snail slime on unwashed lettuce leaves is more of a risk than his snail consumption. He continues to improve on his snail extraction techniques while wishing the common garden snail were the *gros* (20 grams) not the *petit* (10 grams). On inspection of his grisly handiwork he decides tonight's dinner is at least a steak's worth in weight. True to his recycling nature, Trev crushes up the snails' shells and mixes them with the chook food as shell grit.

Snails

Australia's garden snail is also the favourite of the French. It is *Helix aspersa aspersa*, the Petit-Gris. Preparing them is a laborious procedure and not for the faint-hearted.

Collect 50 or so large garden snails from an area where they are unlikely to have had contact with any poisons such as rat or snail bait. Thoroughly wash them in water. Place snails in a well-ventilated, clean container that does not allow them contact with the ground or any organic matter. Leave in a cool spot for a week (this purifies them). Thoroughly hose them down again. Take them into the kitchen and lay down a layer of rock salt on a wide tray, then add a single layer of snails. Place a layer of salt on top of them. They will 'froth'.

Leave them for an hour or so and then remove them. Thoroughly wash off the slime. Boil water in a saucepan and drop the snails in for three minutes (up to this point most of the snails would still have been alive). Remove them from the water and from their shells.

Rinse them off again and drop them into a bowl of brine (120 grams of salt to 1 litre of water). Leave them for 15 minutes. Rinse them off again. They are now ready to cook or to freeze.

To cook, boil in a court bouillon (French for water with herbs and spices) for 45 minutes or until tender, then shallow fry in butter, garlic and cream.

25 April

Anzac day was meant to be an early morning start with a walk down to the War Memorial, but Trev and I both, uncharacteristically, sleep in. I managed to feed the chooks and milk Possum with my eyes closed, and then collapsed back into bed straight after, into a coma that only Caleb with his bed-bouncing boisterousness could bully me out of.

Caleb had a friend sleep over and they are keen to start the fire they spent hours yesterday organising. Under the trees is a campfire circle of rocks they've gathered. We send them off in search of sticks; soon there are two more kids who have heard the word. There will be an Anzac campfire this morning. The front yard is soon cleared of anything remotely resembling dead wood. Bradley's mother donates a couple of bags of marshmallows; Trev makes some damper; we talk about billy tea and how the soldiers would have lived on it. But they are too busy sharpening green sticks and dropping marshmallows into the fire to take too much notice. Once the food is eaten and the fire doused, they ramble around the garden gathering eggs and discovering Trev's unique 'maca' cracker, capable of more than one nut at a time as well as the easy removal of fingers and toes and the waking of the dead. They manage to crack their way through half a bucket of nuts, sparing all digits in the process.

At one stage I hear Caleb repeating with disgust, 'You don't know what parsley is? You've never heard of parsley?'

Parsley and garlic chives are incorporated into every meal around here, either as garnishes or mixed in with whatever ingredients are going. We have around 50 or 60 plants. Garlic chives turned out to be great drought busters, and provide us with greenery most of the year.

After the macadamia cracking I thin the onion seedlings, replanting the thinnings. I weed the pak choi, carrots, peas and broccoli — there are so many opportunistic tomato seedlings growing among them that they will soon be overwhelmed. Trev and I remark how the idea that chooks remove weeds and seeds from almost any given area isn't entirely true, as some seeds just pass right through, the chooks becoming great vehicles for their transport. Hence a large population of tomatoes. I'll never forget feeding the chooks a huge wheelbarrow of cobblers pegs and then discovering a million small seedlings growing once the pen moved on. The soil moisture is good after the recent rain, only requiring a quick watering over the newest sown beds.

I've been undertaking a voyeuristic surveillance of the chook pen. One of them is doing a very good impression of a rooster, not by crowing or strutting, but by rutting. I'm not sure this is normal, but as 'she' has so far failed to pass an egg, and is long overdue, the crowing biz might not be far off. Trev and I have been considering breeding the chooks for eating. We saw another horrid movie about how the poor things live and die, and have decided perhaps the only way is to rear them ourselves, and provide them with a better lifestyle before they are, very quickly, dispatched. Caleb, while sick and slightly delirious, had a good lick of my arm the other night and announced that it, 'looked like it would taste of chicken'. He will continue to need some meat in his diet and if we provide it ourselves in a more sustainable and humane way, we may be able to overcome at least some of our ethical concerns about killing animals for food.

26 April

Back to home school. Caleb is resistant at first — enough threats follow to ensure he starts, and once he starts he discovers it's not so bad after all. We're looking at the digestive system today; at the moment he's drawing and labelling all the various parts of it for a wall poster. He's just watched an online movie and taken a quiz about how it all works. He has a rather interesting viewpoint that he should, at least, be allowed to demonstrate the ingestion part of it and is busy snacking on a cinnamon scroll.

Soon he's going to add 10 new things to Andy Griffiths' list of 101 dangerous things, from the book that he has just finished reading. He laughed so hard I wondered if that might be dangerous too, at least to his stomach. His teachers often thought he wasn't listening, and he often seems preoccupied, but he amazes me with his ability to regurgitate information after only hearing it once.

Considering the tone seems to be all things vomitus, Caleb discovered recently that the Romans had rooms called vomitoriums. The stomach has a 2-litre capacity, and when you were feasting this was considered inadequate, so you could retire to the vomitorium and remove your feast, in order to consume more.

The last day in the life of a hapless soon-to-be-headless battery chook

'It's dark. It's always dark'	Broiler chickens live in permanent darkness. This is to keep them docile and less likely to peck at each other.
'I consider myself a loner, a chook on the fringe, but I am never alone.'	Tens of thousands of chooks live in the same shed. The recommended maximum chook density is 40 kilograms of birds per square metre. The area for an adult chook is around the size of an A4 sheet of paper.
'I don't know if it's day or night. I'm not even sure what they are. But I must have been here a long time. I can tell, it's the arthritis in my bones.'	Selective breeding means the chooks never get old. It takes as little as 37 days to grow to 1.6 kilograms, instead of the uneconomical 98 days of their unselectively bred ancestors. This unnatural growth causes valgus deformation, spondylolisthesis and dyschondroplasia, big names for ways in which the chooks generally spend the last days of their short lives in states of chronic pain and reduced mobility. Around 1–2 per cent die because they are physically unable to reach food and water.
'I'm hungry. I've been thinking about escape. It's not a word anyone uses around here. Most of them just stand around bitching about how their feet hurt. Me, I've got plans. I just have to wait for the right moment. The right chance. The door to the shed is opening. This might be it.'	Food is withdrawn 8–12 hours before transportation to the abattoir.

'There are suddenly lots of the two-legged stinky tall things. They're grabbing at chooks. Pulling at their legs. Everyone is squawking. There's panic. Chooks are flying around upside down and screaming. I try not to panic. I sidle towards the door. I'd run, but my legs aren't like they used to be.'

Catchers walk around the sheds grabbing chooks by one leg. They are bundled into crates with little ceremony, as each catcher needs to grab 300–500 birds an hour.

'I don't see him. He has me. My hip nearly pops out as he swings around to grab more of us. I'm screaming too. We're shoved in with each other, we're bounced around. It takes a long time. Some of us are too tired to squawk any more. Some are so tired they've lain down, shut their eyes and won't get up. I keep mine open. Maybe my chance will come soon.'

Each year 625,000 chooks arrive dead at the slaughterhouse due to heart failure or hip dislocation. Ten million arrive with broken bones, 15 million with dislocated hips.[12]

'I'm pulled out by my leg again, the pain almost makes my eyes pop. I'm upside down, and something with cold claws has me by my feet. Holding me tight. I try to fight. I try.'

Chooks are shackled upside down on a conveyor.

'We're moving. I can see water ahead. I hate getting my head wet. I wriggle up as high as I can and pass through without so much as a drop.'

Chooks' heads are passed through a bath of electrified water, which stuns them. Many lift their heads and pass through, unstunned.

'I'm still struggling when something sharp hits my neck. I squawk, and then notice that the chooks ahead of me aren't squawking anymore.'

Chooks do manage to pass through the automatic knife without having their heads chopped off. They're meant to be caught at this point and have their heads removed by a back-up person. However, this often does not occur.[13]

'My legs are free, I'm flying. I lift my wings and try and move them against my weight. But I'm too heavy. I'm falling, not flying. I hit ...'

Birds that miss both the water bath and the automatic knife are plunged alive into a tank of scalding water.

The Romans had interesting toilet habits. For a start it was a social occasion, with toilets set up as two long rows of planks with suitably shaped holes in which to place your bottom. Anything that was produced fell into aqueducts, and was carried away while he-who-produced reached for a sponge tied to a stick that sat in a pot of salty water. This is the same one that your mate had just used. It's amazing what humans can get used to. In Roman times the toilet arrangements must have seemed positively enlightened compared with other cultures.

I keep harking back to western society's less-than-advanced use of the toilet. We'd probably consider it more sanitary than sharing a sponge on a stick, yet every time the toilet is flushed an aerosol spray of contaminated toilet water forms a mist that adheres to the walls and ceiling and can still be floating around two hours later. We still haven't got the elimination of waste quite right.

28 April

'Burdekin plum', Marguerite announces.

'But I bought a Japanese plum, I thought this horrible black thing was some ornamental throwback.'

But it turns out it's a native plum that is more stone than flesh, and so acidic it's right up there with monster fruit for inedibility. It's been growing for almost seven years before finally producing recognisable fruit. I am not impressed. Do we chop it down and start again, or leave it for the birds? (Though even they seem disinclined.) It takes a long time to establish good fruit trees. One of the reasons it took us so long to gear up for our six months was waiting for various trees to come online. In the years to come, that can only improve. I have a carob tree that should be producing in earnest next year. I'm keen on having a go at producing our own 'chocolate'. There is a neem tree that I've just started making insecticide with. We have coffee bean bushes, although nine of the originals were killed during a record frost in the first couple of years. Only two survived; they have both recovered and are producing well. One of them even survived a bobcat running over it. I'm waiting for the newest arrivals to set good quantities. In the next few weeks I should be able to pick what we have and start the coffee-making process. Something new to learn.

I've been looking sideways at the bananas in the last month or two. They need more shelter, as it only takes one bluster to shred them where they are. I've been clearing away an area on one side of the house that gets sun most of the day but is sheltered from wind and frost. I'd planted large grass plants there. They have to go. Caleb and I give them brutal haircuts and find bits and pieces of Bionicle that had escaped from the verandah wedged in their scalps. We spend an additional and fruitless hour trying to lever them out of the ground with a crowbar. No can do. I've left the crowbar there as an open invitation to Trev. If we can clear the area further, we can transplant the corms of the dwarf banana suckers. Hopefully this will make bagging some of them easier — I can just hang out over the railing (in a perfect world). This year's lot might as well be hacked down and fed to the goat, as lack of water and wind have taken their toll.

We need to consider what to do with the nectarines and peaches. This year my efforts at fruit fly protection failed. We ended up with maybe five out of the 50 kilos of stone fruit. I bagged them all after hand-sewing the bags, but the fruit had already been bitten while small, hard and green. My efforts meant they did not make the ground, but the maggoty bags needed to be boiled to try to reduce the fruit fly numbers. Now I want to get serious about the issue. Hanging thousands of traps around only reduces the male population and, as the females only need to mate once to be good for thousands of eggs (and therefore maggots), the traps are not adequate. Going around picking up other people's fruit is time consuming; I want to invest in a fruit fly 'cage' and grow nectarines and peaches and anything else maggot-susceptible in there. We've tried one before but it blocked out too much light. It's time to find something tough and UV-resistant that won't. Or move to Tasmania. However, I'm not sure Trev's roots could handle transplanting and Caleb would die of hypothermia at the first hint of a cold day.

In response to winter's imminent arrival I've been slowly moving my plantings further up the hill. Carrots and broccoli are fine anywhere, but I'm going to try to keep beans going up in the herb garden, which died over summer as I rationalised the water elsewhere. It has the most beautiful topsoil and I've recently hauled out more wheelbarrows of rich mulch from the goat pen and dug it in. The only issue is that the topsoil has all been imported to the area over the years, so dig down further than 25 centimetres and you hit solid rock. It was the old driveway and someone had put the world's crappiest road base onto it (it's a near-vertical slope), which is also the only reason it doesn't become overly waterlogged during wet weather. The water cannot escape through the soil; it runs off the hill into a shallow trench and is led off down the hill rather than under the house. Having garden beds there slows the flow and reduces the risk of a flood. I've successfully grown herbs there; I went through a herb stage that saw me growing woad, angelica, motherswort and other old-world herbs like soapwort, grown to make shampoo. Now I'm taking a risk on bush snake beans and tomatoes and hope that the area will stay frost-free long enough for a crop or two. Gympie is renowned for being the hottest place in summer and the coldest in winter.

Soapwort shampoo

Dig up and wash 2 packed cups of the roots, stems and leaves of the soapwort plant, and chop finely. Place in a pot with 500 millilitres of water and simmer for half an hour, then leave to cool. Strain liquid, discarding solids. Add a few drops of essential oil of your choice; we tend to go for clove oil, mostly because we have a large bottle, but also because we love the pungency of it.

As the shampoo is a thin liquid, an open-necked bottle will mean most of it will end up down the plughole, so pour it into a squeeze bottle or other dispenser.

30 April

Last day of April, which went so fast we're still spinning. Time seems to be getting back to normal now that the first three centuries of the experiment are over.

We've just arrived home after our weekend jaunt on the bikes. Caleb, after an agonising four months, has saved enough money for a Bionicle. He was 50 cents short last night and insisted on doing the dishes while perched precariously on the side of the bench, doing dangerous high-dive dish drops. I tried everything to entice him away and ended up paying him 50 cents *not* to do the dishes. Something he finds incredible and is still raving on about. Last night he went to bed 10 times, jumping up every five seconds to tell us something else about the soon-to-be-latest acquisition.

'I'm just TOO excited to sleep! My first Bionicle in FOUR months!'

I was excited too, just the thrill of the ride, scoring a good DVD to watch from the library, access to books and $12 to spend in the supermarket. We also managed a social detour to the soccer grounds where every parent we know seemed to be within a 10-metre radius. Caleb was busy sharing his latest prize with his mates while we basked in multitudes of comments about our weight loss and my newly acquired mathematical skills.

'I've lost 8 per cent of my total body weight,' I gloat, 'while Trev has lost 9.5 per cent', which is a great way to say how much without saying exactly how much and having to state our current weight, which, after a certain age and rump size, becomes untenable.

Nearly an inch of rain has topped up the tank and given the garden a reasonable soak. This may well be why time has been kick-started. Our spirits have risen while the rain fell.

Trev has been experimenting with making potato crisps, and ended up with a fair approximation both visually and taste-wise. As a special end of the month treat (or a 'getting towards being on the home straight' slack off), we also shared a bottle of that dark bubbly stuff between us, while Caleb had a chocolate (cow's booby milk) shake. I haven't even experienced an addictive twinge in months, and seem content enough to drink water or one of the herbal teabags that have been gathering dust in the back of the cupboard for the last five years.

And we're saving money, a very nice side-effect of not spending it! But I will repeat — this is not what we did it for. It's all about the environment and enriching each other's lives, which, of course, we repeat incessantly to all those poor souls who cross our paths:

'You too could feel this great! It's not just saving money folks, no, it's much more than that! Roll up, roll up, see the wacky greenies lose weight, reduce their CO_2 emissions and discover 53 ways to eat pumpkin!'

It would only take another three inches of rain and then ... nirvana.

Maybe I'll just go on another near-vertical bike ride and settle for a good whack of endorphins.

Trev's rave

I love meat. I am a dyed-in-the-wool, card-carrying, unconditional lifetime member of the carnivore society. I love it fried, baked, grilled, poached, braised, and will, under some circumstances, even eat it raw. Vegetarians? Get thee behind me, Satan. Vegans? Even worse. But mass production, as in so many other areas, conspires against me.

I had read an article in the paper telling, in (I thought) totally unnecessary and gruesome detail, of the ultimate fate of the poor chickens so toothsomely rendered to us by the Colonel et al. In short, an article about the killing. This charming little missive didn't touch on the terrible lives the poor birds had led up to the day of the long knives (although Linda is always only too happy to fill us in on that), merely contenting itself with creating an ooze of guilt so thick you could walk on it regarding the processing of the hapless avians. It did not make pleasant reading.

As if this were not bad enough, the next day I had reason to visit the railway station. Stopped there, in the hot sun, was a seemingly endlessly number of rail cars, each one chock-a-block with cattle. Walking up and down the line was a railway employee with a cattle prod. Apparently the function of this person was to prod any cattle that had the temerity to lie down, lest the goods inadvertently damage themselves. I asked the Station Master where the cattle had come from and where were they bound. Townsville and the Brisbane meatworks respectively was the answer. I remarked on the prodder and the length of the journey. He agreed, saying it 'seemed a long, hard trip for, well, no result, really'.

And this is my point. Surely it is not entirely necessary that the animals we eat have the essential grimness of their fate exacerbated by appalling treatment during their lifetimes. I don't want to anthropomorphise too much, but it can't be any more pleasant for an animal to spend all their life in a tiny cage (chooks) or suffer interminable, crowded, holocaust-style journeys in the hot sun (cattle) than it would be for me. It must, then, diminish us as a species to subject other species to 'inhuman' behaviour.

I have no real objection to the killing of animals for food. I know this is a vexed question and that I will offend the hell out of a lot of people by saying so, but nature is red in tooth and claw – some species have been food for others since time began, and we have been traditionally on the side of the predators for most of this. This may have to change in the future, given the pressures of overpopulation and diminishing resources, but that is not the (admittedly limited) point here. Which is, do we need the torture? Do we need the feedlot? The micro cage? The shit-covered, cattle-prodded, 1000-kilometre train trip?

The only answer for me was to stop eating meat that had been massed produced in this way. I figure, when the cravings get too much, it's okay to eat a bit of kangaroo. The kanga gets to run free, and is then killed quickly, on the spot, and it's all over – minimal torture. I apologise to all those who are offended by the concept of chowing down on the national symbol, and to those for whom the kangaroo is a species that needs protection, but we'll have to agree to disagree.

However, during our adventure all this is rendered academic, because there's no meat to be had. Except snails. There are a lot of advantages to be had from eating snails. They are nutritious and low in fat. They are a garden pest that would otherwise require either poison or elaborate, non-chemical methods to control. And there's not a lot of sympathy out there for the snail (so far, the only objection we've had was an email from a committed vegetarian, objecting to us encouraging the callous murder of innocent snails). People will be grossed out, will screw up their face and utter an extremely heartfelt expression of disgust upon being informed about what's on the menu for dinner, but very few will exclaim 'oh the poor things!' and call you a murderer. For a man as tortured by guilt as me, that's a big plus.

may

1 May

After a salutary (or is that salary-free) four months it seems that less begets less — less of the wanting at least. I don't have any major lists anymore. A few more resources for the home school, like air-drying clay, would be good. I'd also like new bathroom towels — the current ones seem determined to fall apart — and some new cushion covers. Never let men change cushion covers. I've discovered that my appetite for chocolate, which was rudely reawakened after Easter, has waned. Books? Heck the library has heaps, I don't need to own them. I don't miss the car, and we'd both thought that would be torture. Food, yes, we're not doing without, but sometimes it would be nice to cop a work-free meal, one loaded with saturated fats and unnecessary packaging. Or as Caleb says, 'I don't care what's for dinner as long as it comes with a free toy'.

Overall my desire for 'things' has declined. A weekend spent at home does not feel like bondage.

Which, more or less, says less is more.

Of course I am speaking for myself here, and not for Trev, though I wouldn't hesitate to say his requirements would be nicely covered with a trip to the tobacconist, the bottle shop and the deli and meat section of the supermarket, plus a bag or two of cement.

Caleb and I set off to visit a friend and help them out with their computer. Caleb has arranged to play with their son and has packed his latest Bionicle acquisition in a waterproof bag. Which is odd, as it's made out of plastic and neither of us are wearing a raincoat. I'm looking angry though. As we coast down the hill it starts to rain, but that's not the problem: Trev was the last one to ride my bike, and the seat is so high I'm physically unable to sit on it, and he's compounded this error by taking the spanner to work with him. As I pedal, standing, the end of the seat repeatedly bangs into my back. It's enough to make anyone mad, but it's more than that: I look ludicrous. It pisses down. Both Caleb and I are drenched by the time we get there and I have the beginnings of a whopper bruise. No one is home. We stand in the carport till the rain eases. I coax Caleb, who was keen for a social visit, back onto the bike. I wrench at the seat with desperate hands, then tell him to hop off again, we will walk. Caleb seems to gauge my mood well and insists on repeating the same question 10 times regardless of how I answer him. I invent a small electric gadget and pretend to place it in his brain. He giggles as I tell him, 'Next time you repeat that question, I push the invisible button and, bzztt. Actually, anytime you misbehave from now on, it's gonna be bbzzzzt!'

'So like if I don't stop jumping on the couch, you'll ...'

'Bbbbzzzzttttt!'

'What about if I don't eat my dinner?'

Evil chuckle followed by 'bbbbzzzzztttt!'

This game keeps us occupied till we meet up with our intended social event hosts on the roadside. They apologise profusely. They needn't; it's not that long ago I did the same thing to them. Just one of those things. It starts to rain again. We continue walking, and then something truly profound happens. The leopard changes its spots.

'Look, Mum, someone's thrown a whole heap of cigarettes on the road!'

Around 20 or so slightly damp cigarettes have been thrown from a car window, either by the smoker or, more likely, by the smoker's partner. (I've done it before.) I pause in anguish. What wouldn't Trev give for 20 cigarettes already filtered and smothered in chemicals to make them burn?

'Why have you stopped, Mum?'

'I ... can't ... leave ... them ... there.' I labour over every word. The rain is increasing; I have to make a decision. To scavenge off the side of the road, or not to scavenge? Call it recycling, says my distinctly uneasy inner voice.

'Wanna help me pick them up, Cal? Dad will love these.'

We do. When we get home I tell him never to tell anyone or bbbbzzzzzttt!

BUTT OUT!

Cigarette butts are made from cellulose acetate and can take up to 15 years to break down.

An unknown number of the 3900 chemicals in cigarettes are trapped in the filter of the estimated 4.5 trillion butts littered around the world each year. Many of the butts end up in our waterways. Within an hour of immersion they start leaching lead and arsenic. Many filters take up residence in the stomachs of birds and aquatic life.

Clean Up Australia listed them as the most common form of litter, accounting for 15 per cent of all items picked up in their 2005 community clean-up.

Changes in smoking laws in restaurants and other public places have heightened the issue of cigarette butt disposal as people are forced to smoke off the premises. Footpaths are being used as ashtrays more now than ever.

If you find this is an issue, ask the proprietor or local council for a permanent off-the-premises disposal facility to be placed in an obvious spot. Most tobacconists also sell discreet, pocket-sized receptacles to place butts in.

5 May

We had 1.5 millimetres overnight — every bit helps, but I still use the greywater hose to water the garden. I let the chooks out. They immediately start scratching away at the ground, which they have successfully bared to its bones, though the lab lab has survived. It's on one of the steepest slopes on the block. Trev has ingeniously placed a series of pegs across the slope and used my recent prunings and any dead branches, sticks, banana stems and arrowroot leftovers to make low barricades. Now I call the chooks 'terracists' as their efforts mean that, rather than have all the soil they scratch end up at the bottom of the hill, they go as far as the line of sticks and branches, and form terraces.

GREYWATER

Greywater is wastewater from the laundry, bath, shower and hand basins. Kitchen wastewater is too high in contaminants and cannot be easily broken down by soil organisms; it should be diverted into sewerage or septic. Your ability to use domestic greywater is governed by different state and local legislation.

- Use greywater only during warm, dry periods.
- Keep the outlet moving, and do not allow the soil to become saturated.
- Ensure greywater does not contaminate any source of drinking water.
- Greywater should be drained onto the garden by sub-surface irrigation.
- Never use a sprinkler or create a 'spray' of greywater.
- Wash your hands after gardening.
- Don't use greywater on vegies where the leaves are eaten and may be splashed; where the plant is eaten raw; or where the greywater will have direct contact with root vegetables such as potatoes and carrots.
- Never store untreated greywater for more than 24 hours.
- Never allow greywater to seep into a waterway or drainage system, as it can be detrimental to aquatic life.
- Never allow pets, animals or children to drink or have access to greywater.
- Use low-phosphorus/low-sodium detergents.
- Reduce fertiliser use when irrigating with greywater as it is generally high in nutrients.

Trevor, Caleb and Linda, triumphant at the end of the six months.

TOP: The camouflaged house.
BOTTOM: Caleb marking off the days.

ABOVE: Trev optimising solar-panel efficiency with a quick clean.

LEFT: A full verandah of solar panels. In front is the 'solar oven', great for drying tomatoes and bananas.

ABOVE: Dark Orange and Light Orange, the goat-pen chooks.

RIGHT: Trev using the 'Bentall's Improved' chaffcutter, one of several pieces of old machinery made new again.

TOP: Caleb claiming some watermelons as his own.
BOTTOM: Possum turning her back on yet another feed.

TOP: Grinding up grain for the chooks.
BOTTOM: Loofahs – the new kitchen sponge.

A moment of long-awaited rain. You can almost hear the garden sucking up the moisture.

TOP: Linda's larder. Most meals are based on whatever is abundant in the garden at the time.
BOTTOM: Fresh goat's fetta.

Blackwater is created by the addition of faecal matter to drinking-quality water. It's then considered sewage, and it's dealt with by a septic system or sewerage outlet to create anaerobically (oxygen-deprived) broken-down pollution.

Today is earmarked for cheese-making, doing the washing and working out how to make pyramids from clay. Caleb and I had our first game of Senet, an ancient Egyptian board game, last night. We've made cartouches of our names and hung them on the wall, drawn up a plan for a paper pyramid, written in four facts about pyramids on each of the sides, cut them out, painted them with several different techniques including splattering paint with tooth-brushes, cut them out, glued them together and felt proud of ourselves. One of the best things about home schooling is that often there are connections to the real world — I can point them out to Caleb, or he to me. So far we haven't seen any pyramids.

Trev brought home a block of educational-expenses clay yesterday and that will now be the focus for today's arts and crafts. We make pyramids from clay; tomorrow will be an obelisk, that's if I can get him away from the latest *Captain Underpants* book. I made a show of disapproving of them. They deliberately spell words incorrectly — for example, 'heard' becomes 'herd'. My disapproval has, of course, made them all the more alluring.

I might find myself disapproving of pumpkin soon. I grated it into a quiche yesterday thinking the small flecks might go unnoticed. Fifty-four ways to cook pumpkin and I still can't get him to eat any. Recently he proved how much he hated dinner by creating a Lego mask that forced his mouth closed. Even if he wanted to he wouldn't be able to eat. I took several photos to show Trev, not just the mask, but the arms folded across the chest and the look of scorn directed my way.

Caleb has become my little helper. After school he does such things as collect the eggs and clean and fill the chook water buckets. I have to pay him of course, but these are the days of the Bionicles and there are only a few ways to secure them around here. By virtue of generosity is not one of them — yet. We're on the countdown, only 54 days to go but, strangely, now it's that much closer, I'm not feeling the burden of the days anywhere as much. Trev, though, is exhausted; he needs to take a holiday, but won't. He's promised himself two weeks off at the end of our 'holiday', as he euphemistically calls it.

6 May

Caleb has a brilliant day at school, after which we bike down to the shop to post the letter he has written to his great-grandmother in New Zealand. It's become our weekly event: write a letter, post it and, as an end-of-the-week reward for good effort made, a small 'goodie' is procured. Last week, an ice-cream; this week, one of those contradictory packets of sour sweets. He's happy; it's made all that hard slogging over the school desk worth it. More and more he is choosing to continue with some aspect of his schoolwork after we have officially finished, which is great. I just have to be wary of it dipping into my own time. The peas are being inundated with opportunistic tomato seedlings. My guess would be that if the place was abandoned for 100 years, someone would find a healthy number of tomatoes, chillies, eggplants, potatoes, pak choi and pumpkins on reclaiming it. Environmental weeds? We wonder why they're not.

8 May

It's Mother's Day, but you wouldn't know it. We're up at six, but no mention is made of this auspicious day. By eight o'clock I drop the hint, 'Heck, it's Mother's Day. We should ring our respective mums'.

'I hadn't forgotten', Trev says, 'I was going to do it after I fixed my thongs'.

He goes downstairs and spends an hour sewing new soles he's cut out of a thin rubber sheet found dumped in the rubbish bin at work. He comes in wearing them.

'I feel like I should be walking on the moon with these, or using them as diving shoes. Maybe I could market them to the mafia?'

He tops his previous recycling efforts this week by showing me his collection of lead wheel-balance weights, which he finds on the roadside. He's saving them to make into fishing sinkers.

He rings his mum. Somewhere in the conversation she asks him if I had breakfast in bed. The connection is made.

'I didn't think of it', he explains to me. 'It's not like you're my mother.'

It's not like I had been expecting boxes of chocolates. An acknowledgement would have done just fine. He feels bad. Caleb gives me a hug and half a tree branch (it was flowering), and Ehren pops in with a box of chocolates and gets Stepson of the Year Award. All is well. But Trev still feels bad. Caleb, who watches more TV than either of us and can sing any amount of disturbing jingles, has a plan in which there is some small amount of self-interest involved.

Trev and I milk the goat that evening. It's raining. As soon as he is finished Trev excuses himself and makes the dash for the house, leaving me to finish off my side. I clean out Possum's house, as she's been pooing in it during the drizzly day. I pick eggplants. Tonight's the night for ratatouille — a meal that is almost a swear word around here and, once the experiment is over, will not be eaten for several years.

When I get back to the house no one is there. I start on dinner.

Outside it's nearly dark, but I see the unmistakable shape of our car glide past the window. Now my interest is piqued. It's Trev and Caleb bearing gifts, very oily, chippy and chickeny gifts.

'It was Caleb's idea', Trev is quick to intercept any arguments. Caleb is ear-to-ear grin.

I'm two pieces of chicken and half a bucket of chips through before I start thinking of recriminations. I swallow them.

'The car was due for its monthly start up', Trev defends himself. I nod. I smile. Recriminations are currently being destroyed by large amounts of hydrochloric acid. Caleb, the boy who designed the world's first Lego facemask to prevent food intake, is inhaling his dinner.

Minutes later Trev and I are both sitting there with twin bewildered faces. We say the same thing at the same time.

'My stomach must have shrunk.'

Caleb is lying on the floor quietly groaning while he picks at the packaging on the Sara Lee Chocolate Mousse.

9 May

'It's like Laurel and Hardy', he explains. 'You say how easy it is, I have to say how hard it is. But I don't really think it is at all.'

Trev and I are talking generally about the experiment. I make concessions on the grounds that Trev does do the hard yards compared with Caleb and me. We aren't out there among the temptations anywhere near as much as him and we don't have as many addictions, though Trev has been reducing his considerably. It is almost beyond comprehension that he is no longer a drinker of alcohol. We discuss the possibility that his blow-out, when we finish, will last three years and result in him weighing in at 120 kilos and spending most of his time rolling in the gutter with a bottle in a paper bag.

He says that nothing happens in our life that's really any different from anyone else's, bar the self-denial. Everything is now grafted on so much that it feels normal to milk a goat in your backyard, pick your own coffee beans, resole your thongs, bike in the rain and all the other treasures of our lifestyle. He thinks I overplay the ease; I think he overplays the hardship.

'Who are Laurel and Hardy?' Caleb asks.

'A skinny bloke and a fat bloke who get hit on the head a lot', I tell Caleb while looking at Trev with a glint in my eye and a hand on the 'jam spoon'.

We turn on the solar hot-water booster. We work out that it's the first time in two years we've needed to resort to such measures. I try not to hang around long enough to watch the meter whiz around. Cursed with six months of predominantly overcast days yet very little rain, we are not doing well on the power stakes and a double whammy with the water. Now we can look forward to an early and devastating frost ... that would be nice.

10 May

'Use a chainsaw', Caleb mumbles past the six fingers he has managed to plug his mouth with.

'It will come out when it's ready, Caleb, leave it alone.' So far he has tried to extract his loose tooth with a pair of pliers, a piece of string, vigorous pushing, and biting hard on a tough apple. He has a blister on the end of his tongue from worrying the poor thing.

'There must be a cure', he whines. The problem isn't so much the tooth as the toothfairy and the idea that once the bit of bone has vacated he can turn it into $5.

'The toothfairy gives $5 for the first tooth, I'm not sure she gives that much for the rest', I warn. But there is a Bionicle at stake.

'I'll leave her an invoice', he says.

He wants another Bionicle, a more expensive one than the last. He made himself $14 in jobs in the last week or so. He needs to make it to $40 — hence the pliers. We're keen to teach him the value of money and our weekend bike adventure included a walk into town and to Toyworld, where he put the object of his angst on lay-by. He and I wrote up a plan on how he can obtain the rest, including picking cherry tomatoes, packaging them up for the neighbours and selling them for 50 cents. I've shown him how to choose only the best and present them well. An early lesson in sales and marketing. Other sources of income are egg gathering, chook-shed shutting and opening, doing the dishes, and opportunistic suggestions such as, 'You're folding the washing, maybe I could do that?'

The plan also includes bedroom cleaning, something I'm aware is as much of a myth as the toothfairy.

12 May

The average rainfall for May over the last 135 years is 72 millimetres. So far this month we've had 68, and we're out there mil-gathering right now. Several weeks ago Caleb amused us greatly by going down to collect the eggs and then arriving panting at the door to exclaim, 'There's green stuff on the path!'

'Yes, Caleb, it's called grass.'

I walked out of the goat pen with Trev the other day and paused to announce something astounding: the Earth wasn't showing its bones anymore. It had a verdant coat of green, studded with shades of tomato red, pale squash and yellow flowers. It's amazing how quick the turnaround can be. Plants that were tired and at the point of pull out and compost have revived and are producing. The wildness has outgrown my weeding, which I've kind of outgrown too. The first frost, I promise Trev, will decimate the hundreds of thousands of wildling tomatoes and pumpkins. It's a pleasure at the moment to go into the perky garden, if not a little hazardous. There have been quite a few calls of 'Whoa!' along with frantic grabbing of trees and spare arms as we slip down the hillside. Possum hates it. Wet weather makes her depressed. She hates wet ground with a passion; luckily she is not predisposed to foot rot. She stays in her shelter peering out miserably. When I fill the feeder, she stands with her back legs on her outdoor platform and her front legs on the lower fence line — all hooves clear of mud — and reaches into her feeder to eat. It's a delicate balance, and she's not prepared to muddy herself, but who can blame her. We expect her milk production to dip; it usually does in weather like this. The chooks look miserable too; wet and bedraggled, they sit under shelter and look as reproachful as a chook can. The weather this year has been strongly reminiscent of a New Zealand summer —

hot, dry and stormless — followed by an unseasonably wet winter. I'm kicking myself. If we'd known this would happen we needn't have resorted to town water, we could have scraped through on tank alone.

We found a family of refugee geckoes living in our power meter. We've been concerned they might inadvertently short something out so, over time, we have enticed them from their refuge and brought them inside. We're very happy to have them racing across our walls at night, a great symbiotic relationship. We provide them with free housing, shallow dishes of water, access to exits and an ample food supply in the form of cockroaches. I'm keen to see if there is a reduction in the numbers of the horrid beasts. Trev tells me they don't eat the cockroaches but prefer to munch on the freshly hatched offspring, hanging around the egg until the event occurs, increasing infant mortality rates, hopefully by 100 per cent. At this point my cockroach-killing technique of coating the necks of jars with oil and placing enticing food on the bottom has borne results — we catch some, but obviously not enough to eliminate them.

Trev and I have been on coffee rations for over four months now. Each weekend Trev endeavours to make the world's most perfect cup of coffee and gets pretty close. The quality over quantity compensation theory. The coffee beans we had when we started lasted the first six weeks, after which we learnt to do without. Then Mum started sending relief parcels.

'No, no, don't do that, Mum. Um, yes, coffee would be nice.'

But I've also been watching our own beans grow, oh so slowly, and now they have culminated in a gorgeous red colour. I've harvested two lots, and at least another two are coming on.

There are two, sometimes three beans per fruit. Commercially the casing is fermented off, but there are too few for us to bother with that, so I peel them off and give the beans a good rinse. The green beans are left to dry before roasting. As we don't have commercial quantities or commercial roasting equipment, it's going to be a hot oven roast. A test batch first, so I don't ruin the lot. What I've read on the subject indicates it's very difficult to get an even colour. I've set up a perforated pizza tray on top of a stoneware dish. Hopefully this will shield the beans from too strong a 'glare' from the bottom element and will spread the heat evenly.

In order to make the use of the oven as power-efficient as possible, Caleb and I have spent the afternoon making baked goods. I remember the jam spoon over the back of the hand routine from when I was a kid, along with the cries of 'But Mum it tastes better when it's not cooked!', so I do a lot of back turning to allow for opportunistic spoonfuls to disappear and make only mock attempts to address the wandering biscuit dough.

Then it will be the coffee beans. They're supposed to crackle when they're ready; I'm too deaf to hear anything. The smoke alarm goes off every 2.3 seconds and I'd have to be a giraffe to reach the thing and rip it off the ceiling. The beans emerge smelling good, but are uneven at best.

Hot on the coffee's heels is roast pumpkin, potatoes and onions, to be served with steamed vegies for dinner followed by mini lemon meringue pies.

'Turkey,' whispers Caleb salaciously over my shoulder, 'roast turkey'.

Both Caleb and Trev want their pound of flesh.

The first cup of our own coffee is ... the right colour. It even smells more like coffee than tea ... but the taste has an unusual note to it. It takes a bit of squashing my tastebuds up against the flavour to decide it's a 'very long to arrive and only stays for a brief visit' hint of burnt. Which a few of the beans were, while others were still very light. A few more mouthfuls and the burnt flavour is barely detectable. I'm no connoisseur, and thank god no connoisseurs will be given the opportunity to taste this, but it'll do me fine.

13 May

It's the fifth week of home school. It hasn't been all ups. Most notable was the time Caleb insisted, as part of an experiment, that he be the one to light the match. This was fine up until the part where he went to drop it. I'm yelling at him to let it go, he's shaking his hand and looking puzzled. We discover, post burn, that he has a significant build-up of glue on his thumb from the previous activity. But we've 'matched' it with an equally good time while making up the 10 additional 'really dangerous things' after reading Andy Griffiths' 101 others, and it didn't require any further skin grafts. We've made 3D scarab beetles and used online games and videos to supplement the down and dirty reading parts. Caleb is content with the way things are.

He received a book of letters from his friends at school. They said things like, 'We miss you', and 'Please come back'.

'Make you want to go back?' I asked him when we'd finished reading them.

'No way!'

His concept of school is waiting around most of the time being bored, being told to do things you're not so keen on and occasionally getting yourself yelled at. At home school there is no waiting around and only some boredom, which is generally alleviated by a quick blood rush of bouncing on the trampoline to clear the cobwebs. There are degrees of coercion on occasion, and plenty of getting yourself yelled at. But overall it must have something going for it. I've noticed a radical decline in television watching, and a willingness to extend himself into craft and reading activities in his own time. Originally he wanted me to fill in his time with planned activities, but when that didn't happen he discovered the wonderful art of constructively filling it in himself.

The social side of life seeks him out, and we don't find ourselves having to organise a great deal to ensure he has an adequate amount of time bashing others of similar age with sticks and calling it sword fighting.

It occurs to me that really all we're doing is changing the perspective on how we live. Sometimes it seems I am obsessed with kWh, protein, energy and time, but really it's only replacing our original obsession: money, the lack of, accruing, spending and sacrificing all else to its warping qualities.

14 May

Trev is worried. Will he or will he not die before he gets to eat one last steak. At least, one that he remembers eating, and a beer, a real beer, one that has a guaranteed level of alcohol. This is apropos of his air operations training next month. Trev is not a good flyer. I know this from many observations: a) I've seen him fall before and he does not bounce well; b) he is big (not as big as before, but still verifiably big) and this means he is not aerodynamically sound and is likely to increase the plummet speed of any flimsy bit of falling steel by appreciable amounts; and, of course, c) he's a big wuss. Plus he thinks that this type of emotional currency is worth something.

But jokes aside, I'm not that keen on it either. Andrew, my first love, died in a microlight crash, 17 years ago now, but it's still something that I dwell on and I have a well-developed respect for the butterfly flimsiness of human life. It's why I have this superstitious need to send Trev off with the same lines each morning: 'Bye, have a good day and don't run over any trucks'.

Scrape the joviality away and not far beneath is a great vein of paranoia and fear. So I'm not that fussed about Trev's gravity-defying feats either. But we won't mention that, we'll make jokes about it instead and, as part of that superstition, he will be denied any last steaks. Besides, flying planes is extremely greenhouse gas emitting behaviour.

We get back from our trip into town and Trev announces how much he's struggling, all that resistance required to get there and back without going rank in a supermarket, hauling entire shelf-loads of meat products into a green bag and heading for the counter. I shrug my shoulders, I can't even think of what I would buy. And if I did it wouldn't be because I really wanted it, just because it was there. Trev looks at me with great disdain.

'That means', he says, 'that I am better than you. Because I resist. There is no virtue in resisting temptation when it isn't there'.

PLANES, TRAINS AND AUTOMOBILES

The world's greenhouse gas emissions rose 17.4 per cent between 1990 and 1999, from 390 million tonnes of carbon dioxide and its equivalents to 458 million tonnes. Domestic power consumption, including car use, accounted for one-third of energy-related greenhouse gas emissions.[1]

Atmospheric carbon dioxide (CO_2) has increased 28 per cent since the 1700s. This is due to a number of factors, foremost being a reduction in forested areas, and the increased dependence on burning fossil fuels for energy use.[2]

Jetsetters should be aware that, typically, flying uses the same amount of fuel per person as each individual would use if they drove to their destination alone. However, the fuel emissions (CO_2, nitrous oxides, hydrocarbons, sulphur dioxide, naphthalene, benzene, ozone, formaldehyde and ultra-fine dust particles) are dispersed high in the atmosphere, where their impact is roughly three times greater than those created by earthbound forms of transport. A Boeing 747 flying from London to New York and back again spews out approximately 440 tonnes of CO_2 – about the same as emitted by 80 four-wheel drives in a full year of hard driving.[3]

Vehicle greenhouse emissions per year and trees required to absorb it

TYPE OF VEHICLE DRIVEN	KM/YEAR	VEHICLE EMISSIONS IN TONNES	TREES REQUIRED PER YEAR
Petrol engine under 1.4 litre	15,000	4.05	5.67
Petrol engine over 1.4 litre	15,000	5.25	7.35
Diesel engine under 2 litre	15,000	2.85	3.99
Diesel engine over 2 litre	15,000	3.3	4.62

Electricity usage greenhouse emissions per year and trees required to absorb it

kWh/YEAR	EMISSIONS IN TONNES	TREES REQUIRED PER YEAR
8000*	8	11.2

* Average annual household use

We can make a difference

By using energy-efficient products, households have the potential to reduce their energy-generated greenhouse gas emissions by between 43 and 54 per cent. This would reduce Australia's total emissions by about 5 per cent annually. For example, the most efficient fridges on the market can save 10 tonnes of greenhouse gas over their lifetime compared with the least efficient fridges.[4]

Simple things like buying appliances that are the most energy-efficient available does help. Look for the best energy rating and buy accordingly.

16 May

It arrives. We've managed to track down a device (called a spar meter) that will measure the wattage of any appliance it's plugged into for a specified period, whether it be 24 hours, a week or 30 days. The fridge is first priority – in she goes.

17 May

Out she comes. The fridge used 1kWh in a 24-hour period. This is good news. However, this is the first cold week we've had, so it will be working more efficiently than usual. We're also producing more power than usual – over 6 kWh a day – due to the cool clear days we are experiencing. Caleb and I sit out on the verandah with the schoolbooks, and soak in the sun.

I plug the device into the laptop; 24 hours spin past. Verdict: 350 watts per day when it's plugged in for the whole day. When the 'lid' is down, it's drawing 1 watt per hour.

19 May

I drove the car. We're both getting a little nervous about it having only had one tank of petrol for the whole six months, and Trev has heard that petrol can start absorbing moisture out of the air and end up ruining fuel injectors. It's been two months since I last drove. I find myself feeling a tad nervous about it. What say I've lost the knack? But I haven't. We drive to the feed store and buy another bale for Possum, and grain for the chooks. Caleb spends the trip there requesting a 'goodie'. But I will not budge — he had his goodie yesterday when we biked up to the shop to send a letter he'd written to his grandparents in New Zealand. He had $2 and spent it on Wonka's Long-lasting Gobstoppers. They didn't last long. We drive back home via the art store. We collect more clay and some plaster of Paris. Trev enjoys finding theoretical ways we can extend educational expenses. The latest experiment he is proposing is comparing the textures of five different kinds of meat.

We arrive back home moments before a storm hits, but it's a fizzer, around 1 millimetre of rain. Possum is down in the yard looking pleased about it. I've pulled the plug on the power device; the microwave used just under 500 watts for a 24-hour period. Interestingly, though it says it's an 800-watt microwave, it draws 1200 when on high. Hmmm, what next? The electric jug.

Time spins, and the verdict: around 500 watts a day. Still lots of appliances to go and a lot of 'missing power' — surely lighting the house can't be using that much. I stare suspiciously at the stove, which is hard-wired into the house, therefore I cannot 'spar' with it. Wretched thing.

I type up an Excel sheet. I am going to wrestle with the case of the missing power usage till I've got it pinned down in a figure-four leg lock. This is the worst six months on our records by a long shot and I'm starting to think that Trev's ideas on generating methane from human poo might be a good idea after all. Anything to avoid using more power than we create. We could always go the next six weeks without cooking, just lettuce leaves, raw onion and eggs.

How about it, Trev?

Approximate power use for our house daily/annually

	kWh PER DAY	PER WEEK	PER YEAR
Electric bicycle charging*	0.15	0.75	54.75
Electric kettle	0.3	2.1	109.5
Electric stove	1.25	8.75	456.25
Fridge	1.1	7.7	401.5
Laptop	0.3	2.1	109.5
Lighting	0.2	1.4	73
Microwave	0.35	2.45	127.75
Misc. kitchen appliances	0.1	0.7	36.5
Phone	0.072	0.504	26.28
Television	0.2	1.4	73
Video	0.2	1.4	73
Washing machine**	0.44	0.88	45.76
Water pump	0.253	1.771	92.345
Total	4.915	31.905	1679.135

* five times a week ** twice a week
Note: solar hot-water boosting not included.

Dinner time, and I know Trev, who isn't complaining, is starved for food with a different flavour than that of the past five months. I know I feel like chicken in a lime, coconut and coriander sauce, with vegies served for a decorative effect rather than as a main.

'Potatoes, the other white meat', I mutter.

Then I do it: I make a goat's milk sauce with lime and coriander, holding my breath that it will not curdle. It comes through the heat treatment complete. I add the steamed sliced potato, sweet potato and beans and simmer. It doesn't look half bad. For entrée its cumin eggplant pakoras, this time grilled (I'm trying to avoid the big oil suck-up — perhaps eggplants would be great for an oil spill at sea, they seem to double their own weight in it so easily). Success. They can be dipped in Trev's chilli sauce. It's hot. Everyone chokes on the fumes when he makes it. Dessert will be hot fig and ginger muffins smothered in hot chocolate sauce. This kind of renewed cooking vigour is the result of seeing the bags under Trev's eyes this morning. Tonight I smother him in food — as soon as the last morsel is consumed, the plate he is eating from is replaced with another, full and steaming.

23 May

Caleb volunteers to help me in the garden. This is unusual. I often suggest it, but never expect him to acquiesce. He decides it's his job to take the wheelbarrow down for me. Three squashed eggplants and a pigeon pea on a bad angle, and we're there. We grab a spade each and start to fill it with topsoil from an abandoned garden bed. Caleb finds a number of small potatoes that I'd missed in the recent harvest. He plays 'pinball' with them. My job is to haul the wheelbarrow up the hill. It's so heavy and the slope so steep that I lose my shoes and socks on the trip up as they slide off my feet. I tip the load into one of the beds. I get back down to see a limp Caleb sprawled in the garden bed. He appears dead, except for his twitching lips.

'Heck. He's dead!' I exclaim. 'Lucky it's in the garden, in nice soft ground.' I pick up the spade and shovel a good load over his stomach. His mouth twitches. Another shovel full, this one full of writhing worms. He starts to giggle.

'Keep covering me up, come on, bury me!' he hisses.

We're both laughing. Then I notice a helicopter passing slowly overhead. I lean against the shovel and try not to look guilty while I use my toe to prod him to life.

He helps me pull out arrowroot tubers and feed them to Possum. He thinks it's fun to find ways to swat me with them. They hurt; I swat him back. It's not long before my pockets are full of dirt and my scalp is gritty. I pull out the roots of a dead pigeon pea. Caleb decides the second stump is his, and proceeds to lean his body on it until it collapses in a north, south, east and west direction. The roots snap and pop as he goes. He spends half his time on the ground giggling. He tugs hard on the stump and manages to fall backwards in a series of stumbles and ends up 6 metres away — another squashed eggplant. He doesn't like eggplant. I'm beginning to suspect ulterior motives. He pricks up his ears at the sound of children playing, and is off. I reach over and pluck the stump out of the ground, and finish off our other jobs, taking half the time it would have taken together, and having half the amount of fun. I haul up pumpkin vines that are still bearing. You have to be ruthless with pumpkins, they take over. I've let them go too far. Discipline is not my strongest suite.

Arrowroot flour

Peel tubers and cut into small cubes. Add a little water and puree in a bowl with a stick blender. Leave to settle; the flour will sink to the bottom while the brown fibrous pulp will stay at the surface. Skim the pulp off and drain surplus water away. Spread the flour out in a thin layer on a large tray.

Place the tray in the sun to dry the flour, which takes a day or so depending on how hot the sun is and the thickness of the flour. Two teaspoons of arrowroot flour to a cup of water will form a light syrup when heated. You can use it in place of cornflour; it has more of a glazed effect than the milkier cornflour effect.

I've unscrewed the plates holding sleepers together in the bottom garden, and hauled them up above the goat pen to use as garden borders. It's part of the plan to establish more intensive garden beds in the upper yard and fence off the lower garden as a goat-browsing area. There are lots of pigeon peas and arrowroot growing there already. Weeds too, lots of weeds — since we've decided on this plan I've neglected the area. Possum will clean it up quickly enough. I'd love to get onto it right away, but we'd need to buy posts and dog-wire aplenty, so we'll have to leave it till after June. There are fruit and nut trees in there: pecans, macadamias, fig, peach, olive and a couple of good plums. Trev wants to fence them off too, and use the fencing as framework to hang fruit fly exclusion netting on the susceptible. I'm in favour of relocating those that can be, turning a blind eye to those vulnerable to goat attack and starting again somewhere higher up the block. The chooks can go in there too, although I'm not sure how they will battle out the new pecking order. It's not nice to watch. The advantages will be that a large area will not need to be watered, weeded or fertilised. Perhaps the best part will be that Possum will be further from the house. Every three weeks when she's on heat, or gets into a bad mood, she can drive me insane with her bellowing. Though in the last month or so she has been calm and quiet. She likes it cool and sunny; give her rain and wind, and she becomes the fly on Michael Douglas' face in *Falling down*.

25 May

Caleb trips over the power pack on the notebook. It dies. Caleb doesn't notice, he's busy flying his latest paper plane.

Twenty-four hours later I can conclusively say that I can live without chocolate, potato chips, chicken, pizza, 'yellow cheese' — heck, most things — but I can't handle living without a computer. I'm not sure I can express myself on paper anymore. I certainly can't imagine not seeing a storm approach in five virulent shades of rainfall intensity on a flat screen, nor doing without instant access to up-to-date info on any number of things. I can't imagine educating Caleb without resources like interactive CD-ROMs and websites that effortlessly convey so much and in such a way he not only recalls the information but also enjoys it. And, of course, not being able to contact people all over the world, in an instant, and for nothing. All this is leading up to admitting replacing the adapter at a cost of $110. The natural attrition of goods. Ones that cannot be repaired, for a service that cannot be replaced. At least by relying on the computer so much, we use less paper and what we use is recycled.

RECYCLED PAPER – THE KINDEST CUT

We may not have achieved the paperless office yet (will we ever?), but by choosing recycled paper you will make considerable environmental savings. Consider this:

- 1 tree makes 16.67 reams of copy paper.
- 1 ream (500 sheets) uses 6 per cent of a tree.
- 1 tonne (40 cartons) of 30 per cent postconsumer-content copier paper saves 7.2 trees.
- 1 tonne of 50 per cent postconsumer-content copier paper saves 12 trees.[5]

One tonne of paper from recycled pulp saves:

- 17 trees
- 2.3 cubic metres of landfill space
- 31,400 litres of water
- 4200 kWh (enough to heat a home for half a year)
- 1600 litres of oil
- 26 kilograms of air pollutants from entering the atmosphere.[6]

26 May

I make a habit of logging on to *The Australian* newspaper online each morning to have a quick look at the main news. Today one of the headlines is about thirsty crops. Rice to be precise. The CSIRO has determined that if the water wasn't subsidised rice would cost $21 per kilo. A crisis of conscience: should we support a water-inefficient crop by eating it? We consider it one of our staples. So far we would have eaten at least 15 kilos of the brown variety in these six months alone. I decline to use the calculator again. There are lots of jokes about fundamentalist greenies, those who react at the slightest hint of un-environmentalism. I laugh at them too. So where is the balance? Is choosing not to eat rice the right thing to do? Or is it too extreme a reaction to the news? Is the way we are living now too extreme? Yet we live in luxury compared with most of the world's population.

Trev and I debate the issue. And decide that, rather than not eating rice, we'll support the rice industry by using our barter money for organic rice, which is more water-efficient, instead. It's not that much of a price difference: the cost of organically grown rice in Coles is $3.30 per kilo compared with $2.80 for a non-organic alternative. Fifty cents is a small investment.

If there is an increase in people buying organic rice, it will be more viable for all rice growers to do so, and make it cheaper. We can try to find ways to have the rice and eat it too.

AUSTRALIAN RICE – IS IT WORTH IT?

Wherever possible we should be growing crops suited to our environment, irrigating them using appropriate methods, from a sustainable water source, and instigating improved environmental management systems.

According to *Water use*, edited by Justin Healey,[7] 'Over a quarter of Australia's river systems are close to, or have exceeded, sustainable extraction limits, and two-thirds of water extracted is from these stressed systems. More groundwater is used than ever before'.

The book goes on to say, 'A water audit has found that more than 26 per cent of rivers, streams and creeks had too much water extracted from them, while about 34 per cent of Australia's groundwater was also being overused'.

There are calls to reduce water subsidies as artificially low water prices mean that rice becomes a viable proposition when, really, it's not. Rice requires 11.2 megalitres per hectare (a megalitre is 1 million litres) to grow and a hectare can lose up to 80,000 litres a day in evaporation. Without water subsidies, the cost of rice would be many times higher.

Trev and I often laugh at ourselves. We hold up humour as our protective totem against extremism, fanaticism and fundamentalism. We buy a new fridge by walking along the rows looking at the energy star rating. Without looking inside we say, 'That one'.

We bought a car the same way. We walked around the caryard looking at the fuel consumption labels and without opening a door or taking it for a test drive we pointed at the Pulsar and said, 'That one', and then laughed at ourselves the whole way home.

Trev's daughter, Leela, comes to stay for the weekend and every time she walks out of the bathroom, Trev and I look at each other and whisper, 'Voccers' — volatile organic compounds. Such things are outlawed in the house. We refrain from extending the law to include her — we think that's pretty good of us, even if we can't resist the urge to tease her for wearing petroleum products.

VOLATILE ORGANIC COMPOUNDS (VOCS)

VOCs are substances containing carbon and other elements that can vaporise or become gaseous very easily. They are emitted from various natural and manufactured products.

Even freshly cut grass has been found to emit the VOCs methane, acetone and possibly even formaldehyde. VOCs are everywhere, but the problem occurs when we sit in homes without adequate ventilation, homes that contain materials emitting high levels of VOCs. The levels of VOCs can be as much as 100 times higher inside a home than out.

An added reason for concern is that children breathe in 20 per cent more air per kilo of body weight than adults, increasing their exposure to VOCs. Research has indicated that childhood asthma could be reduced by up to 65 per cent by lowering the level of indoor VOCs.

Indoor pollution is caused by the use of household chemicals and pesticides, and by manufacturing wood products and household furnishings using chemical adhesives and synthetic fibres that leach into the air over the products' lifespans. Particleboard and plywood use large amounts of adhesives that off-gas for years. An employee of a particleboard factory described to me how the boards were once packed into airtight bags, but the practice was abandoned after the bags turned into balloons from the high level of off-gassed formaldehyde. Paint may continue to emit many VOCs (including organochlorines) for years after application.

Bioeffluents (another type of VOC) affect air quality and are produced by humans. We exhale carbon dioxide (CO_2), acetone, ammonia, a large number of volatile fatty acids, phenols and solvents previously inhaled. We also produce gas: between 200 and 2000 millilitres per day. Flatulence comprises nitrogen, oxygen, carbon dioxide, hydrogen and methane.

Reducing VOCs

Along with limiting products that emit VOCs (which will also assist in the protection of ozone layers, waterways and the environment in general), we can make sure there is adequate ventilation in our homes and workplaces, which will reduce VOC concentration.

The best practice is to use natural paints, which are now widely available, and to limit the use of petroleum-based products, such as synthetic carpets. Opt for natural fibres instead and natural cleaning products like baking soda and vinegar rather than attractively packaged bottles of chemicals. Perfumes and other beauty products are made from petrochemicals.

NASA experimented with using plants to clean air and was able to show that certain plants can remove up to 85 per cent of VOCs (based on at least two plants per 10 square metres).[8] Plants are able to do this because the moisture they transpire through their stomata attracts airborne pollutants. The pollutants are then drawn via moisture into the root area, where microbial action renders them harmless.

Formaldehyde

Causing ailments from nausea to nosebleeds, and suspected to be carcinogenic, formaldehyde is found in carpeting, clothes, foam insulation, household cleaners, paper products, particleboard, plywood, water repellents and furniture. Plants that are effective in removing formaldehyde are azalea, bamboo palm, chrysanthemum, corn plant, golden pothos, mother-in-law's-tongue, philodendron, poinsettia, spider plant and aloe vera.

Benzene

Symptoms of chronic benzene exposure may be non-specific, such as bleeding; fatigue; fever due to infection or manifestations of thrombo-cytopenia, such as hemorrhagic diathesis with bleeding from the gums, nose, skin or gastrointestinal tract; and hematologic abnormalities.

Benzene is found in detergents, petrol, inks, oils, plastics, synthetic fibres and tobacco smoke. Plants found to be effective in removing benzene include chrysanthemum, dragon tree, English ivy, gerberas, peace lily and Janet Craig and Warneckii dracaenas.

Carbon monoxide

The symptoms of low-level carbon monoxide poisoning include flu-like symptoms, shortness of breath, mild nausea and mild headaches. These symptoms are usually caused by vehicle exhaust and leaky gas heaters. Plants found to be effective in removing carbon monoxide include spider plant and golden pothos.

Organochlorines

These are chlorines combined with organic substances, usually petrochemicals. Symptoms of exposure include skin irritation, headaches, depression, suppressed immunity, damage to major organs such as the liver, reproductive and developmental impairment, infertility, birth defects and cancer.

Organochlorines are found in plastics, dyes, deodorants, bleaching agents, refrigerants, wood preservers, cleaning solvents, pesticides, synthetic fibres, carpets, upholstery, PVC pipe, paint, vinyl, wallpaper, cosmetics, linens, household cleaners, fabric softeners and vehicle exhaust.

I think being a 'greenie' in today's world is like being a passenger in a vehicle with the worst fuel consumption imaginable. And there's a party going on inside. The driver is drunk, and everyone is singing songs, indulging all of their senses. They're driving at night, with no lights on and straight towards a cliff edge. Oblivious. The greenie is trying to make themselves heard over the noise: 'There's a cliff ahead! Stop the car! There's a cliff ahead! Turn on the lights for god's sake!'

'Here, have a drink.'

'Shut up, wowser.'

'Let me out! I wanna get off!' But there's no getting out of this car. It speeds up, the doors are locked, there is no flinging yourself from the moving vehicle. You can do what you like, but this car is on a set course, and you can either keep jumping up and down knowing you are unheeded, or take the drink that's offered and hope it dulls the pain of the inevitable.

I don't want to be a part of the 'I hate lifestyle four-wheel drives' faction. But I am. The hard part is trying not to group all drivers under the signpost labelled 'evil', though they do epitomise a way of thinking that is the root cause of environmental issues: 'I want, I have, and I don't care'.

Perhaps four-wheel drives should come with warning stickers:

> Health warning!
> This vehicle contributes to greenhouse gas emissions
> at the rate of 2.1 average vehicles, produces 35 per cent
> more hydrocarbons and carbon monoxide, and is more likely
> to result in vehicle accident fatalities.

HEALTH AND ENVIRONMENTAL EFFECTS OF EXHAUST EMISSIONS[9]

Carbon monoxide (CO)

CO reduces the ability of the blood to carry oxygen and can cause permanent damage to the nervous system. Those at highest risk are smokers, or people suffering from heart disease and anaemia.

Carbon dioxide (CO_2)

CO_2 does not impair human health, but does contribute to degradation of the human environment.

Nitrous oxides (NOx)

Nitrous oxides exacerbate asthma, reduce lung function and increase the risk of respiratory infections in the young and the elderly. They can lead to chronic lung damage. NOx react in the presence of volatile organic compounds and sunlight to form ground-level ozone. They contribute to the formation of acid rain and the nitrification of waterways, leading to algae blooms and fish kills.

Ozone

Ozone is formed when pollutants emitted by cars and other sources react chemically in the presence of sunlight. Ozone can irritate your eyes and respiratory systems, reduce lung function, aggravate asthma and lung disease, and may cause permanent lung damage. Ozone also reduces growth rates of vegetation.

Particulate matter (PM)

These minute particles can penetrate deep into the lungs where they may accumulate and then enter the bloodstream. Many of the chemicals are recognised toxins, carcinogens and endocrine disruptors. They can cause lung tissue damage, cancer and respiratory disorders.

Sulfur dioxide (SO$_2$)

SO$_2$ produces acid rain. As it is water-soluble it is easily absorbed through the respiratory tract and can have a depressant effect on lung capacity.

Volatile Organic Compounds (VOCs)

Exhaust fumes contain VOCs that have the potential to cause nerve and lung damage. VOCs react in the presence of NOx and sunlight to form ground-level ozone, a component of smog.

Trev recently tried to understand someone's awkward behaviour with us.

'Ahh', he says, 'maybe they know we're "greenies". They think we think they're unsustainable and they feel guilty and awkward, because some part of them must recognise that we're right'.

I'm not sure if he's right, perhaps it's just that without all those petroleum products applied in the right places, we smell.

Caleb tells me one day, 'When I grow up, I'm not going to be enviro-mental'.

It's his rebellion. It's a threat that gives me pause. We've made jokes that he will come out of the family home ready for conversion to all things requiring consumption. It's a normal reaction to any extremism. I know I came out of my home determined not to eat meat, be a clean freak or respect authority, and I planned to use lots of salt. The same thing applies to each generation. One form of extremism tends to give rise to the opposing form. A balancing act that one only hopes is like the pendulum swing and will eventually come to a median point.

27 May

Caleb joins me in the garden again. He wants to know if any of the chooks have 'pooed' out any more eggs. They haven't. I've fed them oats, milk, garlic and chilli powder today as an egg-laying health tonic. Two of the four chooks in one pen are exhibiting signs of egglessness. I'm sure you can imagine the symptoms. Then it's on to changing chook water. Caleb declines this task and instead pulls a mandarin off the tree and shares it with Possum. I join him and we have a taste test from various trees to see which is the sweetest. He knocks over my 40-litre bucket of assorted animal poos steeped in rotting, mineral-high herbs. He manages to smear himself liberally and then accuses me of smelling bad. I ask him to help gather up the fallen limes, but he insists it should be me to climb under and haul them out; he will be the one to hold the bucket. Only there is a catch — there are levels to this game. The first three I get to throw into an unmoving bucket, the next into one rotating. The next level rotates and has the handle slammed up and down, and any that fail to fall into the bucket roll down the hill and are mine to collect. One of the limes meets the top of his head with a nice little splot. Then it's time to collect peas. We take them upstairs and I wash them well while he washes himself less so under a hot shower. I grab the jar of dried pigeon peas we collected at the last harvest and put some on to soak for a dhal.

Dhal

200 grams red lentils or pigeon peas

¼ teaspoon turmeric

1 teaspoon ground cumin

2 potatoes, peeled and chopped

4 tomatoes, skinned and chopped

900 millilitres water

1 teaspoon ground coriander

1 onion, chopped

4 cloves garlic, crushed

25 grams butter

1 teaspoon garam masala

Simmer lentils, turmeric, cumin, potatoes and tomatoes in the water for 15 minutes or until the potatoes are cooked. Add coriander.

Sauté chopped onion and garlic in butter until golden. Add garam masala and cook a further two minutes. Add mixture to lentils and stir through. Serve with rice.

29 May

The bird life in the backyard is prolific. There are the 'pleased to meet you, let's have a quick squawk-talk' butcherbirds, one of which delighted us immensely by hanging a dead crested pigeon in the carambola tree before tearing it to pieces. It gave us the opportunity to discuss with Caleb the 'red in tooth and claw' nature of nature. Yesterday the butcherbird swooped in and gobbled up a cockroach hanging off the flyscreen to cheers of approval. Caleb often entices him with small feasts, which the bird takes straight from his hands.

The crested pigeons are in far greater numbers, usually standing talon to talon along Possum's pen rail or cleaning up loose grain while the chooks watch on. Whenever I walk past they take off like a flock of squeaky hinges. Then there is the pair of king parrots, vivid green and red. The branches of the pigeon pea sway under their weight as they devour their own in seeds.

My next round of sorghum has gone the way of so many of the others; the peach-faced lorikeets prefer those and only the empty seed heads fork towards the sky.

We have a black spangled drongo stopping by; he always seems to at this time of the year, and he hunts around for insects, something we thoroughly approve of.

The blue-headed honeyeaters probe away at the giant banana bells and magpies warble. Once 40 or more of them used to congregate on the verandah railing. They didn't mind popping inside for a quick visit, usually to remove a piece of toast out of three-year-old Caleb's hand while it was on route to his mouth. Someone across the valley got sick of cleaning up magpie poop on their verandah and poisoned them.

The ibis stalk the garden probing the soil with their curved beaks. A few galahs, but not many right now; peewees, kookaburras, a single pheasant. Caleb, having read Roald Dahl's book about poaching, *Danny, champion of the world*, is interested in catching and roasting the pheasant.

30 May

Trev and I noted that this morning marked the 150th day.

'Has a good ring to it, 150 days without spending too many dollars, don't you think?' I start fantasising about a surprise ending, and getting out there and spending money. There are a few things I want to buy at the end. It's surprisingly mundane, a new pillow for both of us (ours having recently collapsed into the thickness of folded handkerchiefs), ugg boots for Caleb and me, and a dressing gown. I figure if Trev isn't too proud to get large-print books out of the library, I can cope with wearing a dressing gown. Especially since I've taken to wearing his. Some new cushion covers, fencing wire, posts and a week of avoiding the scales while we down every disgusting non-vegetable thing we can lay our hands on.

We've got to the point where we think we've proved what we can. We want to move on and see what life is like post-experiment. One of the things we've been discussing is the meritorious nature of restraining oneself when there is excess available. Those who are forced by poverty to live simply are not necessarily acting any more ethically because there is no choice involved. However, when — in a culture that is swamped in material goods — an average person who could buy more than they need chooses not to, it becomes a more virtuous position. Maintaining a sustainable lifestyle is not that hard, providing there are sufficient points in time in which we can get off the wagon and relieve ourselves. Long journeys are like that.

It's a balancing act. Will we go back to dashing off in the car again, or will we stick to our bike rides? When I was 16 I rode a bike everywhere. As soon as I had my licence and a car, the bike rusted away in the garage. Once the choice was there, the easiest option was always the one taken.

LET'S GET PERSONAL – HOW MUCH GAS DO YOU EMIT?

A litre of petrol contains about 33,000 kilojoules of energy. The same amount of energy is enough to fuel a man for two days. The energy in one slice of bread will fuel a car for a journey of 380 metres (not including starting the vehicle). On the same energy a person could walk 3 kilometres or cycle 14 kilometres. This makes the bicycle over 97 per cent more efficient than a car.

But, hang on, humans breathe out CO_2, right? And the more we exercise the more we emit. Is this an issue?

The average person exhales around 300 grams of CO_2 a day, more if physically active. With 6 billion of us that's 2.03 trillion tonnes a day. Seems like one of those figures to start sighing over and thinking about population control involving draconian methods. But what we are exhaling is fast-cycle CO_2, absorbed from eating plants, and animals that ate plants. Emitting this type of CO_2 doesn't make any difference to the level of atmospheric CO_2 as it would have decomposed and re-entered the chain within a short time anyway.

However, burning fossil fuels, which have been bound up in the slow carbon chain for millions of years, does increase atmospheric carbon dioxide levels.

Every litre of petrol burnt creates 2.4 kilos of greenhouse gas. If you drive a 1.6-litre vehicle and live 2 kilometres away from your school or workplace – that's a potential 480 kilograms of CO_2 per year. Each kilo of CO_2 pollutes over 10,000 litres of air.

The message: get on your bike and don't be frightened to exhale!

We've already made it abundantly clear by our conspicuous lapses that we are not perfect models of domestic sustainability, not the kind of people who can eat green leafy vegetables every meal and never crave a great fat dollop of butter, but we strive to be the best we can.

The difference between self-sufficiency and domestic sustainability is more than semantic.

The 1970s were about moving away from the strictures of the quarter acre, Hills hoists, concrete pathways, apron-wearing wives and closed minds. It was about embracing wildness, espousing lots of idealistic things about peace and love, and divorcing from mainstream society with dreams of 'self-sufficiency'. It rarely worked. Once people had enough of it, most moved on and back to consumer society, some becoming card-carrying members of the yuppies.

We are more about, Yep, we live on a quarter-acre block, let's see if we can do that sustainably while still remaining part of our society and expressing ourselves within that society in any way we see as appropriate, but without drawing on whatever generational 'fashion' is currently happening. This is not a fashion statement, or a phase; this is making solar hot-water as essential as windows. This is a practical reaction to the population explosion. We need to live within our energy means or risk major reductions in living standards right through to dicing with extinction. What we do inside a sustainable house, what we think, what our politics are, is of no account.

We're just trying to make the point in a way that interests people enough to make them want to take the idea off the coat hanger, try it on for themselves, and make as many alterations to the design as they see fit.

If the average person decides they want a fuel-efficient car, manufacturers will stay up late at night burning the midnight oil trying to find a way to burn less. Likewise, governments are sensitive to public groundswells, lest one they have not foreseen knocks them over.

The great consumer ball keeps rolling, but at the moment it's a pinball being driven by mass marketing that tempts us with all things possible, without a word about consequences.

Yet that is changing. A rural radio program recently aired a show informing rural producers that consumers are prepared to boycott sheep to stop live sheep exports; major chicken producers kowtowed to consumer pressure to stop feeding them genetically engineered food; the supermarket shelves are full of barn-laid, free-range organic eggs as a result of the same consumer pressure. It's gradual, but it works. Rural and industrial sectors have been changed due to consumer-driven social responsibility. Unfortunately it also works that consumers want to eat mandarins all year long, so the rural sector has to stretch itself on the rack of consumer 'perceived need' rather than consumers learning to eat fruit only when in season.

Advertising has been carried to lengths never before known. Our mailboxes, telephones, radios and televisions are channels for would-be sellers of merchandise who are hard put to get rid of what the manufacturers produce. There is nothing wrong, of course, with a proper distribution of goods and services. I am not talking about that but about the promotion of superabundance. We need food, clothing and shelter. Even abundance and comfort are gifts of God. But we are no longer his creatures accepting and distributing the goodness he pours upon us but the feverish and slavish worshipers of abundance itself.
JOHN WHITE[10]

Consumers are a huge, largely untapped, power. Like economists, we don't think beyond our own lives, our forecasts are narrowed down to how life challenges may affect our day-to-day ability to experience comfort.

The government relies on economists, who back ideas that pay for themselves within four years — any longer and they are not considered viable. The environment doesn't get the vote, emancipation for it may never come. While it may be billions of years old, the world relies on a four-year economic forecast for its chance at longevity.

I came across the work of Joe Miller, a children's book author. He looked at the history of the Earth from an unusual perspective. The Earth is considered to be 4.5 billion years old. If that were represented by one year, he suggested that life would not have begun until 29 March. The first fish would not appear until 7 December and the first amphibians, 14 December. The dinosaurs would be born on 15 December and die by 26 December. Primitive humans would appear at 6.17 pm on 31 December. The oldest person alive today would have been born within the last second. It could also be added that during that last second we would have used two thirds of the Earth's resources, including the majority of oil.

We age as individuals, and I also believe we age as a species. I'd plot our age range as somewhere in the teens: we're here for a good time, we have the keys to the car, think we're invincible and feel we owe no one and no thing any great respect.

HOW MUCH DO YOU CARE?

In 2004, 8.6 million Australians aged 18 years and over (57%) stated that they were concerned about environmental problems.

The level of concern about environmental problems has shown a continual decline since 1992, when three-quarters (75%) of Australians stated they had environmental concerns.

The Australian Capital Territory had the highest level of concern (69%) and the Northern Territory the lowest (46%).

Those aged between 45 and 54 expressed the most concern about environmental problems (65%), and those 65 years and over the least (47%).

Thirteen per cent of people with environmental concerns had formally registered a concern (via a letter, phone, demonstration, signed petition or other means), and 29 per cent donated time or money to protect the environment. Nearly two-thirds (65%) of people with environmental concerns took neither of these actions.[11]

Ecological living does not imply turning away from economic progress; rather it seeks to discover which technologies are most appropriate and helpful in moving towards a sustainable future. Ecological living is not a path of 'no growth' but a path of 'new growth' that includes both material and spiritual dimensions of life. A simpler way of life is not a retreat from progress; in fact it is essential to the advance of civilizations.
DUANE ELGIN[12]

Trev's rave

I've written previously about the house in the bush and its manifold shortcomings, but it taught me a lot, especially how to fix things and how to improvise. I don't pretend to be a craftsman — more like a farmer or a bush mechanic who can rig something up with a piece of wire and a length of timber. It's never pretty, but it usually works. Well, sometimes it's pretty. The ability to fix things is a useful skill and one I think is, sadly, becoming lost. This is not entirely the community's fault. More and more products are designed to be disposable. The manufacturer will tell you there are no user-serviceable parts inside. Depending on the product, often this is simply not true. I wonder how many items are disposed of because of a blown fuse, or a broken drive belt — often as simple a thing as a rubber band.

The fixing and making required here gets done in the recycling centre. It used to be called 'Trev's black hole', or 'the dog box' and, I admit, it's not the prettiest or cleanest place in the world, but I know where everything is … mostly. There is a tradition in my family to call this sort of place — the bloke's shed or workshop — the doghouse. That was where my grandfather spent most of his time. It wasn't till later, when my own experience with relationships removed the scales from my eyes, that I realised 'doghouse' was something of a euphemism. I remembered the tone of my grandmother's voice and set of her face as she replied to my question as to Grandpa's whereabouts by telling me curtly, 'In the doghouse'. And there he would indeed be, tinkering with something or reading one of his favourite westerns, invariably with the comfort of a cold ale. In my innocence, the doghouse was the place, not the state of being.

My recycling centre serves a similar purpose. While I'm not the author of all my troubles to quite the extent Grandpa was, and Linda is by no means the termagant my long-suffering Grandma could sometimes be, the place can serve as a refuge on those rare occasions the usual amicable détente degenerates into sporadic skirmishing. The emphasis is, however, on tinkering. And there's usually a whole lot of tinkering going on. We already had a tradition of fixing or making whatever we could but during our six-month adventure, when nothing can be replaced, the need to repair things assumes new importance.

And sometimes it's a bit of a challenge. When an egg I was poaching blew itself and the microwave into the following week, a fix was in order; but one pokes around inside electrical appliances at one's own peril, especially when they are festooned with stickers warning one against such poking. I resolved to remove the back cover and if I encountered shielding, or the least unfamiliar thing, I would give it up. An unscrew or two later and I'd ascertained that the cover was just that and incorporated no potentially dangerous bits. From there, it was the work of a jiffy to work out a fuse had blown. Miraculously, I found the exact same fuse in an old computer power supply. Microwave fixed. Admiring looks and whispers of 'My hero' from Linda.

We recycle whatever we can. Jars and glass bottles are used again and again for sauces, cordial and preserves. A broken garden fork and a piece of water pipe becomes a small weeding fork. An old sandpit digger of Caleb's becomes a kid's seat for the back of a bike. A steel bowl from an automatic washing machine and a bicycle tube are turned into a flail, the effectiveness of which exceeds all expectations. I could go on.

I guess the point of all this is that we take pride in being able to recycle, to the extent that we're inclined to take it to extremes – I believe it's safe to say that there are not too many people around who'd resole their thongs – whereas the emphasis in the general community seems to be on pride in being able to throw something out and buy a new, usually bigger one, often for no other reason than that it's no longer the dernier cri.

As a community, we pay lip service with the concept of recycling. This is better than nothing – it shows we are aware, however dimly, that we can't continue to spend resources like drunken sailors – but the aim should also be to use fewer consumables in the first place, and to try to maximise the life of those we do.

june

2 June

Caleb has become a gardening convert. I'd already introduced him to the pea patch and he goes down and clears them out to the extent I haven't actually served any on the table yet. But it's the machete that did it. He's been begging to hack Possum's daily pumpkin. Today I finally let him and the garden became of increased and immediate interest. There are masses of mandarins, next best thing to watermelon in his eyes, and he's under the trees creating castles from the peelings. He counts while he eats them, segment by segment. If his counting is correct, he's over a thousand. For me, seeing Caleb in the garden crouching down and talking to bearded dragons and hand-feeding the goat makes hot summer garden-watering worth it.

We're all out of loofahs for the loo. The next lot are still on the bush and in scanty numbers (mostly due to their suicidal tendency to crawl up the side of Possum's pen). As Trev pointed out, 'She wouldn't eat them if you fed them to her'.

So we're down to phone books. We have 10 — we've only managed to wipe through one book so far. I've taken to reading them before use, and have discovered a local UFO sighting and abduction hotline. Pity I've experienced neither.

3 June

Possum's milk has been dropping off. It's been a bit of a mystery as to why. In May last year we'd loaded her up on the back of the neighbour's ute and drove her off for a romantic interlude. We didn't have a ramp so Trev had to carry her, horns and all, off the back of the ute. He stood in a trail of jumping ants and devised a new sideways dance featuring near collapse.

It was the same place we had bought Possum from two and a half years earlier. The owner told us later that we could have waited around another five minutes and taken her back with us, as that was all it took for the romantic side of business to be performed. However, Possum didn't return for a fortnight and we both missed her presence in the backyard. The next four months were spent going, 'Yes she is', 'No she's not', as her belly swelled with food, or could it be babies? Goats are naturally pot-bellied, and do not 'show' till fairly late in the game. Eventually I was able to give her a bear hug from behind and feel, just before her udder, the wiggle of unborn kids. They were born in September, when we had originally decided to start our adventure, but we'd just gone five months with virtually no rain. Another low rainfall record. We didn't even have tank water left. So we changed the start date to January. Milk production was still peaking in January, but Possum seems to be on the decline now, and will need to be dried up at some stage, given a rest and the process repeated.

Even so, when she appeared to be producing less milk we thought that was the end of the story, she's slowing up. But it wasn't the problem. She'd decided that her 'biscuit' of lucerne wasn't up to scratch and was pulling at it and throwing it around, but not actually digesting much. So I've increased the amount of pigeon pea, arrowroot, lab lab, milk thistle, cobblers pegs and other favoured weeds and she is again on the increase. We're getting over 2 litres a day.

My laptop suffers a major beeping attack. There are symptoms of stroke, to the extent that only every third or fourth letter appears, and sometimes numbers that I didn't touch. We hope to have it repaired and allow it to become the sole property of the sticky-fingered Cal, but I need a working replacement now. So we busted out with an expensive item, which we transported back to the house via vehicle. I could rave on about how essential it is to our daily living, and make a case for its purchase. But I won't. We spent $1000 today — and I feel good.

COMPUTER FACTS

Environment Victoria, a non-government organisation, compiled a summary of computer waste in Australia.[1]

The findings
- Three million computers are sold each year.
- Each year 731,500 are dumped in landfill.
- In 10 years 1.77 million computers will be made redundant each year.
- The Australian Capital Territory is the only place that bans computer waste to landfill.
- In five years, 30 countries will have take-back laws for electronics (Australia has no such law).
- Manufacturing one desktop computer and monitor uses the same amount of chemicals (22 kg), water (1500 kg) and fossil fuels (240 kg) as used when making a mid-size car.
- The biggest computer users are small and medium businesses (28%) followed by large corporates (23%); government (18%); households (17%); and education (14%).

- In just over a decade, the number of personal computers worldwide increased fivefold – from 105 million in 1988 to more than half a billion in 2002.
- A typical computer monitor contains lead, barium and hexavalent chromium. Other toxic ingredients include cadmium in chip resistors and semiconductors, beryllium on motherboards and connectors, and brominated flame-retardants in plastic casings. Seventy per cent of lead, cadmium and mercury in landfill comes from electronic waste.

What you can do

- Make use of purchasing power. Buy or lease a new computer only if needed and choose the most environmentally sound option – for example, look for labels indicating the machine is energy efficient.
- Don't throw away old electronics. Some manufacturers, such as Dell, take back old computers. Ring them on 1800 465 890 for a quote on pick-up. Urge manufacturers to dispose of products responsibly.
- Donate old computers to organisations that can refurbish or reuse the parts. Ask for a written guarantee of safe disposal.
- Write to your federal or state environment minister and local member urging them to take action to bring Australia into line with European standards of producer responsibility.

7 June

Trevor has forsaken the electric bike in favour of the mountain bike. He arrives sweating and out of breath and, like me, spends inordinate amounts of time standing on the scales. We both wouldn't mind dropping a couple more kilos each so we can have the joy of putting them back on in three weeks' time. The end is nigh. Soon I will no longer be able to put telemarketers off by telling them, 'Sorry, but we're not spending any money for six months. You might like to try again in another five months, three days and 17 hours'.

I can't imagine they've encountered this particular strategy before, and they don't have one of their own prepared. It leaves a nice blank silence, in which I can add, 'So, I'm not really in any position to buy anything/take up your kind offer right now. Have a nice evening'.

Yes, there are certainly some things I am going to miss.

Like most challenges, while the rewards are reaching the goal and everything leading up to it was hard slog, for some strange reason you look back at the hard slog and couch it in the sweetest of terms. I sense we will talk about these six months right till the end of our lives. We haven't necessarily succeeded on the terms we set, but we've still managed to reduce our ecological footprint considerably, and have every intention of continuing to do so … after one massive lapse.

THE ECOLOGICAL FOOTPRINT

Australia has the third largest ecological footprint in the world at 7.7 hectares (rising from 7.58 in 1999), with New Zealand coming in at ninth with 5.5 hectares. The ecological footprint is a measure of the amount of resources required to maintain an individual's lifestyle. It's an indicator of how much we consume, taking into account the land needed to grow our food and to mine the materials that go into our homes, cars and gadgets, and the land needed to store our waste. Globally there are about 6 billion people and 10 billion acres of productive land. That means we are all entitled to about 1.7 hectares of this productive land (that is, the ecological footprint of each person should be 1.7 hectares). However, 12 per cent of ecological capacity is allocated to the world's ecosystems, which has been calculated to be enough to protect biodiversity,[2] reducing an individual's ecological footprint still further.

Currently the global average ecological footprint is about 2.8 hectares, with some countries living well below the 1.7 hectare estimate and 'subsidising' the typical western footprint, such as our own. Even so, we're living beyond the means of our environment to sustain us.

According to the online ecological footprint calculator found at www.earthday.net/footprint/index.asp, our six-month experiment resulted in an ecological footprint of exactly 1 hectare, well within the prescribed 'allowance'.

8 June

Curried eggplant burgers for dinner tonight. They turn out to be a raving success, at least with Trevor and me. I've got eggplant pakoras down to a fine art. This time they're sliced lengthwise, dipped in curried batter and pan-grilled with a teaspoon of oil until golden. Then lettuce, tomato, fetta and cracked pepper are sandwiched between two slices. Yum-ouski.

Spent the day pulling up overgrown radish plants and passing them through the chaffcutter. Caleb was around to help. It ended up looking like a big pile of radish salad. We hauled it back down to mulch the bed they'd come from. The smaller pieces should break down more readily than if I'd just tossed them down whole and they will protect against moisture loss at the same time. I pull out the last of the snake beans and gather all the fat pods for next year's seed. I'm notorious for not bothering to label packets of seeds. I have one lot of beans growing that I guessed were climbers, but were actually bush beans and the tepees of recycled tree branches that I installed are being ignored, while in other areas I'm surprised to see pak choi growing when I'd thought it was cabbage. You get that. My slapdash approach annoys Trev immensely.

Last night it started to drizzle.

'Oh hell.'

I'd thrown a bale of lucerne out of the boot and onto the nature strip, but didn't take it down because the wheelbarrow was full of pumpkins, and I'd only managed to carry a few of them up to the house before I got distracted and did something else.

Trevor is unhappy, and he makes several pointed comments about my methods. He's made it clear he thinks I'm lazy.

I stay quiet and entertain myself with thoughts of divorce. The imminent variety.

9 June

I'm already in the goat pen washing Possum when Trev turns up from work.

'Eh-oo, eh-oo', he calls down from the verandah. Ever since his bike horn perished in the sun he's been replicating it himself to let us know he's home.

We get to work bending over Possum's back end and discuss her renewed milking vigour, how Caleb's latest tooth is growing crooked and how the chooks laid eight eggs, the best for some time. When we stand he gives me a funny look. I turn and grab the goat-house scraper and scrape out goat poo balls so she can sleep on a clean floor. When I turn he's still standing there.

'I was going to ring you up and apologise today. You're not lazy and I was wrong to say it. You have heaps to do and you're really good at getting it done.'

I feel instantly appeased. Symptoms of inevitable divorce flutter quietly away and I'm left to thinking about how I do understand what he means. I have slowed down. I am liable to spend time each day sitting in the sun reading, something I would never have done prior to our 'holiday'. When I was working full-time everything was driven, the pace frantic. It took months before I could relax enough during the day to do something so 'lazy' as read. Recently I watched a movie during the day, a first for at least seven years. I had a headache, all right! Why should I feel so defensive about doing nothing?

I spend lots of my time with Caleb and do time-wasting things like building balloon rockets on a piece of fishing line, and I am able to have a yak about things without having that invisible voice at my shoulder urging me to do or die. Pity Trev isn't in a position to feel at ease too.

Having said that, I've been getting up at 4 or 5 am for some uninterrupted time on the computer. It was a great idea and worked for the first day or two, then Caleb would pop out of the bedroom blurry eyed and smiling requesting a cuddle and a hot breakfast. He said it was the light under his door that woke him. So I rolled up a towel and shoved it up against it.

'I heard you and Dad talking', he said this morning. We'll have to ban speech.

The solar hot-water needs boosting again. I flick on a switch for the fifth or sixth time in the last two weeks. This is not good. Last year we only needed to boost twice, but this year, with the cloudy mornings and predominantly overcast days, we've not been doing as well. You can boost with either gas or electricity. Gas is the best environmental choice because it creates less greenhouse gas when used and doesn't have the inherent inefficiencies in transit that electricity does. We haven't gone for gas, as we had hoped to have enough surplus solar power. It's been true of previous years. Not this one. I wonder what percentage of inefficiency electricity has? I vow to track it down. It takes me a few days, but ...

POWER IN TRANSIT

A percentage of power is lost between the power station and its final destination. It depends on distance – for example, double the line distance, double the inefficiency. Typical losses in the Queensland Transmission and Distribution Networks annually are a weighted average transmission of 4.2 per cent and a distribution loss of 6.2 per cent. To deliver 1000 MW to customers in Queensland, 1107 MW is sent.[3] Of course the power loss doesn't end there: add that to all the appliance inefficiencies and the passive solar inadequacies of the typical house (it may not be facing the right way to best use solar energy, for example), which means that over its lifetime it requires high levels of heating and cooling.

10 June

Possum is bellowing even before daylight, so we milk her early. She is not interested in lucerne; she wants to be hand-fed mandarins. I chop her pumpkin and load her up. This keeps her occupied for several minutes, then I take her for a walk. She doesn't seem hungry, just curious to see what's around. I indulge her for over half an hour, but home school is due to start. I drop her off back home and load her up with munchable weeds. She chews on them for all of 30 seconds before continuing the bellowing. Caleb feeds her another mandarin. We retreat back to the house, but before we get a foot inside she's at it again. She is on heat, coinciding nicely with my bout of PMT. Today will not be pretty.

'Almost worth having her on half-milk just to keep the peace around here', I mention to Trev. I start revising our plans to extend the goat pen and wonder if we shouldn't just sell her off to someone who has enough land not to ever need to be within earshot. But it keeps coming back to the milk. Caleb had his first ear infection and bout of tonsillitis at six months and never seemed to stop until we converted to unpasteurised goat's milk. He didn't have another until she dried up and we reverted to organic unpasteurised cow's milk. Back to goat's milk and the ear infections disappeared. The connection doesn't seem the least coincidental. I also had recurring ear and throat infections until I was 13 and it has left me with hearing difficulties, some of which Caleb already suffers.

I go back down and give her a brush — she loves it. I load her up with food, none of which she is interested in. She doesn't want me, she wants a Bbbbbiilllly.

11 June

I've been wandering around the garden looking at everything that is growing and realising that a lot of it is wasted, simply because of our tendency to overlook things like daikon and wong bok. I usually end up feeding them to the chooks or we barter our produce and turn it into potatoes and onions when our own supply is low, and the hot and dry summer meant we were unable to produce more. Caleb is not the only fussy one, though the number one snail-eater would be displeased to hear me include him in this discussion.

We ate arrowroot tubers only once, and sweet potato leaves are supposed to be excellent spinach, but we stick to what we are most familiar with. We do make use of our nasturtiums though, using the flowers in salads and pickling the buds — surprisingly tasty.

Pickled nasturtium buds

2 cups vinegar
1 teaspoon turmeric
1 teaspoon brown sugar
1 tablespoon peppercorns
2 cups nasturtium buds

Bring the vinegar to the boil and add turmeric, sugar and peppercorns. Stir until the sugar is dissolved and then add the nasturtium buds. Simmer for five minutes, then bottle in sterilised jars. Leave for a month or so before eating.

The buds taste like capers, with a peppery, mustard taste, and can be used in salads, pasta dishes and casseroles.

If we'd been unable to barter, some of this produce would have moved from the don't-really-want-to-eat list to the essential food list fairly quickly. Couple this with the difficulties of feeding Caleb something that he is a little more likely to eat and there's the problem.

If we'd done this without him, we would have made less concessions to the standard diet and gone hard on the weeds if we'd needed to. However, we probably wouldn't have done this in the first place if it wasn't for Caleb. He's a part of our drive to make our lives sustainable, part of that cliché about caretaking the Earth for our children's inheritance. It seems society only has a limited capacity to hear the truth in any particular form — the truth needs to be reinvented or clothed in a suitably fashionable way every now and then to keep our interest levels up. Maybe we should be circulating a new idea — only slightly different — that our great grandchildren will no longer want to inherit the Earth, and will be looking for ways to get off this world and trying to hijack another, unless we curtail our environmental expenditure now.

HOW WE MAKE THINGS WORSE

If we want to take care of the Earth for the generations to come, we need to consider our impact on it. According to the World Overpopulation Awareness organisation, these following actions all have environmental consequences, some of which are within an individual's control:

- having too many children
- agricultural burning
- over-consumption of resources
- failure to recycle
- production/disposal of toxic waste
- improper disposal of human waste
- improper disposal of garbage
- misuse of pesticides
- overcrowding
- economic dependence on growth
- depletion of soils by over-farming
- erosion from removal of vegetation
- urban sprawl
- over-fishing
- removal of carbon sinks (trees)
- inefficient use of fuel
- urbanising farmland
- urban growth where water is scarce
- eating meat.[4]

In the afternoon I take Possum for a walk. It's while I'm near the top of the block that a distraught Caleb makes an appearance. He's lost a tiny, green plastic frog on a neighbour's block. No one is home. I try to talk him out of going down on his own and hunting for it, but he can't hear me for his tears. He disappears down the road. Sighing, I decide to take Possum down with me to make sure no one abducts him. I forget about the numerous small dogs on the route. We get there with only a minor fracas. Caleb has his nose to the ground hunting. I peel a mandarin off a nearby tree and feed it to Possum. I am exhorted to assist in the hunt, but I spend the whole time trying to make Caleb see that finding the minute thing in the mulch is going to be near impossible — that is, until he raises his hands in triumph. We walk back home, but the neighbour's dog has been roused, a young terrier with a determined look in his eye. He stands about one-twentieth of Possum's size, but Possum freaks out and I am dragged ignominiously down the middle of the road, my dug-in heels spraying sparks. A neighbour abandons her lawn mower and rugby-tackles the dog. I'd stay to say thanks but I am already halfway down the block, trying to leap over the garden beds that Possum is speeding through.

13 June

The San Marzano tomatoes sprawling all over the garden are heavily laden. They're plump and starting to flush, and stampedes of snails (all of which are small and inedible by anything other than chooks) have trampled the garden to get to them and chewed small holes with their gastropodious feet. Trev and I spend an hour in the garden hammering in stakes and an old piece of wire mesh, and tie the vines up to keep them off the ground. Hopefully this will mean we get to eat some of the 50 kilos or so before the first frost. The race is on. Frost, fruit fly, snails or us: tomatoes make nice, juicy targets.

Trev tackles the terracists. We'd like to put the chooks in the south paddock and give the front paddock a rest. Possum, who turns out to be the only goat known to be frightened of hills, is not taking advantage of the lab lab and, when led in, runs to the top, looks up at the house and bellows in protest rather than make any efforts at eating. So we hand-pick her lab lab (do goats in your backyard sound like more trouble than they're worth?). Trev works at placing old chicken-wire over the top of the dog-wire and around the circumference of the new chook pen. I figure we might as well cordon off the yellow cherry tomato so the chooks don't destroy it and I add in one of the larger garden beds for the chooks to 'improve'. I bully four or five unused star-pickets out of the ground, and spend an hour dismantling chook-wire bean netting, trying to get it to cooperate and snagging it on 60 different branches while moving it 50 metres. Possum is surprised to learn she can be out-bellowed. Trev finishes off the fence while I pull out a row of arrowroot. I've decided to grow goat tucker only where we intend to put Possum in the future, the lower garden. I might plant another long row of parsley there as a border for the garden. Parsley, apart from being a staple, is hardy and attractive stuff. We toss the chooks in and they enthusiastically begin their soil improvement practices. It's a large area; however, in a week or two they will have eaten every bit of greenery and every cringing snail. Bar the taller lab lab, they will turn it into a fertile wasteland of scratched-up mulch, ready for next season's crop. Right now anything I'd like to plant is too susceptible to frost.

Caleb and Bradley visit us in the garden, and present us with small notes that read 'Shop' or, in one case, 'Sop' with little arrows pointing to the house. This means that half the house will be festooned with blankets and my washing line will be naked of pegs. There will be displays of our own fruit on the floor arranged attractively in as many of the bowls and dishes as they can scavenge from the cupboard, and a small noticeboard full of the exorbitant prices we will be obliged to pay. I pay for two mandarins, 20 cents each, not bad. I pay more for the privilege of taking a photo. Trev wants to rob them and ties a tea-towel around his face, but they are determined to hold on to their till contents and he's forced to shoot them. This was a bad move. I am held at gunpoint by two delinquents and forced to buy more mandarins.

Word of the Day is floccinaucinihilipilificationist: someone who deems things of little worth.

15 June

Lapse number 42. I discover, at the last possible minute, that the bowl I'd put the kidney beans in to soak overnight had not had the addition of water. There I was with the food rug whipped out from under me. It was raining, and I'm the only woman in Australia who needs an umbrella to get food from her walk-in pantry. The cupboard (the indoor variety) exposes bags of rice, flour, a container of sugar, potatoes and onions; the fridge is virtually bare, other than five bottles of mandarin and passionfruit cordial, goat's cheese, tomatoes and half a litre of milk. Trev and I milk a reluctant goat in the rain and discuss our various food options. But we digress and instead discuss how we have adopted the 'Are we there yet?' approach to the experiment, testing out our stamina with jokes about packing it all in. I liken it to when nervous swimmers false start, except we keep threatening to false end. Popping our heads out of the water and debating whether we can call it quits before our hands quite reach the side.

We go buy fish and chips. It's been seven weeks since our last meal break-out. It's cold, it's wet, my food imagination fails me. Caleb's face lights up when we tell him. We duck guiltily into the car and disappear down the road. I joke about whether I should drive with the lights off till we're past the neighbours.

16 June

The day starts with more rain. The heavy variety. I can't bear to think of Trev biking to work in it. It's cruel and inhumane punishment. While we milk Possum I organise my argument.

'You know, it would be best if you took the car today, no, no, hear me out, no arguments please. We'll need more chook food before the end of the month. Why don't you get it today? Also you need to take all those books back to work, and you can't get them on your bike and the two cheeses you need to barter. Besides, the car needs some exercise and, look, you're on a month's holiday after tomorrow — it wouldn't be good to go and get run over now.'

I justify our actions by adding, 'Don't worry about it. I'll do what I always do and I'll be honest and come clean about it. And if anyone at work gives you a hard time, do what you always do, blame it on me'.

That settles it. He takes the car.

We have our pet lines, ones that go, 'We've proved our point, the rest is just semantics. We don't want a lot, we just want a few concessions'.

TRIP TIPS[5]

- Plan your route ahead of time. Avoid numerous small trips. Plan to do as much as you can in one. Walk between shops rather than drive.
- Avoid peak-hour traffic as idling is inefficient.
- The engine is most efficient between 1500 and 2500 revs. Change gears before you reach 2500 rpm.
- Avoid the kind of driving where passengers brace themselves on the door – it also guzzles petrol. Aim for smooth driving without incurring G forces on take-off and around corners.
- Explode the myth about how it takes more energy to start the car than to have it sit there idling. When waiting in traffic, turn the car off.
- At 90 kilometres per hour a car uses 25 per cent less fuel than at 110 kilometres per hour. Speed kills fuel efficiency as well.
- Minimise aerodynamic drag by keeping your arms, legs, head and all body parts inside the car. They, like other things, such as roof racks, spoilers and open windows, can increase fuel consumption by up to 20 per cent.
- Keep your car tyres inflated to the highest recommended pressure.
- Airconditioners can use about 10 per cent extra fuel when operating. However, at speeds of over 80 kilometres per hour, airconditioning is better for fuel consumption than an open window.

- Reduce extra weight in the vehicle, such as in the boot, by only carrying essentials.
- Increase fuel economy and reduce environmental impact by keeping your car in good health. Take it for a check-up at regular intervals.
- Buy, borrow, but don't steal, a bike. The bike is 97 per cent more fuel-efficient than driving a car; it is one of the most energy-efficient methods of transport ever invented, beaten only by sailing ships. While it might be years since you have been on one, be brave. There are a few things you should know before perching yourself precariously on a narrow seat – extra wide ones are available. When you are racing down hills and grab instinctively for the seat belt, there isn't one. Don't grow alarmed when, corner in sight, you realise you don't have an indicator. It's imperative to note that there are no windscreen wipers. While you may feel you are in imminent danger the first few times – if not of a heart attack, then of being run over – you gradually discover that it's not the case. Wear your helmet, keep away from loose gravel and vehicles and you'll be right.
- Walking – it's that clever thing we learnt to do when we first jumped out of trees. It's gone greatly out of fashion but, like all fashions, it's swinging around to being the next best thing. (Unlike swinging in trees, which never really came back.) As it is less energy-efficient than cycling, you burn more energy and lose more weight. You also see things, like birds. It is more fuel-efficient than driving a car. After you've huffed your way around for a week or two, you get to remember that the gluteus maximus is a muscle, not handy extra padding for sitting on hard chairs.

18 June

We turn on the hot-water booster — again. I brood. The electricity bill arrived this week. It's the highest ever by a long shot. There are a number of factors involved. At this point we're producing on average around half a kWh a day less than normal. This is the result of a long period of sullenly overcast weather and it adds up quickly. We've also used more than average — solar hot-water boosting has taken its toll. A higher percentage of time spent cooking adds to the dilemma. Everything from making mayonnaise, to baking bread, to heating 10 litres of milk to 70 degrees is all very energy intensive. It's a part of our consumer power use that we don't see when we buy bread and other pre-made and processed products. We also use our household power to fuel our primary source of transport, the electric bike. Not considerable amounts, but they all add up. We do use compact fluorescent bulbs instead of the standard, energy-hungry incandescent bulbs, but we also use an electric water pump, depending on the amount of watering in the garden, and this uses anywhere from 250 to 500 watts a day. This quarter has cost us $27 in excess power. We use 28 cents a day to power the house, while the average household is more in the vicinity of $2–3. Still, it's 28 cents away from the nothing we had set ourselves.

THE BODY ELECTRIC

If we convert calorific energy into electrical energy it would take 4200 calories or 17.5 kWh to power an active man, 2846 calories or 11.9 kWh to power an active woman and 1700 calories or 7.1 kWh for a six-year-old child per day.

The energy I consume per day is enough to power the average airconditioner for two hours. Trev could run our house for three days. (This is more a reflection on the amount of power it takes to run our household than the amount Trev eats.)

LET THERE BE ENERGY-EFFICIENT LIGHT

Annual difference in power use between incandescent and compact fluoro (energy-efficient) bulbs

Incandescent bulbs

Room	No. of bulbs	Watts	Annual cost to run	kg of CO_2
Kitchen	2	100	$35.04	292
Living room	2	75	$26.28	219
Bedroom 1	1	75	$13.14	110
Bedroom 1	2	75	$26.28	219
Outside light	1	100	$17.52	146
Passage	1	100	$17.52	146
Total	**9**	**525**	**$135.78**	**1132**

Compact fluoro bulbs

Room	No. of bulbs	Watts	Annual cost to run	kg of CO_2
Kitchen	2	25	$8.76	73
Living room	2	18	$6.31	53
Bedroom 1	1	18	$3.15	26
Bedroom 2	2	18	$6.31	53
Outside light	1	25	$4.38	37
Passage	1	25	$4.38	37
Total	**9**	**129**	**$33.29**	**277**

These figures are based on an estimated 4 hours of use per day and a tariff of 12 cents per kWh.

Based on this, lighting your house with compact energy-efficient fluorescent bulbs will require only a fifth of the power needed for incandescent bulbs. This will give you an estimated saving each year of around $100. The cost of replacing nine standard bulbs with compact fluorescent bulbs is approx $100 – they will pay for themselves in a year. Because they last around 8000 hours (at this level of use, they will last around 5.5 years), the savings when compared with incandescent bulbs are significant. And not just financially – replacing just one incandescent bulb with an energy-efficient bulb will reduce greenhouse gas emissions by over half a tonne in the bulb's lifetime. (And think of the reduction in landfill waste too.)

Here are some ways to use your lights more efficiently:

- Use bedside or desk lamps where appropriate rather than lighting the whole room.
- Use motion detectors for outside lights.
- Select the lowest wattage bulb required to light a room.
- Try not to have more than one bulb connected to the same switch.
- Wherever possible, paint rooms in light colours, as this reflects rather than absorbs light.
- Turn lights off when not in use.

I make potato, onion, leek, garlic, parsley and carrot soup. Caleb eats it, but will not have a bar of the pan scone. Admittedly there is no butter, but still they're good for dipping. At lunch he'd voluntarily eaten a salad with fetta cheese, making small lettuce parcels with an array of salad items tucked inside and guzzling them. I'm impressed. If it weren't for yesterday's parade of the pegged nose to dramatise his violent dislike of the smell of cooking pikelets, I'd say he was almost normal. It's only been the last couple of years that he has managed to eat homemade chicken nuggets without regurgitating them. Last night he ate five mandarins and an apple to get out of vegetable fritters, steamed beans and potatoes.

The telly goes pop. The kind of pop that is the television equivalent of a death rattle. It remains silent. No small indicator light to show life. Trev and Caleb's mouths drop, and they race to prod its buttons in an erratic battle to restart its cathode-ray heart. But it has gone (again). There will be no resurrections.

Excellent.

Caleb worried me yesterday. We were sitting out in the sun reading when he leaned over and stared pointedly at my prickly legs.

'You too can have beautiful legs with the (insert brand name). No hot wax, no pain, the (brand name) removes the hair, the follicle, it never grows back again!'

I stare at him disconcertedly for several moments.

'Caleb, I don't think you're reading enough books.'

He laughs. I know jingoistic has another meaning, but I wonder what it is you call a language or form of communication that's mostly derived from television commercials.

> *Rich societies such as Australia seem to be in the grip of a*
> *collective psychological disorder. We react with alarm and*
> *sympathy when we come across an anorexic who is convinced*
> *she is fat, whose view of reality is so obviously distorted. Yet,*
> *as a society surrounded by affluence, we indulge in the illusion*
> *that we are deprived. Despite the obvious failure of the continued*
> *accumulation of material things to make us happy, we appear*
> *unable to change our behaviour. We have grown fat but we*
> *persist in the belief that we are thin and must consume more.*
> CLIVE HAMILTON AND RICHARD DENNISS[6]

The rain has not abated; this is an unusual winter weather pattern. It should be dry; it is wet. Summer was dry; it should have been wet. The weather is going temperate on us. We're trapped inside the house all day with Caleb. Trev helps him make origami snakes and sharks. I read him Gary Larson's book *There's a hair in my dirt! A worm's story.* I bake cinnamon scrolls, six loaves of bread, a big bucket of Anzac bikkies. We eat fresh hot bread with melted butter, a special treat; we drink hot cups of tea. As another treat we've bought Caleb a jar of Vegemite. Trev and I vow not to eat his concessions. But by lunchtime Trev has come up with an original twist.

'How about, seeing as this jar of Vegemite will last beyond the end of the experiment, that I eat the stuff that will be left over now?'

He doesn't.

We play endless games of Uno and chess, have luxuriously hot showers and cuddle up in bed. Every now and then someone will wander into the 'green room' and flick the switch on the TV — just in case. While the computer was a 'must fix and replace' item, the TV is not. I catch Caleb standing in front of the blank screen. I stand behind him and tease, 'I think I can hear something, Caleb'.

'What?'

'It's the sound that only a TV that is switched off can make. The sound of your own brain working.'

Don't you just hate mothers?

20 June

The third day without a TV dawns, raining still, with 30 millimetres in the gauge, and gathering more. There is nowhere to go, nowhere to hide. We bring Possum up under the house and milk her. Poor thing. She dodges raindrops the whole way back down, while tearing at passing vegetation. She stands dolefully at her shelter door staring up at us. I've decided to make her hessian curtains for her door to help keep out cold drafts. I tell Trev, who, as usual, wants to do more than is strictly necessary, so he's going to hem them for her. The curtains have now passed their murky way from being one of my jobs to one of his. I will make concessions to Possum's comfort, but hemming hessian curtains for a goat is not my idea of best use of time. I go lie down with a book.

I limit myself to a chapter, and then it's time to clean up the rest of the house and assist Caleb in turning his room into the most elaborate cubbyhouse ever. Blankets are suspended in unlikely places — there is not an inch of unblanketed floor. I leave cubbyhouse food at the door and retreat. Bradley arrives and they disappear into the room and, apart from the sound of muffled voices, are lost. I rouse myself to go down to the garden and do an egg gather. The chooks, defying logic, have renounced their dry sheltered laying box for a shallow rain-filled depression in the ground halfway up a very steep and slippery hill. When I get back I discover the two boys have also renounced their former bedroom position and have laid claim to ours. They are summarily dismissed to the outside verandah. I'm still not out of Trev's dressing gown and, after putting the eggs away, sit down and promise myself another chapter.

Trev and I have a yak.

'How about we have an all-species version of *Big Brother*? You know, they all live together in a kind of merging ecosystem in which they stay in their respective niches, but within sight of each other?'

'Hmm, yes, and by the end of the week the human has tried to kill a sheep and eat it, he's emptied half the pond to pump up to his shower and to flush his toilet, his septic tank has leaked and polluted the groundwater, he's chopped down a tree that shaded his house and has staked out a driveway that will destroy the habitat of four other species.'

'Yep, and the flora and fauna are more than just a little pissed off.'

'I can see it now ...'

What does a great impression of fish eggs, crustaceans and jellyfish, and enjoys great popularity among our marine and bird life? Plastic. A naturalist on Lord Howe Island, Ian Hutton, has been looking at the plastic found in shearwater carcasses on the island; he discovered that the dead birds must have found the non-food items popular too, with plastic that could be spread across an area of 66–182 square centimetres found inside their stomachs. The assortment included pen tops, bag ties, lids, golf tees and strapping tape, but predominantly shredded pieces of plastic. Dr David Priddel, from the Department of Environment, puts the number of plastic items found on the sea floor as high as 4000 pieces per square kilometre. [7]

22 June

The news headline is 'Men urged to drop breadwinner role'.

'That'd be right', I quip, 'another deli choice, the breadwinner roll'.

'It's got bacon on it', Trev grins.

'Ahh, bring home the bacon — very good. Families are being "sandwiched" between traditional roles, with women resenting unpaid work status and men resenting being absent from their children.'

Beyond the joke this has been a hot topic of late. Trev is better at organising his day around the house, constructing labour-saving devices from odd bits and pieces and then using them, than I am. Hemming goat curtains is only the start of it. I do what I have to around here, and a little bit more.

Me, I'm happy to preserve the status quo. I spend a lot of time discussing virtues of various actions on the computer, while not spending a great deal of time instigating them. I did take on the whole home school thing and that has slowed me down. I don't like leaving Caleb completely to his own devices once school is finished and tend to drag it on in the afternoon with experiments like inflating marshmallows by sealing them in a glass jar and sucking out the air inside, creating a vacuum that expands the marshmallow. It was a great way to justify buying a cheap bag of marshmallows and putting it under educational expenses. I have days I spend in the garden and, once the rhythm is established, I'll stay there all day. But if Caleb is around, I'm always worried he's fallen off the trampoline and broken his neck or has been abducted while doing a straddle-jump seat drop. Trev suffers no such concerns. He's happy to park himself in his workshop for the day, coming out only to make lunch. While I don't think I've ever seen him wash windows or clean floors, he does the dishes, is a great cook, makes beds, shares the washing duties and is about the only one around here who cleans the toilet. We have preset jobs and we share things out agreeably. Trev prides himself on his non-sexist approach to cleaning the toilet – better than my sexist version, which states itself in the bold terms of, 'You blokes make all the mess in the first place, so why don't you clean it up?' But generally we share everything around here, even the credit – in Trev's case, his card.

Trev is at the advanced age of 47; I'll be 37 in a few months time. I'm an end-of-summer chicken, Trev is autumnal. I think it's time we looked at reversing our roles and giving Trev the chance to live the laidback life. If he stopped work, he wouldn't have to shift several tonnes of dirt, place it in buckets, weigh them, then put them back in the same place – all in the hot sun. I often point out that being sentenced to 30 years hard labour would come more easily and with a few more concessions to comfort than Trev's job as a technical support officer with the Department of Primary Industries – Forestry. Trev has come home and had leeches drop out of his boots and crawl across the floor; he's arrived completely covered in mosquito bites, even inside his nose; he's been up north swimming in pools of water possibly frequented by crocs. Of course he will tell you it's not that hard, because he is by nature the uncomplaining sort. So perhaps I am left to the inglorious deed of work, and also to repeated assertions that it's his turn to do the morning dishes, educate our son and pull the weeds. But Trev worries about the difficulties of being re-employed. So it looks like the stage is set: Trev will end his days halfway up a steep hillside with a 50-kilo pack on his back, a snake wrapped around one leg and swinging from a bird-eating spider's web. Cause of death: dehydration. Around about then I'll be sitting on the verandah, reading a book and contemplating which plants will provide dinner.

Another cold, overcast day. It's getting to the stage where I can flick on the solar hot-water booster without looking, so much practice have I had at pinpointing its position.

28 June

Trevor has two more non-sleeps to go, a bad bout of insomnia due to over-excitement. It's like Christmas in July. It's rainy — on goes the booster. We have more rain predicted, even the heavy sort. A winter flood? It's very inconvenient: we're getting the rain we could have had earlier, and now don't want or need. The sun we could have done without, we now want and need. Trev shovelled out the goat pen yesterday in an effort to keep the muck levels down. He also removed two tree stumps, and together we lifted an old garden bed edging from its place down in the bottom of the garden and placed it up higher. Trev filled it with wheelbarrows of goat pen muck and liberally limed it. I gave my eyeballs blisters staring at the computer screen, and my fingertips were mushy from repeatedly hitting small black and white squares. Since he's been home, I've abandoned the garden to his devices. He wants nice straight rows, none of that permaculturally messy stuff I do — or, rather, don't do. However, we're harvesting lots of wild food at the moment: lettuces are particularly prolific, and I noticed a new bed of pak choi starting up between my broccoli. Give Trev a year or two of fighting against nature rather than letting it do the work, and he might change his predilection for straight paths through tamed beds to one for a thoroughfare of weeds and impregnable barriers of self-seeded tomatoes.

30 June

The Last Day. We awake eager to eat. But not yet, we have one last torture in store. The excitement level is palpable as Caleb poses in front of the calendar as he crosses off the 181st day. Heartfelt sighs all round. We skip breakfast and drive our fasting stomachs to the doctor's. Caleb has only one repeated thing to say: 'When can I start spending my $200?'

'Soon, Caleb, soon. First the doctor, then blood tests, drop the TV off for repair, drop the car off for a service, we'll walk into town and then you can start.'

We troop into the surgery and have our blood pressure taken. Mine is 110/75, the lowest it's been since before I had Caleb. Trev's is high: 140/90. He's annoyed.

'White coat', he says pointing at the beige-coloured top our doctor is wearing.

She's impressed with our weight loss. We smile smugly at each other. Then it's on to another waiting room. This time for blood tests. The blood is red; it is not pale pink. I'm interested to see our iron levels. It's about the only possible negative thing about our diet.

With blood removed we leave. It's already 11 o'clock. We're walking into town after dropping off the car and I'm already wishing I was wearing my grungy shoes instead of heels (short as they are). Caleb has stripped off his jumper only to discover he never did put on a t-shirt first.

We lose Trev at the first pub.

'Just one?' he wheedles, jumping from one foot to the other like an excited child. I, and the underdressed child, continue on alone. We make it to Toyworld where we peruse the Lego stand. It's agonising, and I'm not just talking about the acid removal of my stomach lining. Trev catches up, and we leave towing two new Bionicles and a half-naked child with a bounce in his step. We stop off at a clothing store and buy Caleb a new t-shirt. Hey, magic! Shoes to replace the frayed and sopping wet ones he left out by the trampoline two days ago. Then it's food: a steak sandwich for Trev, a chicken wrap for Caleb and me, upsized with the biggest piece of caramel slice known to man, and we make a valiant attempt to down it all with mugs of coffee. But how disappointing. It looks great, but we have storage capacity problems, and end up leaving half of it behind. I hate waste, but here we are, wasting already. It's new guitar strings for Trev, a pair of pants that fit for me (size 10, just a tad too big). I've forgotten my pin number, it's been so long since I last used it. We buy books, three of which are for Caleb's birthday and one for me by a favourite author. Trev buys tobacco and a neat wee portable ashtray for when he's out bush. We buy groceries — $250 worth. It seems stunning to think it equates to almost three months' worth of food, and yet we expect to eat it within a week, bar the marinated octopus that Caleb and I won't be touching and the items that have a 100 per cent inedibility factor, such as two new pillows to replace the hanky thickness of the previous two. Trev cajoles Caleb to try the octopus, describing them as 'nice rubber in vinegar'. Caleb is not convinced. There is packaging galore. No matter how hard you try, it's impossible to avoid it altogether. We're in a queue again. We discuss how little we like standing in queues. We look around and add that it feels somehow soulless to be here.

There is something vapid about the lighting, something draining about the endless rows of products. We've also discovered that things have changed since we last went shopping. The number of useless products designed to do things like dispense paperclips has increased and they now sell Elmo socks in men's sizes. It's also expensive, and somehow it isn't as tempting as I thought. I put the Lindor chocolates back on the shelf. I don't really need them. I forget the gourmet ice-cream, but it's not a bother.

We go out to dinner. It costs the same amount as we have gained from bartering in the last three weeks. It's very nice. But somehow it's not quite enough to counteract the cost. I have become frugally minded. This is not something I have ever been accused of. But Trev agrees.

'Let's just make it a week of spending money, not a month. I don't think we need a month.'

He crams the last of his reef and beef in his mouth while I nod sagely. It's too much, somehow, an exaggeration of wealth that is unnecessary. We won't go back to being as stringent as we were. But, and I hope this will remain true, I can't see us going back to squandering money and resources. The rewards are not enough compensation — it sits ill.

We all sit ill. We get home and Trev and Caleb start the great packet-opening ceremony. We all say 'Cheers!' as we toast with packets of M&M's, beer and Skittles. Packets of gourmet chips crinkle. The rubbish bin will need to be brought back inside at this rate. We groan. Caleb is up three times in the night threatening imminent regurgitation and a sore stomach. Trev is complaining of a sore stomach too, and I am burping up a chemical taste. Perhaps even a week will be too long.

1 July

'Well,' says Caleb from the floor where he is assembling his new Lego set, 'that's it then. We don't have to care about the environment anymore'.

Trev and I pause, mostly to swallow whatever high-fat, high-sugar, high-meat mouthful we are currently cramming in, to shake him out of that idea. He doesn't seem stricken by the thought of returning to a state of energy frugality.

We've promised him he can take Bradley to some environmentally unsound takeaway tonight, followed by a cinema visit and a sleep over. We're feeling magnanimous. Anything Caleb asks for, we comply with. At least for this week.

We're aware that this has been a long journey for him. He needs rewards, if only to circumvent the likelihood that he will grow up rampant in his consumerism. He runs down to his friend's house loaded with lollies, keen to share his sudden wealth in artificial colours and preservatives.

2 July

We're clutching our stomachs and groaning as the walls are grotesquely stretched from what amounts to only modest quantities of food. We are clutching at our grotesquely shrinking wallets too.

But with all this indulgence even Caleb has mentioned that the anticipation has not been matched by equal amounts of gratification. It has been nice, but already it's starting to pall. Caleb asked us this morning, 'So, what about our adventure?'

'Well, our adventure is over now.'

'Are we going to have any new adventures?'

'What kind of adventures do you have in mind?'

'Shopping adventures.'

We explain that we will go for a drive down the coast next week and have a final consumer splash, but that we've decided a month of this will kill us and that next Tuesday will see us wading back into frugal waters.

Back on our bikes we will be.

We've started the process of collating figures and finding out just how much power, water, petrol, food and disposable income we've used over the six months. It's too early to start spouting firm numbers, but it wouldn't be too far off to say it's around 5 per cent of average household use on all counts. We had been aiming for zero but have had to come to terms with worse than average climatic conditions and the decision not to eat grass. One of our conditions was to be able to say it was an agreeable lifestyle.

Trev's rave

Well, that's that, then. And not a moment too soon. As I sit here, surrounded by empty pizza boxes, beer cans, and cigar butts, it's probably time to reflect on what we achieved, and why. But I can't be bothered, so I'll confine myself to telling you how good that first beer, that first visit to the Colonel was. If I could.

The much-looked-forward-to, much-vaunted blow-out was, as we'd predicted to each other many times, an anticlimax. Don't get me wrong – it was good, but it wasn't a transcendent, orgasmic, Homer Simpson drool moment.

This is because there was nothing to transcend. During our six-month adventure, we lacked nothing. Virtually any physical or spiritual comfort was available (well, we couldn't go on a pilgrimage to Lourdes, but you know what I mean). The food was excellent: low fat, chemical free, tasty and nutritious. We had an unlimited supply of entertainment in the form of books, videos and DVDs from the library. We could visit friends. We had access to the world via the Internet.

Still I chafed. I asked myself why on many occasions. I made all sorts of excuses and rationalisations: 'It's the awareness of the restriction; a gilded cage is still a cage', I'd say. This certainly had something to do with it, but I think it's more that. I've become used to jumping in the car and heading off for some diversion or some retail therapy every time I get the slightest bit bored or restless; my attention span has gone the way of that of the rest of the TV generations', along with the concepts of rectitude and self-discipline.

And now I sound like an old Presbyterian minister, thundering from the pulpit, but this combination of a natural human urge to flout a ban and a lifetime of easy indulgence is all I can come up with to explain why I found it so irksome to restrict myself to a lifestyle that was still about a hundred times more opulent than that of most of the world.

However, there is a real sense of achievement in having done what we said we would (95 per cent of it, anyway). After what seems like years of talking about it and planning (although it was only a couple of years), it was good to get the thing on the road. And it wasn't that hard – more about patience than hard work, although there were times when we felt more like Sisyphus than Job, especially when weeds grow as fast as you pull them out. Linda's eventual weed solution was to say, 'Weeds are feed; the permaculture theory is to let it all grow wild and harvest the edible stuff for us and feed the rest to the goat'. This sounds like an excuse to be lazy to me, but I wasn't going to argue if it let me out of weeding (or, at least, feeling guilty about leaving most of it to Linda).

Family bike rides, losing weight, lowering cholesterol, being able to eat a meal and realise that not only had we produced the food but also the power required to cook it, feeling fitter, achieving something together as a family – none of these things made up for the desperate craving for some KFC chips that I felt every day. Sorry, I couldn't resist that. These things, coupled with a desire to investigate the ways in which suburban living can be made environmentally sustainable, are exactly what it was all about.

And the KFC chips? Every day, on my way to and from work, I ride the bike past the Colonel's estimable emporium. Every day, during our adventure, I would smell the delicious smell of hot chips — pumped out of the store in great fragrant wafts, I was convinced, just to tempt me. Every day I swore that when we had finished, I would take the first opportunity to stop on my way home and grab a hot bucket. We've been finished for quite a while now, and I've ridden past a number of times without being the least bit tempted. I'm hoping this means I'm not a lazy, self-indulgent bastard, and just that I like to flout a ban more than most.

5 July

We've been lying around, being lazy, reading books and eating for the last few days. We break out for brief forays into the consumer world to hunt and gather gourmet foods before retreating. But today we have stirred ourselves for our big trip. It's an hour and a half to the shopping plaza. I watch the needle on the fuel gauge do a slow-motion dive. Somewhere in the next few days we'll be able to say we used the same amount of petrol in six months as we had in one week. I can grimace all I like, and it doesn't matter if I feel bad about it or not, the greenhouse gas effect is the same. This, however, is to be a rarely repeated trip and by the time we play cat and mouse in the car park for 10 minutes before we finally pounce on a vacant 4 by 3 metre spot, I'm ready to go home.

SNAPSHOT OF A HARD-DRIVING NATION

In March 2004 there were 10.3 million registered passenger vehicles in Australia, up from 8.3 million in 1993.

There are more of us driving.

- Every year Australian's drive the equivalent of 235,000 round-trips to the moon. That's over 180 billion kilometres.
- In 1947 the average person drove 1200 kilometres a year.
- In 1998 passenger vehicles travelled an average of 13,400 kilometres a year.
- By 2002 that had risen to 14,200 kilometres. By 2004, 15,400 kilometres.

We're driving further.

- Since 1950 our fuel consumption has increased 4.7 times.
- In the last 20 years our fuel efficiency based on per unit of weight (GVM tonnes) has decreased 1.3 per cent each year. Despite having more efficient engines, the extra weight of our vehicles has increased our fuel usage.

We're using more fuel.

- This is mostly due to larger engine size, and a sharp increase in the use of four-wheel drives as passenger vehicles. In 1979 only 3 per cent of new vehicle sales were four-wheel drives; this figure rose close to 20 per cent in September 2004.

And we're getting bigger.

Fuel facts: A fuel-efficient car can travel 8.5 kilometres on 1 litre of petrol at 50 kilometres per hour. Around 26 tonnes of prehistoric plant material created that 1 litre of petrol. Each litre of petrol produces 2.24 kilos of CO_2 when used, and pollutes 10,500 litres of fresh air. Each year we use the equivalent value of 400 times all the plant matter that grows in the world.

We walk in and begin the dodge and weave associated with commuting with large numbers of strangers, all of us owning metres of personal space we don't want invaded. We hit the toilets; there is a long queue. I resent the queue, and then recognise that this is not a new feeling, I have always resented the queue. I flush.

Trev and Caleb sit down for a drink, but I have no time to replace fluids — there is a bookshop in close proximity, I can smell it. I careen into remarkably few people on my way to find it.

I rediscover that shopping centres are full of beautiful things. I want all the beautiful things. Everywhere there are enticing sales banners. I am enticed by them all. Caleb discovers all the Bionicles he can buy, and buys them all. Trev takes the full green bags back to the car and returns with them empty. We fill them a second time, and then discover an abandoned shopping trolley and start on that. First item is a bored child. He's spent his money and is looking forward to the seal-breaking moments of joy. We find more things than we have need for, but somehow we find reasons to own ponchos, dangly earrings galore, shirts, shoes, Caleb's birthday presents, gadgets and a table runner for a table I don't even own. It's an exhausting business. We conclude it well before closing time. We wander, foot-sore, back to the car where we cram ourselves and our new belongings in. We are more than replete, we are intoxicated with consumerism, engorged with goods. We drive home feeling slightly sickened by our splurge.

7 July

We buy a table to put under the table runner. Hey, it makes perfect sense. It's beautiful. We check out its environmental credentials. Plantation timber? Yes. Locally made? No. Grimaces all round. More of that anxiety-producing guilt that has no environmental impact reduction and ultimately does not alter our decision to buy it anyway.

'Can you deliver?' Trev asks. 'Today?'

The instant gratification disease has us in its grip. There is more than one reason for its purchase:

a) we don't have one,

b) it's absolutely beautiful,

c) it suits our home,

d) my computer might be called a laptop, but really it would be better as a tabletop otherwise I risk having a hunchback in several years' time. But it's

e) that has us convinced. We must find a way to get Caleb to sit still long enough to eat a meal. As it is he tends to wander off and get distracted while the ants do advanced army manoeuvres on the contents of his plate. Now we will sit together and stay together till all of us are finished eating.

One good thing about a wooden table is that we are locking up potential greenhouse gas emissions as we keep the wood preserved and stop it breaking down and releasing its CO_2 during the decomposition process. We could be choosing to see the best out of the situation, as buying a locally made table would have done the same and reduced the need to transport it so far. It's all about reducing embodied energy as the majority of it is sourced from fossil fuels.

EMBODIED ENERGY

Every product we purchase has a level of embodied energy beyond that of its physical self. For example, a medium-sized apple has around 80 calories. Yet there are estimates that for every one calorie of food in Australia it takes another nine calories of energy to produce it. The extra nine calories were consumed during the processes that occurred while the apple grew, such as spraying, weeding, watering, harvesting, storing, packing and transportation to the supermarket. The apple may also have a portion of energy allocated from the creation of the machinery that was used to implement these processes, such as the spray equipment and the refrigerated truck. The apple could have an embodied energy of 720 calories by the time it arrives in the family fridge.

Everything we own inside our house has an embodied energy, not just the food on the plate, but the plate itself, the bottle of detergent we use to wash the plate, the tea-towel and the dishwasher (which has a far higher embodied energy than a tea-towel). Incorporated into the price of any product is the cost of the energy it took to manufacture it; we take not just the product, but partial responsibility for that energy use. Most of that energy will be derived from fossil-based fuels, such as oil and coal.

World energy use by country[8]

	ENERGY USED (Kg OIL/PERSON/YEAR)
Australia	5543
Developed world	4505
Developing world	803

One of the biggest things we will ever own is a house. CSIRO research estimates that the average home uses around 1000 gigajoules of energy in its production (one gigajoule is a million kilojoules – around 3000 million apples), which is a considerable amount of energy and monetary expenditure (price of apples not included).

There are some materials that are intrinsically higher in embodied energy, making a house more energy-intensive to build. Fired clay bricks use around 2.5 megajoules/kilogram compared with kiln-dried sawn hardwood at 2 megajoules/kilogram. A kilo of timber is also likely to 'cover' a larger area than a kilo of brick, requiring less overall. Brick homes also require higher levels of internal cooling during summer than timber homes and therefore may have greater ongoing energy demands in hotter climes.

The transportation of the materials to the building site and the longevity of the structure must also be taken into account.

Concrete has a low embodied energy compared with timber. However, it may end up hogging most of the embodied energy invested in a building simply due to the larger amounts used compared with that of timber. It's not necessary to have a precise reckoning; in most cases a fair assumption can be made on energy requirements of different building materials (see Appendix 4, page 269).

Recycling materials can reduce the overall embodied energy of a home or structure by up to 95 per cent. LCA (life-cycle analysis) takes into account the recyclablity of a given material, because a portion of the original energy expenditure can be reclaimed through the recycling process. Some materials can be recycled more efficiently – for example, aluminium sits pretty on 95 per cent, while glass shatters at 20 per cent, and the damages in bricks and tiles drop them to just 30 per cent.

Some household structures may increase the initial embodied energy of the home, such as pelmets above windows, but they reduce the amount of heat loss through windows and therefore also the heating requirements over a period of time in which they negate the extra energy use. The same applies to wall and ceiling insulation and verandahs.

Trev presented me with a bouquet today, of broccoli flowers. I've really missed broccoli and he knows I wouldn't thank him for a bunch of flowers cut off in their prime to slowly die on my kitchen table. Something that fruits and has roots is much better but if not that, a box of chocolates will always be welcome.

During the day I drop by for our medical test results. I am blown away. If these were end-of-year exam results, we've just topped the ranks. Our iron levels are phenomenal. I have been worried that they would be the thing people would be bound to ask at parties: 'So, after six nearly meatless months, how were your iron levels?'

Now I won't have to say they were cataclysmically low, though they were close to that at the start of our experiment. Trev scored a 13, I scored an 11, with 10 being the lowest cut-off point and 30 the highest. Now, six months later, we score a more respectable and respective 23 and 19.

Higher by 76 per cent and 72 per cent. But how? We ate lots of eggs, beans and greenery, yet goat's milk is lower in iron than cow's, and we drank tea and the occasional coffee, both good at reducing the absorption of iron when accompanying a meal, which they generally did. It just doesn't make sense. It flies in the face of what we know of dietary iron.

9 July

The scales make a small groaning noise when we stand on them. I make a high ear-piercing shriek to accompany it. Trev has just gone through the same painful process. Already we are putting on weight. It's Saturday, traditionally library day via way of bikes. We are on them soon after. I take the yellow bike, the one with a conspicuous lack of motor. I pop my credit card in my jeans pocket. You never know when it will come in handy. It's got to be one bonus, in that it's always easy to make your bank account lighter.

Is it some sign from the universe that fate plucked the card from my pocket and littered with it? We were down the main street, I was contemplating a large slice of cheesecake (there are still a few luxury items I'd promised myself and have yet to partake of), when I noticed the card was no longer in my pocket. We retraced our steps but, alas, it was gone. I biked home on the wrong side of the road keeping an eye out for it. Once home, I rang up and cancelled it. The moment I put the receiver down it rang again. It was the police saying it had been handed in. Too late. It will be another week or so before it is replaced. A good sign to stop spending now and get back into our dollarless habit.

Many wealthy people grow tired of being defined by their wealth and convince themselves they could do perfectly well without it. And most of us, at times, fantasise about living a simpler life, unencumbered by 'stuff'. Until we test ourselves, though, these are just comforting stories. This is why the emerging group of downshifters — people who have voluntarily reduced their income — is so important. Each downshifter has, so to speak, put their money where their mouth is.
CLIVE HAMILTON AND RICHARD DENNISS[9]

There is this strange thing happening. The contents of the fridge and pantry have become a mystery to me. Even though they are full they never seem to have the right things in them.

Secondly, I find myself increasing the embodied energy of loaves of bread by hopping in the car to go to buy one. And Caleb was caught out using three-quarters of a roll of loo paper for one bottom wipe. This trend has now been identified, isolated and cryogenically frozen (Caleb's bottom not included).

We have a story-telling tradition, provoked mostly by Caleb's requests of, 'Tell me a story about when I was little'.

Last week I told him about one morning three or so years ago when he was snuggling up to me for his morning cuddle and he'd said, 'Mum, your face is very ugly'.

I'd smiled at him, 'That's very kind of you to tell me'.

Puzzled he'd asked, 'No, it's not, why would you say that?'

'It's called sarcasm, Caleb. I don't really think it's kind of you to tell me I'm ugly.'

'Oh.'

At least 20 times during the day he'd spotted it.

'Ah, that was "sartasm", wasn't it?'

'Um', recalling what I'd just said, 'well, yes it was'.

I'd taught him what sarcasm is, and he'd taught me how much I use it. One of those examples of reciprocal education that always foils me. Like how I've taught him the art of cheese-making and he's taught me that hard, yellow, plastic-covered cheeses that melt are far superior to soft, white, possibly even goaty-flavoured ones, some of which, excuse me, are covered in thin white layers of mould.

Which sums up our adventure in domestic sustainability — it started out as a personal quest and ended with us wanting to change the world. While we succeeded in experimenting with a different lifestyle, we learnt more about our limits, boundaries and ourselves then anything else.

This morning I pulled the six red calendar pages off the fridge with a sense of finality. I had to laugh when their removal revealed 181 permanent black marker crosses that had bled through the paper and onto the fridge. Analogy? While the pages are gone, the mark of those days is still upon us. There are some things you can't come back from.

We will never be as stringent in our moneylessness as we were, but nor will we go back to our profligate practices, either monetarily or environmentally. The rest of our lives are here, and we're keen to keep on finding interesting things to do in them.

But, the six months are over.

Epilogue

A month later and we've discovered that life without an adventure is unfulfilling, so we've filled the vacuum with a new one. Sell up, move to Tasmania (where the likelihood of dying of hypothermia far outweighs that of heatstroke), buy a suburban block and attempt to build one of Australia's lowest embodied-energy homes — a strawbale house. I'm even threatening to write a book about it.

the results

Our power report

We reduced our coal-produced household power use by 92%.

While a summertime deficit in our power production is typical, we usually make up for it over winter. Not this winter. While we did have cooler temperatures, we also had months on end where we barely saw the sun. This resulted in low power creation and higher use, as we had to use the solar hot-water booster every second day or so to maintain a comfortable water temperature. The comparison between the six-month experiment and previous years can be seen in the table below.

We also required more power over the period to cook, prepare and preserve food than we would normally use. Baking day happened once a fortnight, but would use between 4 and 5 kWh of power — power we would normally outsource in products such as loaves of bread.

We also used the electric bike. While it did not draw a lot of power (typically around 150 watts five times a week), it added up to an estimate of 15–20 kWh over the six months. So while we used household power for household appliances, it also doubled as a major provider of transport-related 'fuel'.

The average Australian household power use over a six-month period would be 4000 kWh. We use between 920 and 1100 kWh over the same period, less than or equal to 25% of normal usage. We are able to use solar power to cover the usage, or in the worse scenario (our six-month adventure) we create 92%, leaving an 8% gap, which is filled by coal-produced power.

Our average power use/production (kWh)

PERIOD	AVERAGE WEEKLY USE	AVERAGE WEEKLY PRODUCTION	TOTAL USE	TOTAL PRODUCTION	AHEAD (+)/ BEHIND (−)
July–Dec 2003	35.3	36.1	918.0	939.5	+21.5
Jan–Jun 2004	38.3	35.1	996.0	912.5	−83.5
Jul–Dec 2004	35.7	36.1	927.0	938.0	+7
Jan–Jun 2005	48.0	33.7	1103.0	776.0	−327

Over the 2004/2005 year, we used a total of 320 kWh of mains power. This is 4% of normal Australian coal-produced power usage over a year (8000 kWh).

THE COMFORT ZONE

Q: Linda, did you have to do without the convenience of labour-saving appliances? Did it mean doing things by hand, and taking longer?

A: I guess in some cases that would be true. The only thing that comes to mind is using the chaffcutter instead of a mulcher. But while it was physically harder (but not much), it was quieter, and quite an enjoyable job to do.

I never thought I would see the day that I'd voluntarily give up the vacuum cleaner. I used to think a three-times-a-day habit was OK (which might be more of a reflection on living with a small child than being a cleanliness freak). However, when we were trying to reduce our power consumption it became obvious that it was one habit I'd need to break. We bought a wide woolly mop-broom thing and, as we have wooden floors, use it around the entire house. The unexpected bonuses weren't long in coming or in being recognised. No heavy thing to lug around, no horrible cords to tug around, no plugs to plug in, no noise to mug our ears. We were able to converse while sweeping the floor. Everything was swept into a corner and then a dustpan and brush used. Level of inconvenience – zero.

Apart from that there isn't really anything that we do without; we use a TV, video, stereo, two laptops, pie makers, toasters, sandwich presses, microwave and oven. Trev even uses a welder. We might be careful about our oven usage, but it's not something that has a serious impact on convenience or diet.

Once the experiment ended, nothing really changed; we didn't pull out any electrical gear that we'd stored for the six months. On balance I'd say that nothing took any longer to do by being power frugal – if anything it makes life a little quieter.

Having a grid-connected solar system means we are effectively using mains power, while exporting power the panels create into the grid system. There is very little maintenance required apart from periodic cleaning of the panels and I do a one-minute monitoring of power use and creation each week. No special appliances or conversions are required, apart from choosing energy-efficient appliances when purchasing fridges and so on.

I think it's a pity we didn't have a good year – it would have been great to say we reduced our reliance on coal-produced power by 100%.

Q: OK Trev, is she full of it?

A: The short answer is no. The inconvenience lies not in what you use, but how carefully you use it. For us, being power frugal meant that you don't leave every light in the house on, even if they are power-saving bulbs. You turn the TV, video player and other appliances that use standby power off at the wall. If you fire up the oven, you make good use of the heat and do a week's worth of baking. I don't think having to flick a few more switches off or a bit of forward planning is inconvenient.

Our water report

Over the six months there was a total of 61,800 litres available through rooftop rainfall to harvest. Unfortunately, an estimated 5000–8000 litres overflowed when the tanks were full.

Our average rainwater use per day was 325 litres, which is 36% of the national average.

We also used town water during the long, hot, dry summer — a total of 10,350 litres, or 6% of the national average mains water use. Spread out over the 181 days it amounts to 57 litres of town water a day.

Taking into account both town-water and rainwater usage we used a total of 42% of the Australian norm. Of this, 6% was mains or town water.

I don't have the ability to calculate the amount of 'virtual water' we saved by growing the majority of our own fruit and vegetables using water-efficient methods. We would have used only a fraction of water compared with their store-bought competition. Nor can I calculate the amount of water we are responsible for with our bartered goods, such as the amount of flour, sugar, rice and so on, as the equations get messy when we also have to consider the amount of water we used to create the goods we bartered with, such as tomatoes, coriander and pumpkin. It would be true to say that our virtual water use during the six months was a fraction of the usual family's total.

It became obvious during the weeks we weren't watering that our daily household water use is around 200 litres (22% of Australian daily average). With our overall daily average of 325 litres, our garden water use is around 46% of that. The town-water usage was 100% garden.

We reduced our reliance on the mains water system by 94%.

Since 1870 the average rainfall totals in the Gympie area have looked like this:

RAINFALL AVERAGES FOR JAN–JUNE IN LAST 135 YEARS
COMPARED WITH 2005 RAINFALL

	Jan	Feb	Mar	Apr	May	June	Total
135-year average rainfall (mm)	163	168	145	85	73	59	693
2005 rainfall	115	28	21	84	73	122	443
Difference	−48	−140	−124	−1	0	+63	−250

We had two-thirds less rain overall than average; however, February and March had one-seventh of the average rainfall.

Another 250 millimetres of rainfall (to meet the average) would have topped up the tanks with 37,500 litres of water.

If we'd had the extra 250 millimetres in February and March, as we should have, that would be 545,000 litres of rain on the entire block, reducing our household water usage considerably through less garden watering. February and March are usually the peak growing months. The record low rainfall totals had a severe impact on our ability to produce food for ourselves and, especially, the animals.

THE COMFORT ZONE

Q: Come on, be honest, Linda, was it uncomfortable using less water, was it inconvenient, did you feel so water conscious that you felt water poor?

A: No. Now that we're off the experiment, the water usage remains the same. Not through any stringent regime, it's just normal. We have showers; we wash the dishes and clothes just the same. There is no sense of doing without at all. I often feel quite the opposite, that sometimes I'm squandering our water and could do better. I do things like leave the tap running and walk away for 20 seconds, or wash vegies under running water, that kind of thing. Reducing our total water use to less than half of the national average has not been difficult. When we're suffering from severe drought I'm quite capable of rationalising water usage in the garden so that some areas are left to struggle on without assistance. To expect to keep the whole place green in such conditions is unrealistic and unsustainable.

Q: What about you Trev? I don't quite trust Linda, she's always so annoyingly positive. Did you feel water poor?

A: No. I've spent most of my life using tank water in one way or another. As a child, my grandmother, at whose place I spent a lot of time, was on tanks, so water consciousness was a big part of my early education. Then, when I moved to Queensland in my early twenties, we also had only tank water. There's a big difference between using water and wasting it. We're not water poor, we're water smart.

Our transport report

The average Australian drives 15,400 kilometres a year, creating 5.4 tonnes of vehicle emissions (in a petrol-fuelled vehicle over 1.4-litre capacity). Given the experiment went for six months, we're looking at what proportion of the 7700 kilometres we drove, and the emissions we created.

Our first use of the car was in mid-February when we saw the local GP regarding Caleb's heart problem; the second was to Brisbane and back on a similar mission. All up, those two trips account for around 310 kilometres.

Over the remainder of the experiment we visited the doctor four more times, 45 kilometres in all.

When we were forced to buy animal food, we used the car (cycling with a 40-kilo bag on your back also looks a little silly). We estimate there were six such trips, at 11 kilometres each, so a total of 66 kilometres.

We had our lapses – the less said about those the better – equalling 30 kilometres.

It was raining hard one morning and I forced Trevor to drive to work rather than risk life and limb on the wet, slippery, low-visibility, heavily trafficked highway – 18 kilometres.

**We reduced our transport-related emissions by 94%.
We drove 469 kilometres in six months – 6% of average vehicle use* –
creating 156 kilograms of vehicle emissions, compared with 2.6 tonnes.**

* Without the trip to Brisbane we could have kept it to 2% of national average.

Bicycles

Trev's electric bike odometer is sitting on 2100 kilometres. But in the last two months he's opted for the mountain bike, as he has to work harder and finds it more rewarding, especially when standing on the bathroom scales. His mountain-bike travel accounts for another 230 kilometres. My old treadly would have done far less, around 550 kilometres in trips to and from school and some of our weekend jaunts. Most of our excess weight was shed while perched on top of a bike.

Approximately 2880 kilometres were cycled, which accounts for 37.4% of average vehicle travel over the same time period and saving 1.95 tonnes in vehicle emissions.

We reduced our transport usage to 43.4% of national average, 86% of which was on the back of a bike.

THE COMFORT ZONE

Q: Linda, I guess this is where I get to ask you whether it was difficult getting on your bike and sweating your way up hills and you get to say that you really enjoy getting red in the face and think you look groovy with helmet hair?

A: Ah, well, I'll try not to sound like we were having too much fun. I really didn't enjoy it much the day it rained, the bike seat was higher than Mount Everest and I managed to almost punch a hole through the base of my spine. But as for the rest of it, I did have initial concerns about safety. It had been a long time since I'd ridden a bike – I envisioned all sorts of gory accidents involving me doing far from graceful gymnastic manoeuvres and exiting over the handle bars, while Caleb was busy being pulverised under a passing truck. I guess it's like the first time you drive a car – 40 kilometres an hour seems like the speed of light and you find yourself breathing into a paper bag at busy intersections. It does pass.

Once it did, we gloried in the lurid shades of red we turned when pumping up a hill, and the joys of whizzing full-speed down hills with our week's groceries bouncing behind us. It's exhilarating. This strange thing happened to my thighs: the muscles tightened up and when I walked I felt like I could have two children hanging off either leg and still overtake speeding cars. I lost weight, which tapered off once I stopped riding Caleb to school.

The family thing: it was great and rated so highly that it counteracted the helmet hair. There was something special about watching Trev biking away in front of me swearing at Caleb who was attempting to make himself lighter by standing up on the pegs. Going to the library in the car is 'so what', whereas tackling the road on a two-wheeling bit of rubber and metal ... well, it really was great (and this comes from a self-confessed couch potato). It was hard in the beginning, but I'm so glad we stuck it out.

We were surprised to find that we didn't miss the car. Most of the destinations one can think of involved spending money at the other end anyway. As this was definitely out of the question, it reduced the amount of travel required.

Q: So, Trev, you've got the general flow of things by now. Go ahead, play the devil's advocate.

A: Nothing to advocate. I can't say I really enjoy the day-to-day slog of biking to work. I hate it when the wind is a northerly in the morning (in my face) and a sou-easter in the afternoon (again, in my face – this happens a fair bit), but the weekend family trips are pure joy. There's no pressure to get there on time; we can dawdle or hurry as we like; it's time spent together; it's good exercise; and there's no greenhouse gas produced. What more could you want?

Our waste report

This is very difficult to quantify, particularly given that the vast majority of things that were thrown out were actually purchased prior to the experiment and were abandoned mostly as a result of my awakening desire for simplicity (they had no resale or give-away value). I was going through a phase of re-evaluating what it means to own 'things'. I even went through a very determined stage to empty out every half-full bottle of forgotten sauce from the back of the cupboard. I wanted a minimalist cupboard space; I got one.

The rest comprised flour, sugar, rice, packaging from our bartered goods and junk mail. We received junk advertising newspapers that the junk mail deliverer seemed to think snuck past the 'no advertising material thanks' sign. We'd save the rubber band – I even slotted cinnamon rolls into the tubular bags – but the newspaper was dumped in the recycling section. If I had been really keen, I would have composted them.

Our neighbour Shane was good about donating brown glass bottles for the recycling section.

We put the wheelie bin out five times over the six months. Only once (after cleaning Caleb's room) was the bin full (of broken toys that dated back to when he was two); the other four times it was pulled up to the curb half-full. Our lack of consumer spending directly correlated to the reduced level of waste.

We (in particular Trevor) diverted material from the rubbish bin by finding new lives and identities for things and relocating them (think of Trev's famous thong makeover). So while reduction was the primary method of waste control, Trev has recycling down to a fine art.

It didn't take us long to realise that it was no longer necessary to have rubbish bins in the house, so we removed them, taking the short extra walk to the wheelie bin when we had something to plonk in it. The only bin we had in the house was the chook bucket for food scraps.

Approximately 5% of a household's CO_2 emissions are generated from waste decomposing in landfill.

Green waste was dealt with on-site. The remaining items were non-recyclable plastics and recyclable glass. It is impossible to quantify without having weighed and classified each item before disposing of them, but our emissions through waste would have been negligible.

As we put the bin out only five times out of a possible 26, it puts us within 20% of normal household waste, but doesn't take into account the levels of waste in the bin. So, in my excruciatingly non-scientific look at the issue, we'll just say we reduced our waste a hell of a lot, and leave it at that.

The second aspect of waste (and you thought looking into our rubbish bin was gross) is that of human waste. We utilised the composting toilet both as a means of reducing water usage (by around 24,000 litres for three people over six months), and to find a way to use our digestive by-products as a soil nutrient.

We have a little game we play with visitors, it goes like this: 'Look at these two lemons. Note one is twice the size of the other. They're the same variety, but they just come from two different trees. All the lemons on one tree are this big, and all the lemons on the other are this big. Wanna know the secret?'

You guessed it: a nice influx of composted human poo has produced the biggest, juiciest, tastiest lemons I've ever made lemon meringue pie from. Your poo could do that too. I won't go into what your poo is currently doing instead. You already know that stuff.

THE COMFORT ZONE

Q: Linda, I don't think I can bear to ask these questions. Was pulling the wheelie bin up the hill only five times out of 26 difficult to handle?

A: Only if I was wearing my slippery slippers.

Q: And what about your poo, was it enormously difficult to handle?

A: Dealing with human poo is not really a hands-on kind of job. It smells a little bit when we change over the chambers, but no worse than a farty smell that persists a tad longer than the usual farty smells. I guess I'm not that squeamish. I probably would be if it were other people's composted poo. But it's not and it doesn't look like poo anymore anyway. Besides, Trev, by virtue of the glorious distinction of being male, does most of the dirty work.

Q: Anything further to add, Trev?

A: As with the water question, I've been dealing with my own shit (on all sorts of levels) for a long time. Grandma had a thunderbox; likewise my house in the bush. I gag a bit at the changeover, when things are a bit raw (caused more by imagination than any actual smell), but by the time the composting cycle is complete, well, it's just fertiliser and smells less than chook poo pellets. As for the general rubbish-type waste, that is self-explanatory. Buy less crap from the shops, have less rubbish.

Our health report

The blood tests are back and we're able to do a before-and-after comparison with some surprising outcomes.

The doctor labelled Trev's pre-adventure cholesterol readings as 'simply shocking'. His triglycerides were over four times higher than the recommended levels.

Trev's cholesterol was reduced by 42% and his triglycerides by 77%.

Near the end of the experiment Trev's cholesterol was tested at work, and resulted in a reduction from 7.0 to 4.9. The greatest difference came in his triglycerides, which went from 8.3 (the recommended level is below 2) to 1.9.

Mine were high too, but nowhere near Trev's levels. I started off with a 5 in cholesterol and ended with a 4.9, and my triglycerides reduced from 3.4 to 2.5.

Before we started, my blood pressure was a screamer at 140/90 — Trev's holding steady at 140/80. Trev's did not improve over the period, resulting in an increase (we still go with the white-coat syndrome and the anticipation of the end of the experiment). Mine was 110/75 — a gratifying result as I had been diagnosed with high blood pressure three or four years ago and had not been able to reduce it. My guess is that it was a stressful job teamed with poor eating habits (eat now and not for another three days, then pig out on chips) and the highest award for sedentary habits.

My blood pressure went from a moderately high 140/90 to a healthy 110/75.

Iron levels were the rock on which we expected our adventure to founder. Yet it is one area we have had the most dramatic improvement. To begin with, our iron levels were on the low side. I don't normally eat red meat, but do eat chicken and fish. Trev had for some time declined red meat other than kangaroo. His reasoning was that they are wild and native, and had relatively natural lives up to the point they are shot and turned into highly preserved kanga bangas and steaks in a plastic meat tray. He also eats fish.

Our iron levels improved by 75%.

This may have been partly because we both started off with low iron levels. However, at the end of six nearly meatless months, with only a couple of chicken meals, a few feasts of snails and one of fish, our iron levels improved by 75%, which contradicted everything we believed about iron.

Amanda Benham, an online dietician at www.veg.onestop.net, told us she wasn't surprised that our iron levels increased, saying:

It is a myth that meat is the 'best' source of iron or that it is needed to increase iron levels. Many plant foods are richer than meat in iron (on a milligrams of iron per kilojoule basis, which is the only proper basis for comparison of nutrient levels) and also vitamin C increases iron absorption. If your diet was rich in natural plant foods, such as greens, legumes, wholegrain cereals, nuts, seeds, and you were getting vitamin C from fruit and lightly cooked vegetables, then it is no surprise that your nutritional status improved. If you used cast-iron cookware to cook meals then this too can add to iron intake.

We do cook predominantly with a cast-iron pan, and probably used it more over the six months than before, mostly because we used the oven less due to power considerations and because we ate every meal at home. We ate parsley with every meal too, not just as a garnish but also as a green. We also ate a lot of pak choi, pumpkin and red kidney beans, which have high levels of iron. Cocoa was a bit of a surprise with a 10% RDA level of iron for every tablespoon. I knew there was a good reason to make it a staple.

This is all good news for would be, should be and already are vegetarians.

Also being able to eat fresh organic food (potatoes are more like apples in texture) is a great bonus. Some studies show a vitamin and mineral content 10 times higher in fresh organic food compared with the supermarket-bought equivalent.

The most elaborate diet in the world was successful.
Over the six months, Trev lost a total of 11 kilos and I lost 6.

Because we had adopted many elements of this lifestyle before the six months, the benefits have been spread over the past two years. In that time, Trev and I lost a total of 16 kilos and 11 kilos respectively. We also wonder how other health indicators in the blood tests may have been affected as our diets improved over the same period of time. Over the six months our fitness increased due to biking and walking rather than always opting for the car. Our general weight loss, increase in fitness and reduction in stress would account for a general boost in health as well as a reduction of the risk of heart disease, arthritis, osteoporosis and a host of other diseases that our high-fat, highly processed western diet, matched with a sedentary lifestyle, engenders.

Nutritional value of the typical foods we ate over the six months (meat included as a comparison only)[1]

	Size (g)	Calories	% of RDA* iron	% of RDA fat	% of RDA cholesterol	% of RDI** calcium	Protein (g)	% of RDI vitamin A	% of RDI vitamin C	% RDI fibre (g)
Apples	100	52	1	0	0	1	0	1	1	10
Beans (green – cooked)	100	35	4	0	0	4	2	14	16	13
Beef	100	205	12	26	20	1	20	0	0	0
Chicken (roasted with skin)	100	300	8	32	29	2	26	7	0	0
Chillies (red)	100	40	6	1	0	1	2	19	239	6
Cinnamon	5	20	10	1	0	0	0	0	0	4
Cocoa	7	18	14	0	0	8	0	0	3	15
Eggplant	100	35	1	0	0	1	1	1	2	10
Eggs (2 poached)	100	147	10	15	141	5	13	10	0	0
Fish (baked)	100	105	2	1	16	1	23	1	5	0
Flour (white)	100	364	6	2	0	1	10	0	0	11
Flour (wholemeal)	100	339	22	3	0	3	14	0	0	49
Goat's milk	100	69	0	6	4	13	4	4	2	0
Mandarin	100	53	1	0	0	4	1	14	44	7
Onion (raw)	100	42	1	0	0	2	1	0	11	6
Pak choi	100	12	6	0	0	9	2	85	43	4
Parsley	100	36	34	1	0	14	3	168	222	13
Passionfruit juice	100	97	9	1	0	1	2	25	50	42
Peanuts	100	585	13	76	0	5	24	0	0	32
Potatoes (baked with skin)	100	198	39	0	0	3	4	0	22	32
Pumpkin	100	20	3	0	0	1	1	100	8	4
Red kidney beans	100	127	12	1	0	4	9	0	2	26
Raisins	100	296	14	1	0	3	3	0	9	27
Rice (brown – cooked)	100	111	2	1	0	1	3	0	0	7
Strawberries	100	32	2	0	0	2	1	0	98	8
Sunflower oil	7	4	0	7	0	0	0	0	0	0
Sunflower seeds	100	570	38	76	0	12	23	1	2	42
Swiss chard	100	20	13	0	0	6	2	122	30	8
Tomatoes (raw)	100	21	3	1	0	1	1	12	43	4
Watermelon	100	30	1	0	0	1	1	11	13	2

*Recommended dietary allowance **Recommended daily intake

THE COMFORT ZONE

Q: Linda, do you think the health benefits of your six months will continue now you are back in the land of the people who cut chips in a specific shape to absorb more fats and oils and then coat them in salty, artificial and supposedly chicken-flavoured dust?

A: Within a couple of weeks we had both shovelled enough in to notice a sigh of disapproval from the scales. However, our indulgence-deprived appetites have levelled out and we're now back to a healthier diet. The exercise we hope to continue with. So far (four weeks later) that has stayed true. However, it is clear to us that we will have to be harder on ourselves now that we have a choice compared with when we didn't. When you tell yourself and the rest of the country (or whoever is listening) that you intend to spend six months without spending a dollar on food, then you do feel a trifle hypocritical if not uneasy when standing in line at Pizza Hut. Now, without the possibility of a public outcry and full enquiry into the contents of our stomachs, it's easier to slip back into bad habits.

Q: Trev, have you anything to add to that loquacious rave?

A: The main attraction of pre-prepared or takeaway food is that it's easy. It never tastes better than a home-cooked meal, it's never cheaper, and it is certainly never more nutritious. But it's very easy, when everyone's been flat out all day and can't be bothered doing one more thing, to jump into the car and hit the Colonel. Having said that, I think we'll try to stretch out the health benefits accrued during the last six months for as long as we can, but will succumb fairly often to laziness. I like to think that, should we find ourselves succumbing too often, we'll give ourselves a shake, and remember that the garden is where the best tucker is.

Our financial report

We once had one income, very little of which was disposable: we felt impoverished. We've just spent six months on virtually no disposable income and felt enriched (though sometimes famished for a few cheap and tasty treats).

Saying we wanted to go six months without spending a dollar was a gimmick — a slightly deplorable one, it's true — but we figured it would attract a wider audience than saying we were going to go six months without relying on mains power, mains water, petrol or supermarket-bought food. And it was a lot shorter too.

So, while we didn't set out with saving money as a priority, we did save. We don't like to give a sum, mostly because people have a tendency to pinpoint that aspect of the experiment and run with it, despite our fervent pleas to consider the money of no great importance. I've been introduced on a radio segment, as 'part of a family desperate to do anything to save a dollar' and, despite cringing badly and taking as many opportunities as possible to knock that particular idea on the head, I was finally sent out with the line, 'An experiment, all about saving'.

Over the six months we spent $305 on animal food and our occasional lapses. This equates to $11.73 a week.

Foremost we wanted to know how far we could reduce our environmental impact, and how domestically sustainable it is possible to be on a suburban block. We discovered that, while you need a large area of land if you intend to derive an income from it, you can support your family in food on a reasonably sized suburban block.

You rarely buy a car with the idea that it will eventually pay for itself. In fact, it's quite the reverse. But if you invest in turning your house into a sustainable haven, you increase the value of your home; your power, water and food bills plummet; and sometime in the future you will reach that unmarked day on which all the modifications have paid for themselves. Being sustainable is a long-term financial investment.

We saved 44% of our income.

If you plonk $5000 in a savings account at a 5.5% interest rate for six months, you earn a taxable amount of $275. If instead you were to divert the money into sustainable products, the result would be much better. Here's an example.

- Buy an electric bike (and use it instead of the car, riding 50 kilometres a week) – an upfront cost of $1300.
- Replace your current fridge with a power-efficient model (from 900 kWh a year to 400 kWh) – cost $1500.

- Purchase a solar hot-water service — $1900 (after RECs rebates).
- Replace standard incandescent lighting with compact fluoro bulbs, and install low-flow showerheads and tap fittings, and a couple of garden water-saving devices — a very generous $400 allowance.

This would cost you a total of $5000. In six months, through less use of petrol, power and water, you'd stand to save:

CHANGES	AMOUNT SAVED
Electric bike	$150.00
Solar hot-water	$230.00
Fridge	$32.50
Bulbs, water-saving devices	$60.00
Total saved	$472.50

The investment will continue to pay for itself (in the case of solar hot-water, for around 25–40 years). It may also result in an increase in home value. The use of a bike, electric or not, may mean the sale of a second car is possible, making considerable yearly savings in rego alone. This example cannot take into account the increase in health benefits from regular exercise (and the associated financial savings), or the value to the environment.

And remember — these savings are non-taxable.

We spent an additional 9.3% of our income on animal feed (1.4%), junk food (0.6%) and computer-related costs (7.3%).

PERCENTAGE BREAKDOWN OF MONEY WE SPENT OVER THE SIX MONTHS

Bank fees	0.5
Medical expenses	0.5
Food	0.6
Animal feed	1.4
Education	1.5
Phone/Internet	3.7
Insurance	4.3
Rates/rego	6.9
Other (computer)	7.3
Mortgage	29.4
Savings	43.9
Total income excluding tax	100.0%

COST OF THE INFRASTRUCTURE PRIOR TO STARTING OUR EXPERIMENT

Solar hot-water after rebates	$1500
18 x 80-watt solar panels and invertor	$11,500
2 x 5000-gallon tanks with pump and plumbing	$6000
Composting toilet	$2200
Goats and chooks	$250
(Garden costs have never been collated)	
Total cost	**$21,450**

The amount of $21,450 is a considerable sum; we like to characterise it by saying, 'It's about the amount you'd save by choosing to drive an average sedan compared with a four-wheel drive'.

Endnotes

January

1 L Woodrow, *The permaculture home garden*, Penguin Books, 1996
2 www.permacultureinternational.org
3 Figures from Professor J W Kimball, http://users.rcn.com/jkimball.ma.ultranet/BiologyPages/N/NetProductivity.html#Net_Productivity
4 Australian Bureau of Statistics, *Yearbook Australia: environment, water supply and use — 1301.0-2005*
5 Worldwide Wildlife Fund, *Living waters: conserving the source of life*, www.wwf.org.uk/filelibrary/pdf/thirstycrops.pdf
6 *New Scientist*, February 1997, cited by www.animalliberation.org.au/vegconf.php
7 Worldwide Wildlife Fund, *Living waters: conserving the source of life*
8 Dr D Eamus, *The Australian dream — is it killing us?*, Institute for Water and Environmental Resource Management, University of Technology, Sydney, 2002
9 Volunteer Now, 'Consumerism: the problem', http://volunteernow.ca/take_action/issues_consumerism.htm
10 Adapted from A Hayes, *It's so natural*, HarperCollins, 1993
11 B Murphy, *Breeding and growing snails commercially in Australia*, Rural Industries Research and Development Corporation, www.rirdc.gov.au/reports/NAP/00-188.htm

February

1 J Foss, *Ocean outfalls — there is a solution to ocean pollution*, National Board Surfrider Foundation, August 1998, and personal communication
2 J Foss, personal communication
3 J Gordon, 'Credit card debt drives spending binge', *The Age*, 17 December 2004
4 Professor D Crawford, The Heart Foundation, www.heartfoundation.com.au/downloads/res_prof_dcrawford.pdf
5 'Glued to the Screen', *Sydney Morning Herald*, 30 March 2004, www.smh.com.au/articles/2004/03/31/1080544536008.html?from=storyrhs&oneclick=true
6 Department of Environment and Heritage, www.deh.gov.au/settlements/waste/organics.html
7 *Landbank Consultancy Report*, 1991, cited at www.rwh.org.au/wellwomens/whic.cfm?doc_id=7691
8 T Flannery, *The future eaters*, Reed Books, 1994
9 A Bartlett, 'Environmental sustainability', paper presented at the annual meeting of the American Association of Physics Teachers, University of Colorado, Denver, Colorado, 1997, www.hubbertpeak.com/bartlett/envSustain.htm
10 C Haub, 'How many people have ever lived on Earth?', *Population Today*, February 1995, www.prb.org/Template.cfm?Section=PRB&template=/Content/ContentGroups/02_Articles/oct-Dec02/How_Many_People_Have_Ever_Lived_on_Earth_.htm

11 D Attenborough, *The life of mammals*, BBC Books, London, 2002

12 Environmental Protection Authority, 'Survey and audit of kerbside waste and recycling practices and recommended kerbside service standards', 2002 (prepared for the EPA by NOLAN-ITU Pty Ltd)

13 Clean Up Australia, *2004 Rubbish report*, www.cleanup.com.au/annualreport/

March

1 T Flannery, *The weather makers: the history and future impact of climate change*, Text Publishing, Melbourne, 2005, p. 83

2 Cited in S Leary, 'Wasted food', ABC radio report, 9 May 2005, www.abc.net.au/westernplains/stories/s1363389.htm

3 Australian Greenhouse Office, 'How do households contribute to global warming?', www.greenhouse.gov.au/gwci/how.html

4 United Nations Development Programme, 'Biodiversity in crisis', www.undp.org/biodiversity/biodiversitycd/bioCrisis.htm

5 United Nations Development Programme

6 Eamus, *The Australian dream — is it killing us?*

7 Agricultural and Resource Management Council of Australia and New Zealand (ARMCANZ), 1999

8 Australian Water Association (AWA), 2003

9 New South Wales Environmental Protection Agency (NSWEPA), 2003

10 Energy Supply Association Australia 1999, cited on www.actewagl.com.au/education/electricity/generation/#overview

11 Energy Information Administration, http://eia.doe.gov/oiaf/ieo98/ele.html, cited on www.actewagl.com.au/education/electricity/generation/#overview

12 Australian Greenhouse Office, *Renewable energy commercialisation in Australia*, 2003

13 Flannery, *The weather makers: the history and future impact of climate change*, p. 77

14 R Sanders, 'Standby appliances suck up electricity', *Cal Neighbors*, Spring 2001, University of California, Berkeley, and Lawrence Berkeley National Laboratory

15 *Revised minimum energy performance standards and alternative strategies for small electric storage water*, prepared for the Australian Greenhouse Office by George Wilkenfeld and Associates Pty Ltd, August 2003, www.energyrating.gov.au/library/pubs/200309-riswaterheaters.pdf

16 Australian Greenhouse Office, *Your home technical manual: design for lifestyle and future*, www.greenhouse.gov.au/yourhome/technical/fs42.htm

17 Adapted from A Hayes, *It's so natural*, p. 172

18 Animal Liberation, *Vegetarianism: questions and answers*, www.animalliberation.org.au/vegoqa.php

19 Animals Australia: The Voice for Animals, www.animalsaustralia.org/default2.asp?idL1=1273&idL2=1293

April

1 Australian Bureau of Statistics, *Yearbook Australia: environmental issues: people's views and practices 4602.0–2002*

2 Soil Association UK, *The biodiversity benefits of organic farming*, www.soilassociation.org/sa/saweb.nsf/0/80256ad800554549802568e80048af3d?Open Document

3 T Marshall, horticulturist and founder of the National Association for Sustainable Agriculture Australia (NASAA) and the International Federation of Organic Agriculture Movement (IFOAM), 2005, www.livingnow.com.au/food/s1foodstories2.htm

4 Marshall, 2005

5 Organic Retailers and Growers Association of Australia, 2000, cited in *Pesticides and You*, vol. 20, no. 1, Spring 2000, Beyond Pesticides: National Coalition Against the Misuse of Pesticides, Washington

6 Australian Bureau of Statistics, *Yearbook Australia: environment water supply and use 1301–2005*

7 Commonwealth Scientific and Industrial Research Organisation, cited at http://bulletin.ninemsn.com.au/bulletin/site/articleIDs/56FC9A6D92739D89CA256C0F0016CE28

8 Water Services Association of Australia, www.wsaa.asn.au/download/2005/IRTSSupplementV1_1.pdf

9 Adapted from www.thisplace.com.au/eco/tt_waterusage.htm

10 Commonwealth Scientific and Industrial Research Organisation, Manufacturing and Infrastructure Technology (CSIRO MIT), *Embodied energy*, www.cmit.csiro.au/brochures/tech/embodied/

11 D Elgin, *Voluntary simplicity*, Quill, William Morrow, New York, 1993, pp. 28–29

12 Animal Liberation South Australia

13 Australian Bureau of Statistics, 1997, cited at www.animalsaustralia.org/default2.asp?idL1=1273&idL2=1293

May

1 Australian Bureau of Statistics

2 ActewAGL 2005, www.actewagl.com.au/education/electricity/generation/

3 S Davidson, 'Air transport impacts take off', *Issue Ecos*, 123, 2005, CSIRO, pp. 15–17

4 Australian Greenhouse Office, 'White goods fact sheet', www.greenhouse.gov.au/yourhome/technical/pdf/fs41.pdf

5 Conservatree – Paper for the Environment, www.conservatree.com

6 UK Environment Agency, www.environment-agency.gov.uk

7 J Healey (ed.), *Issues in Society, volume 189: water use*, The Spinney Press, Thirroul, 2003

8 F Ronn, 'Indoor plants taking up volatile organic compounds', ABC radio report, 29 August 2005, www.abc.net.au/melbourne/stories/s1448510.htm

9 www.idontcareaboutair.com/facts/health.shmtl

10 J White, *The golden cow*, Inter-varsity Press, Illinois, 1979

11 Australian Bureau of Statistics, *Environmental issues: people's views and practices* *4602.0–2002*

12 Elgin, *Voluntary simplicity*, pp. 28–29

June

1 Environment Victoria, 'Computer waste summary sheet', www.envict.org.au/inform.php?menu=6&submenu=532&item=905

2 World Wildlife Fund, *Living planet report*, 2002

3 Department of Energy, Queensland, www.energy.qld.gov.au

4 World Overpopulation Awareness organisation, www.overpopulation.org/solutions.html

5 www.greenvehicleguide.gov.au

6 C Hamilton & R Denniss, *Affluenza*, Allen & Unwin, 2005

7 J Woodford, 'An ocean of old plastic stuck in seabird craws', *The Sydney Morning Herald*, 3 November 2004, www.smh.com.au/news/Environment/An-ocean-of-old-plastic-stuck-in-seabird-craws/2004/11/02/1099362148877.html?oneclick=true

8 Eamus, *The Australian dream — is it killing us?*

9 Hamilton & Denniss, *Affluenza*

The results

1 Derived from www.nutritiondata.com, sourced from the United States Department of Agriculture (USDA)

Appendix 1

Rainfall in the Gympie area 1870–2005

(figures in bold indicate below average rainfall)

Decade	Jan	Feb	Mar	Apr	May	Jun	Jul	Aug	Sep	Oct	Nov	Dec	Total
1870s	164	179	209	**85**	102	78	89	78	53	77	92	134	*1339*
1880s	**111**	189	**102**	92	82	**41**	**48**	47	**44**	79	**83**	**126**	*1042*
1890s	264	243	226	**79**	**59**	80	**47**	**39**	64	**62**	**86**	145	*1393*
1900s	**133**	**115**	155	**79**	102	**38**	**45**	46	54	**69**	**65**	130	*1032*
1910s	168	**123**	**122**	**60**	**53**	64	**39**	**32**	58	**61**	**73**	**84**	*936*
1920s	190	167	144	131	**37**	97	58	**26**	48	**64**	**75**	202	*1239*
1930s	**138**	168	144	86	**67**	63	**49**	**35**	47	74	113	134	*1117*
1940s	**139**	172	**136**	86	73	**50**	**35**	**20**	55	91	99	**125**	*1080*
1950s	**150**	211	191	87	**69**	62	68	**39**	**27**	68	**89**	**122**	*1180*
1960s	214	**110**	**138**	**63**	**67**	75	**44**	44	**37**	78	**86**	134	*1089*
1970s	231	195	**111**	**68**	**50**	**41**	84	**35**	51	95	135	**124**	*1218*
1980s	**115**	**93**	**102**	126	109	68	71	46	**30**	**72**	**75**	159	*1066*
1990s	**116**	235	**131**	**65**	92	**36**	**39**	**25**	50	**57**	**85**	146	*1095*
2000s	**140**	**130**	**85**	87	**42**	**37**	**12**	48	**7**	80	91	**104**	*839*
Average	162	166	142	85	72	59	52	40	45	73	89	133	*1119*

Appendix 2

Bureau of Meteorology map of Australia and its annual rainfall

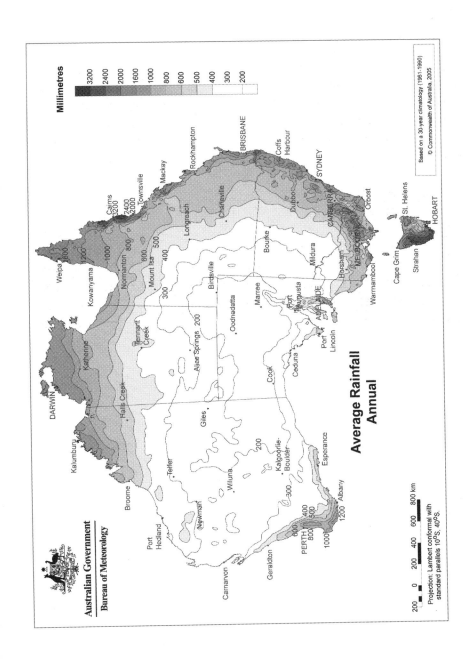

Appendix 3

City driving compared with highway driving and their relative inefficiencies

Vehicle year/model	City consumption (L/100km)	Highway consumption (L/100km)	Engine size (Litres)	% difference in fuel economy between city & highway driving	Annual fuel cost*	Annual CO_2 total (tonnes)
2003 Toyota Prius (10 Series) Auto sedan 4dr	4.6	4.2	1.5	10%	$802	3.7
1998 Toyota Starlet Man. Hatch 3dr & 5dr	6.6	4.8	1.3	38%	$1074	4.8
2002 Nissan N16 Pulsar Man sedan 4dr	7.2	5	1.6	44%	$1157	5.1
1996 Holden SB Barina City Man Hatchback 2dr	7.6	5	1.2	52%	$1204	5.3
1995 Toyota Corolla 4WD Auto. Wagon 4dr	9	6.4	1.6	41%	$1455	6.5
2002 Hyundai Elantra LaVita Man 5dr	9	6.2	1.6	45%	$1443	6.4
2003 Nissan T30 X-TRAIL 4WD Man wagon 5dr	9.5	6.6	2.5	44%	$1526	6.8
1996 Ford HC Mondeo LX Auto Sedan 4dr	9.5	5.8	2	64%	$1476	6.4
2002 Honda Accord VTiL Man sedan 4dr	9.5	7	2.3	36%	$1551	6.9
2002 Honda *Prelude VTiR Man coupe 2dr	9.5	7.6	2.2	25%	$1589	7.2
1989 Ford KE Laser TX3 EFI Turbo4WD Man. Hatchback 3dr	10	7.6	1.6	32%	$1647	7.4
1998 Mazda 626 Man. station Wagon 4dr	10	6.6	2	52%	$1585	7.0
1993 Ford KH TX3 EFI DOHC Turbo 4WD Man. Hatchback 3dr	10.5	7.6	1.8	38%	$1706	7.6
1986 Mitsubishi GN Sigma Auto. Wagon 4dr	11	8.5	2.6	29%	$1821	8.2
1992 Toyota Tarago GLS 4WD Auto. Wagon 3dr	12	8.5	2.5	41%	$1938	8.6
2003 Nissan R50 Pathfinder 4WD Auto wagon 5dr	13.5	10	3.3	35%	$2208	9.9
1997 Ford Explorer ATW XLT 4WD Man. Wagon 5dr	14	NA	4	NA	$1642	NA
1998 Holden U8 Jackaroo 4WD Monterey Auto. Wagon 4 dr	15	NA	3.5	NA	$1760	NA
2002 Ford AUII Utility XL Chassis Cab Man. Dedicated LPG 2dr	15	10	4	50%	$2384	10.5
1996 Mitsubishi NK Pajero 4WD GLX Man. LWB 4dr	16	NA	3.5	NA	$1877	NA

* Based on 100 km highway driving and 188 km city driving per week (a total of roughly 15,000 km per year, just a little under the annual average) and petrol cost of $1.20 per litre

NA: information has not been provided by manufacturers as 4WDs operate under different ruling than passenger vehicles. Information derived from www.greenvehicleguide.gov.au

Appendix 4

Embodied energy of building products

MATERIAL	EMBODIED ENERGY MJ/KG
Kiln-dried sawn softwood	3.4
Kiln-dried sawn hardwood	2.0
Air-dried sawn hardwood	0.5
Hardboard	24.2
Particleboard	8.0
MDF	11.3
Plywood	10.4
Glue-laminated timber	11.0
Laminated veneer lumber	11.0
Plastics – general	90
PVC	80.0
Synthetic rubber	110.0
Acrylic paint	61.5
Stabilised earth	0.7
Imported dimension granite	13.9
Local dimension granite	5.9
Gypsum plaster	2.9
Plasterboard	4.4
Fibre cement	4.8
Cement	5.6
In situ concrete	1.9
Precast steam-cured concrete	2.0
Precast tilt-up concrete	1.9
Clay bricks	2.5
Concrete blocks	1.5
AAC	3.6
Glass	12.7
Aluminium	170
Copper	100
Galvanised steel	38

Figures from Dr Bill Lawson as cited at
www.greenhouse.gov.au/yourhome/technical/fs31.htm

Appendix 5

Worldometers

This information was adapted from www.worldometers.info. It was taken from the website around June 2005, so yearly figures, i.e. births this year, are representative of only half a year. All figures are based on data that is said to be somewhat correct for 2003–04.

POPULATION

6,488,258,165	current Earth population
64,200,713	births this year
281,993	births today
26,398,833	deaths this year
115,953	deaths today
166,040	absolute population growth for today (births minus deaths)

GOVERNMENT & ECONOMICS

17,807,497	cars produced this year
54,047,316	bicycles produced this year
41,707,033	computers sold this year

EDUCATION

468,618	book titles published this year
259,302,151	newspapers circulated this year

ENVIRONMENT

5,623,420	forest loss (hectares) this year
3,124,122	productive land loss through soil erosion (hectares) this year
11,676,407,081	topsoil erosion from farmlands (tonnes) this year
11,059,392,928	carbon dioxide (CO_2) emissions (tonnes) this year
7,341,687	desert land formed due to mismanagement (acres) this year
6,593,745	Earth's weight in trillion tonnes
4,500,642,531	age of Earth (years)
1,562,061,148	lightning strikes to Earth this year
64,406,093	tonnes of biological waste from living things this year
45,299,773	tonnes of fish caught this year

FOOD

1,249,649	tonnes of food produced this year
3,079,140,715	millions of calories consumed this year
82,603,043	millions of grams of protein consumed this year
16,839,019,175	dollars spent on diet in the USA this year

ENERGY*

5,903,029,078	energy produced this year
5,596,865,093	energy consumed this year
2,158,362,371	oil consumed this year
1,790,590,694	coal consumed this year
1,357,415,517,000	solar energy that has reached Earth this year

HEALTH

31,562,061	people currently infected with HIV
7,181,031	deaths caused by HIV (total)
3,124,122	deaths caused by cancer this year
499,860	deaths caused by malaria this year
1,562,061	deaths caused by smoking this year
2,741,636	millions of cigarettes produced this year
9372	deaths caused by pesticides this year
591,006	global government spending on health care ($US millions) this year
495,330	world spending on illegal drugs ($US millions) this year
65,357	US spending on alcohol and tobacco ($US millions) this year
2374	US spending on perfume ($US millions) this year
134,493	automobile accident fatalities this year

*Energy figures are measured in tonnes, coal equivalent

Index

Don't feel overwhelmed, don't feel guilty, don't feel you
need perfect knowledge, a lot of money or heaps of time.
All that does is compound the problem and stops you from

feeling empowered.

Your actions will not save the world.
Who cares, it was never the goal. It's about doing the things
that are within your power to do. That's all you can do.
Don't think of it as an obligation, think of it as an adventure.